100

No-Nonsense Things that ALL Teachers Should STOP Doing

Compiled by
Rick Jetter, Ph.D.

Edited by
Rebecca Coda

This book is available at special discounts when purchased in quantity for use as premiums, promotions, fundraisers, or educational purposes. For inquiries and details, contact the publisher at pushingboundariesllc@gmail.com.

Published by Pushing Boundaries Consulting, LLC
Tonawanda, NY
www.pushboundconsulting.com

Cover Design by Rebecca Coda
Editing and Interior Design by Pushing Boundaries Consulting, LLC

The interior icons were designed by Stop Sign (Surang), Hand Drawn Arrow (Freepik), Success (Wichai.wi), Danger (Freepik), Trophy (Freepik), United (Freepik) and Winner (DinosoftLabs) from Flaticon.com.

Library of Congress Control Number: 2021934225
Paperback ISBN: 978-1-7370390-0-6

PUSHING
BOUNDARIES
CONSULTING, LLC

Dedication

I am grateful for all the wonderful educators I have had the blessing of meeting, knowing and working with throughout my career. This book is written for you and for those I have yet to meet.

Disclaimer

Don't let the word "STOP" scare you away. If you think that this book should have been about what teachers should "START" doing, that's your opinion, but sometimes, it is OK to say "STOP." It creates *urgency*. It creates a *shock value*. Yes, we want to *shock* you into becoming a better teacher NOW, rather than waiting until LATER.

How many times have you learned a new technique or strategy during professional development only to add one thing to your plate while never eliminating the malpractice? Sometimes efficacy requires you to "STOP" practices that don't impact students. YOU might be an incredible teacher, already, but just haven't found the right words to help a colleague. Until NOW. We think that we found the right words. Sugarcoating everything in the teaching profession is not what we wanted to do with this book. Using the word "STOP" means that we love teachers enough and respect the profession so much so that we are willing to flip the typical educational narrative to ensure award winning results that all students deserve. That's why we wrote this book with helpful insights, so that you don't have to repeat our mistakes. It is our hope that you will optimize your talents, passions, and knowledge to create award winning classrooms!

Plus, this book is not just for NEW teachers. It is for anyone, really. It is a platform for leading realistic conversations to establish norms, beliefs and expectations using a common language. It may even guide families, substitute teachers and community stakeholders to better understand what should and should not be occurring in award winning classrooms. There are many incredible teachers out there AND there are some terrible teachers out there too. You know that and we know that. It is OK to encourage a colleague to "STOP" doing something if it will make them a better teacher to better serve our students. Sometimes doing what's right requires stopping bad habits altogether.

Contents

STOP Doing These Things with Students
This Type of Nonsense Impedes Five-Star Classrooms

STOP Doing These Things at Your School

This Type of Nonsense Blocks Synergistic School Culture

STOP Making Everything About You
This Nonsense Prevents Dynamic Off-the-Charts Achievement

A Plea for Collaboration and Truth

DOUGLAS REEVES, Ph.D.

With bracing candor and insights born of deep professional experience, the authors give advice that educators–especially those joining our profession–rarely hear. These insights range from what we do in the classroom to how we influence the boardroom. Some of the chapters may make you wince. I know that I did when I saw myself in some of the chapter titles. As the late Rick DuFour liked to say, "I offer a public apology to my students who had me in class before I knew what I was doing." I feel the same way, regretting every moment that I thought it was my job to show that I knew more algebra than a 14-year-old. I wish that my first-year teacher-self would have read this book. Therefore, I hope that readers will not react defensively, but rather see in these pages a clarion call for professionalism and self-care. The message of the book is not that teachers should be heroes. Heroism is not a sustainable strategy. I have seen too many teachers, especially during and after the global pandemic led to school closures, who are exhausted, stressed out and reconsidering their professional choices. But the words in this book, including advice about how teachers can save time, emotional energy and money, will help you finish reading the book with confidence and relief. My great hope is that readers will consider these pages not an attack on educators but rather a repudiation of actions that often threaten the profession of teaching. Moreover, I hope that future publications will consider what administrators, board members and officials at the state and federal level should stop doing.

The Focus Imperative

This wonderfully collaborative effort gets to the very heart of what so many teachers and administrators find overwhelming: the tendency of educational systems to start new ideas without any thoughtful reflection on what to *stop* doing. The authors challenge us not just to slow down or yield or perhaps find a traffic circle so that we continue the ride, but rather come to a full stop. This challenge is particularly relevant for the post-pandemic era in which well-intentioned federal funds are flowing into school systems. Anyone who remembers the proliferation of programs following Race to the Top funding in 2009-2010, will recall the futility of requiring an "evidence-based program" that teachers did not have time to implement. That funding was a little more than $ 4 billion; the funding under the CARES Act exceeds $81 billion. If Race to the Top led to a flood of programs, then the CARES Act will deliver a tsunami–unless, of course, educators and school leaders are willing to *stop* and decide what not to do before adding more programs to the classroom. If teacher morale is low now, try asking them to add more programs in the fixed number of hours in the day and, by the way, still require them to cover every sentence of state standards. In a study I conducted of more than 2,000 school plans, my colleagues and I found that, as Michael Fullan described in his foreword to that book, the proliferation of programs was inversely proportional to gains in student achievement. Once the plans had more than six or seven priorities, the ability of teachers and administrators to focus on what mattered most was lost. We found individual schools claiming to have more than seventy-five priorities and school districts with more than 200 of them. This is why, I say with deep respect to superintendents who live and breathe with strategic plans, that many of those documents are counterproductive. *When everything is a priority, then nothing is a priority.*

The Power of Collaboration

Collaboration sounds good until my fellow collaborators disagree with me. The hard truth is that collaboration is a challenging process and one in which we do not always get our way. I grieve when someone tells me, "we tried to have collaborative teacher teams, but it didn't work." I wonder how many times they had tried these collaborative efforts. The astonishing answer is rarely more than one or two, after which collaborative processes were abandoned. I still see the after-effects of this today, when "collaborative" meetings are little more than a 1950's style faculty meeting, with one person talking and others pretending to listen. ***When this project began, it was a risk.*** The editors did not know if work would be submitted, if it would be practical and useful, or if anyone would read it. By its very example, the book makes the critical point that, while collaboration is a risk and takes some time to get right, the result is worth the effort. May we all have the patience and persistence to approach every collaborative effort in our schools with the same effort, tolerance and goodwill reflected in these pages.

I do have a respectful request of the readers . . .

If you find even a few of these ideas as thoughtful and useful as I did, please share it with administrators, board members and, most importantly, with the student teachers you will mentor. My deep thanks and respect go to the authors, perhaps some of whom are seeing their work published for the first time. I hope that this will be only one of many contributions you will make to our profession in the years to come.

Dr. Douglas Reeves is the author of more than 40 books and 100 articles on education and leadership. Twice named to the Harvard University Distinguished Authors Series, Doug is the recipient of several national and international awards for his contributions to education. Doug Tweets @DouglasReeves.

Cut to the Chase: We Can do Better

RICK JETTER, Ph.D.

This no-nonsense, cut-to-the-chase, running-out-of-time perspective is meant to stop you in your tracks so that you can achieve your most audacious goals within education. Promoting five-star classrooms, synergistic school cultures and magnetic off-the-charts dynamic success is the aim of every author who jumped into this project. To achieve the highest possible level of classroom success, educators must STOP with the bad habits. This first book in the 100 STOP Series is a pro-teacher book. Think of it as a toxicity cleanse from anything holding you or your school back from high and masterful achievement. Although this book is written in the "negative" ("stop" or "knock-it-off") perspective, don't let that scare you away as the disclaimer warns you. This series was written in this manner to address issues powerfully and passionately for current and practicing teachers. Recently, a teacher was candid with me and said, "Why do we always have to sugar-coat everything?" My eyes lit up and I said, "You're right, why do we?" No-nonsense means there is no time to mess around. The clock of achievement is ticking.

The chapters are organized in such a way that they could be read in isolation as your curiosity is piqued, or read cover to cover, with threads of you feeling the same way we might be feeling. This mindset is the perfect way to launch your school year as you create school-wide norms and faculty social contracts. What a great baseline to start with! If you are a school leader or an administrator, why not head off the problems before they even begin? These insights are also essential for new teachers within university or district level induction programs all the way up to highly aspiring award-winning grade level teams seeking Blue Ribbon School or Disney Teacher of the Year status. More than anything, the ideas in this book are for the courageous, bold, and excellence-seeking boundary pushers that are willing to be intentional, disciplined and strategic.

Over a four-year period, I started to notice a trend with teachers as my interactions broadened within social media. I took notice to the types of questions and trends that started to emerge. I noticed that teachers primarily focused on new methods and sharing ideas, but they also wanted to express what their colleagues should STOP doing. From there, I decided to start tracking responses by simply asking the following, basic question:

What are ten things that teachers should STOP doing?

That's it. That was the question. This book reports the findings of over 1200+ teachers, like yourself, who want to know the top 100 tips to help new teachers, veteran teachers, school administrators (who help train teachers) and anyone looking to lead their school or team to highly effective schools.

The chapters are story-based and are gathered from real educators telling it like it is. Some chapters are funny. Some are serious. Some are tear jerkers. Some are wake-up calls. Every author in this book narrativizes from a perspective of we-can-do-better and you-can-learn from my mistakes. I bet you will find that you follow many of our contributing authors on social media and find them to be forerunners of excellence, uplifting, inspiring and innovative educators doing transformative work in the field of education. They have spectacular advice--just amazing insights! A huge thank you goes out to all our authors who have made this book a reality.

Every author in this manuscript is in your court cheering you on to your greatest classroom success. Our 100+ authors masterfully provide realistic advice collected from authentic been-there-done-that experiences. It is our aim that you will do incredible things and achieve with such impact that your success is not only contagious, but it will permeate throughout your entire community. It is time to make sense of our past nonsense!

Sure, we came up with 100 "things," but I'll bet you can think of more.

STOP Doing These Things with Students

This Type of Nonsense Impedes

Five-Star Classrooms

Stop Teaching the Students You Want &
Teach the Students You Have

KEN PATTERSON

The perfect class doesn't exist. Read that sentence again. The perfect class doesn't exist. Some teachers tell the story of growing up, dreaming of becoming a teacher. Often, these mini teachers in training just want to play school. You may have even been that kid using siblings, neighborhood friends, or even stuffed animals as the ideal, make believe classroom filled with make believe students. In that moment as a child, dreaming of one day being a teacher, everything was perfect. The best part of role-playing school was that even the behavioral disruptions were planned. These childhood experiences of playing school became a utopia of perfect teaching in a perfectly orchestrated and controlled context. Although these childhood experiences are many times the inspiration for becoming a teacher, someday, it can also create a naïve, fairy-tale perception of a real classroom with real students with backgrounds far different than mine.

More times than not, students are not like the perfect ones that were dreamed of when new teachers started out in a teacher education program at a college or university. We weren't necessarily prepared for the real students with cultural differences, emotional struggles, social biases and learning deficiencies that can easily ruffle your feathers if your skillset didn't extend past your childhood utopia version of school. Unfortunately, what some teachers do is rather simple: they ignore these challenges. Unskilled teachers act like these students don't exist. This causes amped-up frustration because the students who show up to class are not only ignored, but they make teachers say, "These kids just don't get it!"

A "Band" Encounter

In my second year as a High School Band Director, fresh out of college, I prepared to take my students to the district-wide performance assessments where our performing groups would be rated by top clinicians and instructors in the field of music. This was certainly a high-stakes event that was one of the most stressful times of the year for performing arts teachers. This was going to be a walk in the park for me because I had gone above and beyond to ensure I was prepared. I spent countless hours working with my students in class. As funny as it sounds, I spent even more hours in the bathroom or in front of the mirror practicing my graceful baton work. I visualized conducting the most beautiful and riveting symphonies that the ears would ever hear.

On the day of the performance, I had it in my own mind that it would be the performance of the ages. In just two years, I had completely turned this music program around into one everyone could be proud of. So, I knew the performance had to be riveting and off the chart spectacular. I worked hard and I thought I deserved accolades for all the time, effort and talent that I had invested.

Two weeks later the scores came back.

"Failure...Poor musicianship...Unsatisfactory." These were the ratings that were given to me by the top clinicians in the field. I was livid. I demanded to know why. Clearly, they could not recognize the *genius* of my artistry–even if they had held their doctorates longer than I've been alive. But, I practiced in the mirror! I prepared my students the best that I could. In my mind, the stupid judges couldn't appreciate my greatness. I called one of the judges to give them a piece of my own mind: "My conducting was impeccable. How could you?" The judge responded:

"Your conducting is truly marvelous. The passion, the movement and the expressions you delivered were certainly remarkable and noteworthy. However, you were not conducting the students who were in *front* of you. It was as if you weren't even listening to them. In your mind, you were looking right past them and conducting one of the most beautiful orchestras in all the world. You were not conducting a hodge-podge of 14-year-old orchestra students struggling with relationship issues, peer pressure and zits. You thought you were on Broadway. As a result, it was clearly all about you and not at all about the students."

Mic drop. Ego crush. Touché. I let that advice sink in before I came around to reflecting.

This is what often happens with teachers. We make it all about us and overlook the students we have sitting right in front of us. If we aren't careful and thoughtful, our classrooms can become more about teaching the students we want, rather than the ones we have. This needs to stop. This problem also extended beyond my personal orchestra conducting experience.

I Didn't Want that Student in Class

Teachers must also stop deciding before the school year even starts to exclude certain students from their new rosters. These negative conversations happen all the time.

I will never forget as an administrator, receiving an email in August–before the students would even arrive–from a teacher insisting that she did not want to teach Dwayne because she already talked to his previous teacher and heard that he was a lot to handle. She proposed to us that she did not feel she would be effective with this student and suggested we give this student to another teacher on her team! In fact, she had already explained to the other teacher that they would do a "trade" and she claimed to be merely looking out for the student. I kept thinking, "you cannot suspend, complain, or bully your way into the perfect class." You must begin each year grounded in the reality that no matter who is on the roster, it is your honor to have a class in the first place.

Teach the students you have with dignity and acceptance knowing that you believe in them as scholars. There is no other possible outcome other than academic success. As you slow down, get off your high ego horse like I had to and focus on the students in front of you.

The students on your roster, the actual ones with names on your class list, will have a teacher fully committed to their growth and development, regardless of how long it takes, and YOU will be that teacher for all. There is no such thing as a perfect class. To deeply succeed, you must resolve that the students placed in your care will be the most perfectly imperfect students for you because you aren't perfect, either. It isn't about you. It is about you applying your passion and gifts to the students who show up in your classroom each day. Who knows, the more you slow down and focus on the students in front of you, the more likely they will develop into a more impactful group of students than you could ever dream of. Every student deserves you to be their greatest conductor, mentor, cheerleader, innovator and support system. If not you, then whom?

Ken Patterson is a father, Culturally Responsive Teaching evangelist, PhD Student, Middle School Assistant Principal, and champion of kids. His passion is fighting for equitable outcomes for minoritized populations and can be found tweeting, speaking, and writing on the subject.

Stop Unintentionally Harming Students
CORI ORLANDO

If you ask most educators why they entered the field of teaching, many would emphatically respond, "To help students." So, why would there ever be a need to have a chapter about NOT harming kids? Because it is needed. To assume positive intent, I believe that teachers do not set out to harm their students. That goes against the very nature of our teaching profession. We are empathizers and nurturers, after all. As teachers, we have tremendous impact, power and influence over students' lives. So why am I writing this? Because I believe that when we know better, we should do better. At times, there are unintended consequences simply due to a lack of awareness. Students perceive teachers much differently than teachers perceive themselves. When teachers lack perception it often leads to unintentional harm. The perception gap narrows as personal narratives are shared and students are understood. Our stories connect us and our BAD stories connect us (even more) when we are vulnerable with our past and determined to set a thriving course for the future.

Shutting the Door

Prior to implementing instruction, I like to think about student perspective and how my actions will impact my students. I like to predict misconceptions and "if/then" type of responses. I'm very conscientious about what I say and do because I know that it has ripple effect that reaches out far beyond the moment of any given day. As I reflect on my 19-year (and counting) career in education, I have found many blind spots where this has happened. I'd like to share the tale of a recent incident.

I was instructing a third-grade class inclusive of many diverse learners. In an effort to foster a love of reading, (and move beyond compliance measures), I decided to provide my students with some choice in sharing something about their own reading. I had created something called the "Shelfie Station." This would be a place to display pictures of students holding the book that they completed independently. For them to get their picture taken, they would complete an activity from a choice board that I created. The choice board had activities that students had developed themselves throughout the year which included high interest activities such as vlogs, book talks and posters. There was also a "free space" for anything else they could come up with. I was so excited to announce this new venture to my students: "Every time you finish a chapter book, you can choose one of these activities." And as soon as the words escaped my mouth, I wanted to suck them back in! Why did I have to specify "Chapter Books"? I knew my students so well; I knew exactly how and what each student was reading. And I knew very well that a handful of my students were reading at a Prek-1 level. I just shut the door on that whole group before they even had a chance to touch the handle. I honestly can't remember if I back peddled and restated at that point. What I do remember is the day that I saw Sharla recording herself reading her Biscuit book (TK-K level) for the "vlog" option of the choice board. That sight, that moment, brought me to tears. Thank goodness she didn't listen to me. Thank goodness she believed in herself. Thank goodness she busted down that door that I closed on her, unintentionally. Sharla was beaming as she read the book that she had practiced all week and she was beaming when I watched her video with her and praised her on how far she had come in reading!

A few days later, a colleague came into our room to visit. I was so excited to share Sharla's success! I showed this visitor the video. With a smile, the visitor called Sharla over to tell her how impressive her reading was. Sharla was once again beaming. Then the visitor followed up with "And what Lexile reading level is that book?" And with that, my heart stopped beating and my stomach turned because Sharla was reading 3-4 years below grade level. Then, the next statement the visitor made was, "Why don't you try a higher-level next time"? Sharla smiled and just said "ok," but my mouth was glued shut without the words to even respond.

The Power of Words

In Sharla's case, I knew her disabilities, I had data on her reading levels, and I knew her next intentional step that ensured productive struggle for her reading growth. When my classroom visitor spoke, she conveyed unreasonable expectations given her deficiencies in reading. It was painfully inconsiderate. Her unintentional words carried power. As I write this, I want to convey to fellow educators that there is a data driven art to knowing your students, when to accelerate learning and when to back off just as I did with Sharla.

Words have power–whether we are jumping too far ahead academically or holding them back with low expectations. This leads me to one word that I hear so often in education. The word is "can't." What happens when we use this word? What is the power? Deflation, negligence, recklessness? Student devastation?

I believe that when we use the word "can't", it automatically puts a stop to ALL possibilities, and it puts an end to forward progress. It is one thing when a student says, "I can't," but it is a whole other-more powerful thing when educators say that their students "can't." This is the polar opposite thinking of a data-rich, strategically planned teacher. The "I can't" thinking teachers go around chanting phrases, "But my kids can't... focus, understand, do the work, figure it out, use this, pay attention... etc.

Do you really think a teacher who uses phrases like this professionally knows their students? Phrases like that do not demonstrate a deep understanding of a student's home life, social emotional well-being, learning aptitudes, dreams, goals, strategic individualized instruction nor preferences. Who are we to decide what our students are not capable of doing? By making that decision for them, we take away their power of possibility. Our students have already had many doors closed on them before they even walk in through ours, so let us not be another door-closer on their self-esteem and strategic academic progress.

The Remedy

So how do we remedy this? We can reframe our thinking. Rather than focus on what we perceive students cannot do, we should take a strengths-based approach. We must shift our focus on figuring out what they can do and use students' strengths as the starting point to move them forward. We will never truly know what our students are capable of unless we provide opportunities for success, growth and dreaming big. It is our job to know what is going on inside their brains by giving them a voice. We are not mind readers, so how do we make thinking visible? We listen. Really listen. We start conversations. We make intentional connections in building a trusting relationship. We need to know them to grow them. To do this, we need to be intentional with our *time* with students, our *talks* with students, our planning for students and our *tasks* with students. We need to make students' thinking visible and audible, not only to us, but to help facilitate this with their peers. Then and only then, can we help them unlock their own learning and their own potential.

I would like to offer one way to stop harming kids, unintentionally: think before you speak or act. Our circle of influence over students is massive and our actions can carry unintentional consequences. So, when we do fall into this trap, notice it and rectify it. It is through reflection that we can build award winning teachers. Students deserve us at our best.

Cori Orlando is an instructional services specialist, co-moderator of #SVTChat and founder of Leading in Limbo. www.leadinginlimbo.com.

Stop Believing Some Students Cannot Learn

HAL ROBERTS

"There is no such thing as a lazy student or a student who cannot learn." This statement can evoke an internal response of either agreement or disagreement based on what we see or don't see happening. There are always two classrooms in your room; the visible and the invisible. The visible classroom is the most obvious because you can actively see students writing, note-taking, talking, designing, taking a test and/or creating a product. The visible classroom is actively engaged in learning and if we do not "see" something happening, we think students are lazy or they cannot learn.

The invisible classroom is covertly learning so it is hard to know what is going on in a student's mind. It may be hard to know what students are thinking when their behaviors involve relationships, emotions, or negative behaviors. Often, the invisible classroom can appear to be and environment of distractions or disruptions to learning. When this happens, hidden emotional, relational, and neurological factors come into play and wield a powerful influence on what will be learned. Invisible classroom behaviors involve neurological human connections that create the contexts for teaching, learning, and living. Emphatically, the invisible classroom holds the most power.

What I have learned from neuroscience is that when a student is engaged in a relevant lesson, learning will occur. In other words, any student can learn, but they might not choose to learn for so many different reasons. Neuroscience shares that encountering new information, especially during the act of reading and learning, the human brain is searching to make connections (patterns) to what is personal, relevant, and meaningful. This is what we all call schema. The human brain seeks to connect new learning and experiences to what they already know. This is how we as humans make meaning to store in long-term memory. The students in your invisible classroom are always unconsciously engaging in a cultural frame of reference. These are the unspoken interactions that determine how students will construct their own relevance and meaning.

Unlocking Invisibility

To unlock the students within the invisible classroom, teachers must intentionally consider getting to know each student's cultural frame of reference. This may involve recognizing socio-economic status, gender, hobbies, ethnicity, religion and so many other factors. Have one-on-one conversations, utilize personality quizzes, create social contracts, and invest in fireside chats and community building activities. Any time you can connect with students' frame of reference it becomes a catalyst that activates connected learning. To inspire meaningful change, you must make a connection to the heart BEFORE you make a connection to the mind. Then, we can dismiss laziness or the lack of capacity to learn as the root causes of students' problems.

Lean Mean Searching Machine

The brain is a lean, mean searching machine. It searches for four things continually: patterns, pleasure, people (relationships) and prediction. If you can get your students to satisfy all the 'Ps' then you can hook and engage your students to the targeted learning. When learning is associated with pleasure, dopamine is released. This surge increases focus, helping the brain stay attentive or engaged. To get learning to stick, classroom instruction must be relevant to the student (the P's) and relevant to the content. You may want to consider sharing the end of unit standards and involve students in the initial teacher lesson plans. Co-construct, co-plan and then add all the strategic planning behind their ideas. Give students choices and connect to their emotions. Share how you felt as a student once upon a time.

Giving Hope, Not Labeling Them

Some of our students are hemorrhaging hope! I believe that ultimately it is our job to kindle hope. We should strive to change the odds to change our students' trajectories in a positive upward path. We must be merchants of hope! We should strive to make hope building pervasive for every student, every day, and in every period. We also know that if we plant hope, ambition and success will grow. If we plant grit, a person of commitment will grow. If we plant honesty, integrity will be harvested. So, you see, what we plant daily is of utmost importance. It is the investment of enhancing our students' lives that we must commit to a daily mission. We must be intentional every day because every instructional minute matters. The 2017 Student Gallup Poll says this about hope:

> *Hopeful students are 2.8x more likely to say they get better grades than their discouraged peers. Hope: The ideas and energy students have for the future. Hope has also been linked to student success in school. Hopeful students are positive about the future, goal-oriented and can overcome obstacles in the learning process, enabling them to navigate a pathway to achieve their goals. Gallup measures three constructs (hope, engagement and well-being). Gallup measures these three because their research shows these metrics account for one-third of the variance of student success. Yet schools do not measure these*

things. Hope is a better predictor of student success than SAT scores, ACT scores, and grade point average.

Among the 808,521 2017 Gallup Student Poll participants, 38% STRONGLY AGREE that the adults at school care about them. Of students who participated in 2017, 4 in 10 students STRONGLY AGREE they feel safe in their school!

We must connect with the soul of each student before we can move into improving performance. The only way to heal the soul is through intentional relationships and authentic love and if there is not a desire to give loving hope, you will only invisibly guess that students just don't care much about anything when it really is your failure to go deep into the waters of getting through to every student.

Hal Roberts is a retired school superintendent after serving 38 years in education. His book, Make Waves! Was released in October 2019. Hal speaks on leadership, neuroscience, and lesson design. He is now leading a team to create a faith-based school for kids whose parents are incarcerated.

Stop Listening to what Previous Teachers Said about a Student

ALICIA RAY

"Can I see your class list? (Pauses while reading.) You have her? She was in my class last year. I had to stand right beside her desk to get her to complete her morning math. She was barely reading on grade level at the end of the year. She blurted answers without raising her hand and absolutely would not walk down the hall; it was either skipping, jogging, or impersonating a dinosaur. And let me tell you about an incident on the bus…"

That is Someone's Child

Wait a minute! That's my daughter you're talking about! Seriously. Her Kindergarten teacher could have easily said every single one of those things about my own daughter (including the impersonation of dinosaurs). Her first-grade teacher could have taken every single one of those things to heart and, as a result, may not have given my child a fighting chance at a great year.

During the summer between kindergarten and first grade, we went to our family physician for a well-child appointment who referred us to a pediatric psychiatrist. After some discussion, observation and a Vanderbilt rating scale, our daughter was diagnosed with Attention-Deficit/Hyperactivity Disorder (ADHD). We chose to try medication and found that the right dosage worked wonders for her! In first grade, she completed most of her morning math as she was not as easily distracted by the morning buzz of activity. Books held her focus long enough to allow her to sound out words and comprehend what she read. Her impulses to blurt out answers in class and run down the hallways were better controlled. Once we got home, the dinosaur impressions lived on, though.

My daughter's teachers are incredible educators. Both went above and beyond to support their students. Both would have had vastly different descriptions of my daughter as a student at the end of their respective years, however. It is absolutely not fair to my child or any other student to have to be the subject of discussion about what a previous teacher says. Thankfully, neither of her teachers took part in the scenario described above, but sadly, terribly similar conversations are happening in education everywhere. It needs to stop.

Placing Undue Pressure on High Performing Students

This rule does not just apply to situations like the one above. It also applies to the, "Oh, you'll love them; they are such a smart student!" conversations. What is the worst that can happen, right? That student sits in class all year not receiving the help they need with concepts they do not understand because they are the "smart" student. They have heard that they are the "smart" student which puts additional pressures on them to perform. Perhaps they do not ask questions because they are not comfortable showing their misunderstandings. They see the doubt on a teacher's face when their grades begin to drop.

I know this happens because I was that kid. I excelled in math until they put letters into equations. I was a "gifted" student in an advanced math class, and I was told, "Oh, you'll get it; just keep trying." No! I needed a teacher to sit down beside me and walk me through the steps in the same way they did with the girl in the other group. Thankfully, I had a teacher who was willing to put in the work with me and I was able to excel in math again. Yet, the shake in my confidence remained with me for years.

Things Change from Year to Year

Circumstances change, family dynamics may change and nothing is guaranteed for either a student or a teacher from one year to the next. The student who leaves one teacher's classroom at the end of the year is not the same student who joins the next teacher's classroom. No two years are alike. No two teachers are alike. No two classroom cultures are alike. We are all human; personalities can clash. Tolerance levels for behaviors and rules/norms that are non-negotiable vary from room to room. Teachers can have subjective views of our students. When we share our subjective views, we limit what a student can accomplish with a new teacher and a new year. Every year presents a new opportunity for students to redefine themselves. Let us give them a chance to do just that!

Stop listening to what other teachers say about a child. Better yet, let's agree to stop talking about our former students unless it is to encourage and uplift them! When a previous teacher wants to share objectively what worked in support of a former student, I listen. If it's a subjective summary of that child's experience, it's nothing more than gossip. It is a waste of valuable time. If a discussion is not going to directly lead to the success of that student, it doesn't need to be said or heard.

Alicia Ray is a veteran educator from North Carolina. She has taught PreK-8th grade students and currently serves as a digital learning coach and media coordinator in a STEM magnet middle school. She is the author of Educational Eye Exam: Creating Your Vision for Education.

Stop Listening to Colleagues Who Mock Student Work
PAMELA HALL

Let's take Alicia's chapter one step further and talk about student work and take a stand, together.

"If we don't fight hard enough for the things we stand for, at some point we have to recognize that we don't really stand for them."
–Paul Wellstone

"Beauty is in the eye of the beholder." The trouble is sometimes trusted teachers, adults and role models display dissatisfaction toward beauty. It is deflating and disheartening.

Some Call it Scribbling, I Call it Art

One day after school, a colleague came to my room waving around one of her student's pieces of work. It was what some people call art, but most call scribbles. My colleague was erring on the side of scribbles. She indignantly said, "Look at this illustration." I replied, "Well, at least she used paper. It's not on the floor, her desk, or her body." She rolled her eyes in utter disgust.

The student's illustration was for a class book that my colleague thought was sure to ruin the entire book if her illustration was included. My colleague's world was so rocked by this alleged bad illustration (by a six-year-old), that she went on to notify the six-year-old's mom.

My colleague droned on and on about how she couldn't believe the student's mom was going to purchase the book with, pointing to the student's illustration, "This garbage in it." She went on to say, "I warned her mom about it, so she'd know." But, the mother replied, "It's colorful." Siding with the student's mom, I said, "I agree. It's colorful." My colleague stomped off.

Some Teachers Get It While Other Teachers Don't

It was a beautiful masterpiece created by a six-year-old. It disturbed me to think about how my colleague's discontented attitude affected her precious student. I defended the six-year-old incredulously trying to find the reason my colleague would have been so upset by an illustration when it's our job to bring out the best in all students. Be the teacher who GETS IT and stop listening to those who don't! Beauty is subjective. Who are we to judge? We might be looking at the next Picasso, Rembrandt, or Michelangelo.

Imagine what life would be like if Albert Einstein's mom believed his teachers. Humanity would look a lot different. We'd miss what he's best known for: his theory of relativity which holds that measurements of space and time vary according to conditions such as the state of motion. We'd miss his formula E = mc2, which has been dubbed "the world's most famous equation." We would miss the Pythagorean Theorem he discovered at age 12. We would miss his life changing contributions to physics and science. Einstein, a brilliant mathematician, was labeled "slow" by his teachers. They said he couldn't do math. They were right, he couldn't do THEIR math. Thankfully, his mother saw his inner beauty. His potential. She stood up for him, removing him from school and bringing him home to educate. Later in life, Einstein coined a truism: "Everybody is a genius. But if you judge a fish by its ability to climb a tree, it will live its whole life believing that it's stupid." His mother saved him from the label of stupidity. She put the fish in water instead of forcing it to climb a tree.

Don't Let it Just Go, Defend Their Honor

Educators and caregivers must defend students' work being condemned by colleagues or others. We must defend students' gifts and talents and steer them toward the appropriate habitat which fosters growth and achievement. If we don't, everybody loses. What if you allow the future cancer cure inventor to be berated and they give up? They stop dreaming, trying and doing. Instead, stop colleagues and others who belittle and berate. Stand up for students. Help all students believe in themselves instead of judging their deficits. Amplify potential. Water what looks weird to most and lead them to the right habitat for growth, and they'll believe they're smart. They will achieve. It's the responsibility of every educator and caregiver to defend and nurture students' beauty: gifts, talents, and character.

Stop injustice.   Stop belittling.   Stop comparing.

Then and only then will every stakeholder see all students' abilities. Benjamin Franklin eloquently penned in Poor Richard's Almanac: "Beauty...is supported by opinion." Stand firm for all students. Steer your opinion toward their potential. Defend and empower their current and future beauty. You're the beholder.

Pamela Hall, a multi-national award-winning educator, is a speaker and author dedicated to helping educators consciously connect with and grow all learners. She helps educators go from the brink of burn-out to being STRONG and inspires thousands of students and educators all over the world.

Stop Blaming Poverty & Families
REBECCA CODA

Stop blaming student home life for their lack of success. There are times when we are humble enough to learn and open enough to embrace to new ideas. Other times, lessons slap us upside the face whether we like it or not. And sometimes, just sometimes, profound shifts happen through serendipity. These are the moments that stop us dead in our tracks, palm to the forehead style, and grow from it.

I experienced a palm to forehead moment shortly after the book *Let Them Speak* was first released. While on social media platforms I was grateful that so many educators were vocally advocating for student voice. I was new to authorship and consulting, but I felt I was serving my purpose. It was fulfilling to engage with such passionate educators from around the world. One day I received a social media message from Dr. Erin Lynn Raab. She earned her Ph.D. from Stanford, had founded a library and education center in South Africa as a Rotary Ambassadorial Fellow and co-founded REENVISION*ED* here in the United States. She reached out as a fellow social justice warrior seeking to transform education through student voice. Dr. Raab wanted to explore how our work was connected and how we could support one another through student voice advocacy. I was star struck to say the least. After the initial niceties of getting to know one another over the phone, she paused for a time and then asked me,

"So, what would you say is the purpose of school?"

I thought for a moment and then rambled on explaining that students should succeed academically and create a future with a thriving career to support the community. That was the mark to hit. I hadn't ever been asked that question before. As soon as I inhaled after my long winded answer, I had the feeling that I had profoundly missed the mark.

Gracefully she replied with a question, "What do you think it means to live a good life?"

She shared with me the interviews and videos she had created asking hundreds of students, parents, and educators that very question, and notably (her dissertation was titled, Why School?: A Systems Perspective on Creating Schooling for Human Flourishing & Thriving Democracy). As she shared the student responses and outcomes my wheels were spinning. I soaked up every ounce of wisdom she had to share. Little did I know that one phone call would, forever, establish a paradigm shift in my thinking. Palm to the forehead. Growth incoming.

I realized that for my entire career I had been placing my perspective, my expectations, my state and districts expectations and my version of end-outcomes on my students and their families. I knew that I had to change how I interacted with students and families so that I could intentionally get to know their version of a good life, their version of happiness and their mark of success. After all, it is their life to live after graduation, not mine. I learned this principle from the resources on REENVISIONED and through collaboration with Dr. Erin Raab. When young people interview one another and adults in their lives, learn to qualitatively code these interviews, and develop a shared vision for their classrooms and communities, happiness and success occurs. If students were to truly succeed, it was up to me to seek answers to these questions. I rolled up my sleeves and was on a mission to seek out these answers.

Families Want Their Students to Live a Good Life

The greatest partnership we can ever invest in is our families. When we stop viewing our students of poverty as unhappy or unmotivated or inept (and thus unsuccessful), then, and only then, can we begin to define their version of success. Teaching is about facilitating a learning pathway that leads students to THEIR version of a good life, THEIR version of success and THEIR future. This begins with highly intentional relationship building, incorporated into the way we facilitate learning. How many times have you asked one of your family members this question: "When you close your eyes and see your child ten years from now, and they are successful, happy and living a good life, what does that look like and sound like to you?" Asking every family this one question will set you up for individualizing a mutual definition of success. This one question makes it personal, attainable and meaningful. When students and families paint the picture of success for us (and not the other way around) and we work with them to meet their version of a good life, it breathes purpose, partnership and strengths-based success. And believe it or not, it gives purpose and meaning to the expectations of our state and district-wide student achievement goals. I am grateful for the likeminded collaboration and similar visions that Dr. Erin Raab and I had surrounding our purpose in supporting all students to live a good life. The greatest gift we can give, as educators, is understanding our families' versions of a good life and co-creating a plan of success, together.

Families Send Us Their Very Best

The most profound perception that we must hold, as educators, is understanding the value of students and their families. I vividly remember Salome Thomas-El during a small breakfast pre-session at the 2019 ASCD conference in Chicago. I had a cantaloupe chunk on the end of my fork and as I went to take a bite, he approached my side of the room, using proximity, and he pointed and looked me square in the eyes and said, "Families send us their best. Family members don't get up and put their children on the bus and say, "I'm sending the dumb one to school today and I'm keeping all the smart one's home. Heaven forbid, when they get up every morning, they send us their absolute best." I gulped and wiped the corners of my mouth and sat up tall. He had my full attention. Once more, I was put in my place and I knew that I must intentionally ensure that every one of our families know that it is an honor to teach their child.

Salome Thomas-El is a principal of an inner-city school of poverty and he doesn't make excuses, he doesn't lower expectations, but he does ensure that students and families know that we are grateful for the honor of teaching their children. It is a partnership to distinguish success and we should do everything within our power serve their absolute best. Regardless of poverty or circumstance, we have the power to provide award winning educational learning experiences. Students are worthy of me appreciating their backgrounds. Students are worthy of positive relationships that are laced with mutual and high academic expectations. Students are worthy of us adapting to their version of a happy life.

Families are the CEO of Their Student

One of the greatest pieces of advice I had ever received as a parent of special needs children was that I am the "CEO" of my children. I remember having to use my family advocacy group to attend an IEP meeting because I hadn't felt heard by the special education team. Right before the meeting, my community agency advocate looked me in the eyes and said, "You will always be the CEO of your child. Nobody knows your children better than you and just as any healthy thriving company is run, you must schedule regular team meetings and establish checks and balances. Just because you may think things are going well does not mean that we don't check in. As educators, we cannot use any excuse regarding families, poverty, culture, or the background of our students as an excuse. There is no practitioner, assessment, medical professional, or previous teacher that knows our children better than their families. Families experience students' first steps, first words, likes and dislikes, happiest moments, saddest moments and how they respond to every scenario in life. Whether our students' upbringing or lifestyle matches our version of a good life, it doesn't matter. What matters is that we respect our families enough to rely on them for advice and to voice what is working and not working at school. Academic success begins when we are open to growth, reflective enough to listen and convicted enough to change to adapt our interactions to students and their life experiences. Five-star award winning classrooms are developed when we truly listen and intentionally engage in relevant conversations with families and students about their version of a happy life. This is where sustainable community happiness and success is born.

Rebecca Coda is the co-founder of Pushing Boundaries Consulting, LLC, founding publisher for Encodable Impact, LLC in New Orleans, author, speaker and a faith-based ambassador of hope.

Stop Calling Families with Only Bad News

TERI M. PREISLER, Ed.D.

[Four weeks into the school year scenario.]

[Phone rings/buzzes: Parent answers phone.]

"Hello?"

"Hello, Mr. Davis?"

"Yes, this is Anthony Davis."

"Hello Mr. Davis. This is Kelly Lawrence, Dakota's 6th grade teacher. I'm calling to make you aware of Dakota's (disrespectful behavior) (failing grades) (lack of paying attention)." The list could go on and on.

[Long pause.]

"I knew I shouldn't have answered the phone," Mr. Davis thought to himself.

[Call ends.]

In a frustrated tone, Mr. Davis says to himself (or other parents) (or his spouse) (or a random acquaintance to the school), "Why can't anyone ever say anything good about my kid? I'm so sick of everyone only seeing the negative. I'm done with these teachers and this school."

Imagine yourself as the parent in this scenario. How would you feel if this was the first direct contact that you received from your child's teacher? Now imagine that this is the typical type of direct contact you receive from your child's teachers year after year. Call after call.

Build on Strengths Not Rap Sheets

Perspective, empathy, and strategic communications matter, especially in bridging home to school partnerships. Let us look at this concept in another context: I doubt that you would want a parent or guardian ONLY calling you with bad-news-only situations. Or, let's look at it in an even more personalized context: How do you feel about administrative evaluations that are only focused on areas that you need to improve upon? How do you feel when the post-observation conversation is merely deficit-based? Can you imagine how defeated you would feel if you only ever received a rap sheet year after year? Nobody could thrive in that type of toxic fixed mindset environment. Not one of these scenarios sends a message of a strengths-based positive partnership for growth for the student or for you as an educator.

The only thing worse than ONLY calling with bad news about student behavior, academics, attendance, or any other student related topic, is to not call at all. When families do not receive any communication (especially no positive communication), this establishes a nearly irreparable partnership of success. Families must be viewed as the driving force in a partnership of strengths-based focus on success. Nobody will win if you become the foe.

A Garden of Success

Let's be brutally honest: partnerships take time and require planning and intentionality. Intentional positive interactions build a foundation for success. Another truth is that teachers must take the first steps in activating these positive relationships right from the beginning. The good news is that even before a new school year begins, you can be proactive and act. Postcards, positive phone calls (with the intent of learning one thing about each student), videoconferencing (to share your favorite pet or hobbies you like to do-and vice versa) can work wonders. This is the good stuff, the human stuff, the common denominator that builds community. These positive interactions are the seeds of thriving partnerships that will come into full bloom. Your (classroom) garden of success will take root and reach for the sky as each relationship is nurtured, given nutrients, and watered in just the right dose. Growth is inevitable with positive strength-based interactions.

They are Children First

The only reason there's a connection between a teacher and families is because of their child. I intentionally use the word child instead of student. Upon birth, families fell in love with their child whether biological or not, and certainly didn't view this tiny person as a student. They see birthdays and milestones, friends and neighbors, graduations and happiness. When teachers come at families with a compliance-based mindset focused on standardized tests, the relationship is over before it even begins. We must believe and act like they are someone's child and our future.

Four Ways to Make it Positive

Here are four simple ways to improve your partnership building with parents:

1. Be proactive and make a positive call early in the school year. That's it. Carve time into your schedule to call parents early in the school year and make a deposit in the positive "relational bank account" with no reference to 'but' or 'and just to make you aware' statements. Don't settle for the "I don't have time" excuse.

2. Change your mindset from, "I don't have enough time to make positive calls to all of my parents", to, "I'm determined to cultivate and nurture partnerships, one parent at a time." You will either make time in a proactive, productive positive action now, or you'll have no choice but to spend time later in a reactive, repair-focused loop of despair. Hopefully, the latter situation is even still repairable. Another option is to, at least, make positive phone calls to some of your parents and use a different mode of communication for positive contact to all when possible.

3. Start the school year by introducing yourself to parents, directly, not just at the back-to-school year open house. These personal introductions can be done through email, letters through the mail, or use of the student management communication system. Let parents know who you are as a person, that you care about their children and that you are accessible and receptive. Better yet, include a short survey to honor them in this partnership and ask parents to let you know about their child's interests, school experiences and how they would like to be contacted. We need to stop assuming that parents just know that teachers want to partner with them.

4. When it is inevitable that there is no getting around a "bad news" call, stop putting it off. When a situation has occurred, make the call, not an email or student management system notification. Make the call and lead the discussion with strengths, first. Delay only compounds the crisis. Make the call to the parent before the child does. Give yourself the opportunity to provide the full information before emotions start to evolve with the possibility of a slanted version. Plus, even with "bad news" situations, this is still an opportunity, to begin and end the conversation with positives. Let's consider an alternate version of the phone call that was used at the beginning of this chapter:

Take Two: [Four weeks into school year.]

[Phone rings/buzzes.]

"Hello?"

"Hello, Mr. Davis?"

"Yes, this is Anthony Davis."

"Hello Mr. Davis. This is Kelly Lawrence, Dakota's 6th grade teacher. I hope the start of the school year has been a positive one for Dakota and your family. I'm just calling to let you know how much I enjoy having Dakota in our class." (Continues to share some positive things.)

[*Short pause*]

"Really? Is that the only reason you're calling? Is there a 'but' coming in this call? Like Dakota's great to have in class but …."

"No, Mr. Davis. It's important to me that our parents know how much their children are valued and cared for and that I'm honored to be his teacher."

"This is the first time I've ever received a call like this. Thank you! If there is ever an issue involving Dakota, please let me know and I will work with you to make things better."

Now, you've set the stage for an award winning classroom and possibly one of your best years yet.

Dr. Teri Preisler served as a teacher, principal and superintendent in Minnesota preK-12 public schools for over 30 years. She is currently an Assistant Professor in K-12 Secondary Programs in the College of Education at Minnesota State University, Mankato. She is a firm believer in: "Every Student Every Day."

Stop Speed-Reading Student IEP's
REBECCA ZIEGLER RUPNICK

Learning is a progression not a grade in the gradebook, a reading level, or a grade level. We teach students, not content. No two learners are alike and our instructional and academic materials cannot be identical for all students. Students do not learn in the same way or on the same day. Yes, you signed up for this job, you have a heart for students and, no, you may not have realized that it is a LOT of work to keep up with every student, especially in regard to the legality of an IEP, but the reality is that it is still your job to meet the needs of all learners.

IEPs are Not an Option

There is no doubt that the meetings and paperwork are precise and time intensive. It requires a practitioner skillset and a lot of attention. Whether it comes naturally or not, we are obligated to know and follow through with this legally binding document. Implementing and adhering to an IEP is bound by a court of law, so stop speed-reading it. Your title might not be that of a special education teacher, but you better believe it is your moral, ethical and legal duty to implement the individual accommodations and modifications required by any student that you serve. Speed-reading is unacceptable and dishonorable to the students being served under these IEPs. It's cheating if you don't. It's complicated if you do. But it is impossible to succeed if you don't learn. Set up time at the beginning of each year, to read each child's IEP. Read the entire document, not just the section that correlates to the class you teach. Take notes. Highlight. Note questions. Create charts and spreadsheets that are filled with anecdotal information about how the IEP should be applied to your classroom. Keep this document in your lesson plan and take it into consideration for all planning. Read these notes often and in depth. Whatever you do, don't speed-read.

If You Don't Understand, Just Ask

Doing what's right matters, so you may want to set up meetings with the special education team so that you have a full and concrete understanding of each of your students' IEPs. Your special education team may or may not be proactive or thorough. Take the initiative and reach out and schedule a meeting with your IEP lead teacher. IEPs are living, breathing documents not to be tucked away in a file or in a cabinet never to be seen again. They are working documents that deserve your time, your expertise and your understanding. Students with IEPs and their families are counting on you and the merit of your time. Ask for help instead of shirking your professional and legal duties.

Parents Are Biased

My own daughter has an IEP. Does this make me biased about this chapter? ABSOLUTELY! 100%. But it also pushes me further to make this chapter cut and clear. Families are often biased toward their child. They see hope, they see a thriving future and they see success, not disabilities. I am an educator, but I am also honored to wear the title of a mother of a child with special needs. I am privileged to parent a child who is so astonishing, brave and determined that I would never let anything stand in her way of academic success. She is my driving force for writing this STOP chapter.

Have you considered how families feel when their child's IEP is not followed? I do. Do you know the feeling when you learn your child could not participate in a classroom activity because accommodations were not planned? I do. Do you know the feeling when your child comes home in tears because they were left out at school? I do. Do you know the feeling when your child was ostracized and treated unfairly at school? I do. Trust me here, you don't want to feel these feelings let alone cause these feelings. They are gut-wrenching, heartbreaking and soul crushing. As a parent-educator, I am particularly sensitive to fully carrying out IEPs, so I put systems in place to ensure that it never happens on my watch. I verify that every activity and instructional methodology is clearly aligned to the accommodations and modifications on each and every one of my students' IEPs.

Avoid Fury

The one thing you won't ever want to face is a furious family that knows the law and legally catches you dodging their child's IEP. Imagine an angry family member furiously emailing the special education team while carbon copying the director of special education and school principal questioning and demanding the lawful implementation of their plan. Yes, there may be families that are complainers or who demand perfection, and then there's the well-versed family so focused on equity that they will not let anything get in their child's way of an individualized and equitable educational experience. It is our professional obligation to have deep understanding of EVERY students' IEP, even if it feels daunting.

Families of children with special needs hold unique circumstances. I guarantee you will encounter a parent just like me throughout your teaching career. Don't fear us because we are here as a reminder: do your legally obligated job. Stop speed-reading student IEPs. Give students with IEPs everything they need, everything they fought for and watch them flourish and develop into powerful, brilliant future leaders of the world.

Rebecca Ziegler Rupnick is a middle school language arts coordinator and teacher in the suburbs of Chicago who is passionate about student voice and student advocacy. She is currently working on her dissertation dealing with providing EL students with corrective feedback and repair.

Stop Having Parent Conferences without the Student Present
JULIE WOODARD

Imagine it is time to go over your mid-year teacher evaluation and your boss schedules a meeting with your mother or father, or even your spouse to go over your teacher evaluation form. "Hi Mr. Woodard, I'd like to go over Julie's teacher evaluation form. Her lessons are well-planned, and her learning targets are spot on. She works well with her grade level team; she integrates technology with her students which is so engaging. But one thing we would like her to work on is her depth of questioning throughout the lesson. What do you think her goal should be and how can we partner together to help her grow?" What? Are you kidding me? You may think this is a completely absurd scenario because it is a completely absurd practice!

Seriously, how would you feel to learn that the most important people in your life were gathered around a table (or collaborated on a video conference visit or on the phone) and all they talked about was you? And to top it off, you were never even invited to this behind your back closed-door discussion! I can't imagine any educator comfortable with their spouse and boss addressing their issues, challenges, struggles, emotional battles and then how best to deal with them. And all the while you aren't even in the conversation. This concept is pure madness when we take it out of the context of school. Unfortunately, this is exactly what we do to our students. As teachers, we must stop having parent conferences without the student present. Just stop.

Students in the Driver's Seat

Can you imagine your spouse and boss developing your improvement plan and deciding when you will read, what you will read, how long you will spend lesson planning and with whom to plan? Who knows the most about how you learn, and how you study, and what motivates you to be successful and what distracts you from your plan? I bet it is YOU. Students know themselves, too. Even at a very young age, students understand where they are most comfortable sitting to read or write, what lighting helps them to focus, or even what snack is great for a study session. Planning, preparing and hosting conferences with students in the driver's seat leading the discussions, is significant.

Ownership

Student-driven classrooms begin with ownership. Students are ultimately responsible for work quality, their engagement with learning and their own classroom and school behaviors. When we make students the leaders of parent conferences, then families and educators become the support system supporting student happiness in learning. Imagine a NASCAR race where students are the drivers and we become the pit crew willing to support in any way possible. This pit-crew-team-mentality places ownership in the hands of students so that they can meet their personal goals or reach classroom expectations. If we are to meet our targets and objectives that were written for or designed by us, educators, wouldn't it make sense to also include students in the planning picture? A NASCAR driver certainly wants to give input into the design. I don't know any colleague who enjoys their supervisor sending a SMART goal without their input and consideration.

Students succeed when they have a voice in setting the expectations on how to achieve them. Student-led conferences don't just happen on their own. It requires knowing your students ahead of time, having all the information that will be shared and providing a protocol or sequence for the conference. When the driver meets with the pit crew to debrief the race, they still need a checklist to go over. The student needs to know the post-race checklist (topics and information) that will be presented in their conference about their learning. Ownership leads to empowerment and empowerment leads to more wins.

Imagine a pre-planned student-led conference that sounded like this, "Theo, thank you for sharing your current reading levels with your family and me. What are some ways we can help you meet your goal of improving your comprehension? I know you came up with some great ideas when we were planning for your conference. What is your plan to increase your reading proficiency by mid-term? How do you think we should break this apart to make our end goal attainable?" This pit crew approach to goal setting and success gives students full ownership over their learning.

Planning for Success

Does preparing for student conferences with the expectation that the student participates look different in the planning phase? Of course. Student age also plays a role. We cannot expect every student to be able to articulate what is on their minds, but we should try to guide them to do their best.

I meet this challenge in one of several ways. Using an app or online digital survey, I am able to schedule conferences at a time selected by the families that works best for them. I like to ask some simple questions on my survey, such as: What time slot on the date list is best for you? Would you prefer in-person, video conference, or a phone conference? By utilizing a digital scheduling app or tool it will handily set up a digital organization structure for incoming responses with labeled categories and time-stamps for family responses. This makes for a nicely organized method of meeting with both your student and their parent or guardian at the same time, a time-slot they chose.

I know I don't like when people talk about me behind my back or when I'm not in the conversation. We should not be talking about students without ever including them either. Plan to include students. Plan to provide ownership. Plan to improve communication and build trust. Plan your conferences as student conferences, not family conferences.

Julie Woodard is an award-winning educator, artist, speaker and affiliate consultant with Pushing Boundaries Consulting, LLC. She also designs art for authors and speakers.

Stop Comparing Students to their Brothers and Sisters
BRYAN MCDONALD, Ed.D.

Families of more than one child fully understand and appreciate that no two kids are alike. One child may act coy and shy while the other one is vivacious overflowing with a bubbly personality. One may be active and the other passive. One has the attention span to sit while you read a countless number of books and the other you barely get through the first few pages and they are squirming to get away. Families fully understand these differences. And, boy, do teachers understand the difference too!

They are Not a Younger Version of Their Older Sibling

When teachers see a similar last name to that of a former student, why do they start associating characteristics of the younger sibling? Typically, teachers either become enthralled because the sibling was a dynamo student in the class, or they roll their eyes in irritation because they can't believe they have to deal with "another one" from "that family." It happens. Just because the older sister loves science does not mean that the younger sister loves science. The incoming student may hate science and when we assume connections about them, without any real justification, we increase the possibility that they may dislike science even more. Students walk into our classrooms as individuals, as unique people, who are like no other. Incoming brothers and sisters are not a younger version of their older sibling. They have their own likes and dislikes. Every student possesses their own strengths and areas where they are challenged. We must stop comparing children from the same home to one another. When we connect academic achievement or behaviors from one sibling to another based on the academic achievement or behaviors of another sibling, we are flat out wrong.

Why Do We Set Expectations Based on a Last Name?

Below are, what may be the most common examples of how we tie expectation from one sibling to another.

Sloan Farnsworth

Regina Farnsworth is a great reader. When she was in 6th grade, she tested at a post-high school level on the reading assessment given to the students each year. Regina would have 3-4 different books in her backpack that she was reading at any given time. Any free moment that she had, she was with book in hand, and she was always reading. She often took a book out to recess to finish it when she was near the end of a story. Her teachers always commented in family conferences about how good of a reader Regina was and how impressed they were with her vocabulary. They talked about how her writing was exceptional too because of that extensive vocabulary.

Regina's sister Sloan was not a reader. As a matter of fact, she would rather do 100 other things than read. Yet every year she would hear the same thing repeatedly. "Oh, you're Regina's sister. I have some books you will love reading." Sloan went home day after day hating reading even more. She was reading at grade level, but not at a post-high school level like her sister. Teachers did not say it, but Sloan read their actions as if they were disappointed in her for not being like her older sister. Many tried to kindle the fire like her sister had but it never did work. Sloan would rather have gone outside running around than reading a book. She would rather have been doing hands on experiments in science or using manipulatives in math. Sloan's teachers did not catch on nor recognize her strengths because they made an unfair connection to Regina. Later in the year, Sloan's teachers realized that, as a student, she was not like Regina at all. All those months went by while Sloan was frustrated and even angry with her teachers. By the time the teachers recognized Sloan's strengths and vast from her sister, the relationship was already doomed–all because of her last name.

Colin Blickham

Jacob Blickham was a holy terror. Every teacher who had him always dramatically noted that they have never had a student like him. Jacob was unable to even sit in his seat. He was loud. He did not do well in school. He was aggressive with other students and could not follow directions. The list went on and on. The teachers in the next grade level prayed that he didn't show up on their class list in the fall. Some teachers' even requested to teach in the grade level below so they didn't lose in the Jacob Blickham lottery.

Jacob had a younger brother named Colin. He was active. Colin struggled sitting in his seat, as well, but was not aggressive or rude and he consistently followed instructions. However, when teachers saw another Blickham show up on the roster, tears began to well up in their eyes. Jacob was such an exhausting challenge that they threw up their hands and declared that they would quit if they got Colin. Nobody wanted to have another year like the one they endured with Jacob. To prevent another catastrophic year, rules were put in place specifically for Colin because of anticipated behaviors. Colin's teachers started the year looking for things that Colin was doing wrong (anticipating he was just like his older brother) and they found them--not because Colin was like Jacob, but because the teachers were looking for any hint of misbehavior. Eventually, Colin rose to their expectation of negative behavior and became more aggressive. He stopped following instructions and started to become just like his brother. If his teachers had a strengths-based approach and tried to catch him being good, would he have morphed into a mini-Jacob? Of course not. Students rise to our perception and expectation of them. If they think they are the most special person in the world capable of any goal, that is what they will believe. Colin deserved a teacher that welcomed him as a scholar, fully capable of success.

Mark Franklin

Montel Franklin was a struggling student. However, he truly put forth the effort to get better each day. He wanted to be a strong reader but was struggling more than one year below grade level. In math, he struggled with basic computation and just could not remember multiplication facts or understand them conceptually. He had been tested for special services but never qualified. Teachers loved Montel because of his bright beaming attitude, big contagious smile and his athleticism. Montel's sister, Eleanor, who was a freshman, also struggled. Her reading was even lower than Montel's and in math she was still struggling with basic addition and subtraction. The following year, their brother Mark would be coming to the high school. Teachers were looking forward to having him in class because they were sure he would be so well behaved with an understanding that he would struggle in school academically. Just like his older brother and sister, the teacher anticipated needing to provide lots of support and, even then, knew he would most likely struggle. The low academic expectations were set before Mark even set foot on his high school campus.

During Mark's freshman year he received the following schedule: algebra, a lower-level ELA class and a basic science rather than advanced science class. At the dawn of the semester break, Mark's teachers were surprised that he was so accomplished in all his classes even though during the middle school transition meeting, they heard that Mark was successful in school. They just chose to not believe it. They knew the pattern, firsthand: Mark was the sibling of Montel and Eleanor and he was sure to follow suit. Mark had started the year in lower-level courses and this held him back from the possibility of taking the advanced classes he wanted to take before going to college. Their perception altered Marks's opportunity to take the upper-level math and science courses he was hoping to take in high school.

Do we really do this? Judge students on the performance or behavior of their siblings? I don't believe it's done intentionally but, I do believe it happens. It happens at all levels and it may get worse when we have had more than one sibling who is similar. We need to look at every student who walks into our classrooms as their own self. There are strengths and challenges for every student we teach. We MUST stop intentionally or unintentionally comparing students to their siblings.

Dr. Bryan McDonald is a retired teacher and administrator from Missouri. He is currently an Assistant Professor in the Educational Leadership Program at the University of Central Missouri.

Stop Boring Students at All Costs
LIVIA CHAN

I asked my teenage daughter, "What makes school boring?" Her response was, "Teachers. If you are a bad teacher, the class is guaranteed to be boring." How many times have you heard students say an activity or school overall is boring? Why do students find school boring? Is it the teachers alone? Is it partly the students because of disengagement or their mindset about learning? What exactly makes something *boring*? Why is it that some students find the same task boring while others see it as fun? Or maybe it somewhere in between boring and fun?

Boring is Worse Than Not Interesting

Boring is such a nebulous word that can be interpreted differently depending on perspective. Some understand boring as: unvaried, unstimulating, unoriginal, unimaginative, uneventful, and unexciting. If students are bored, then you may be the root cause (or part of it, at least). You are the teacher. You plan the lesson and the learning for the day. You possess the power to stop boredom and infuse curiosity, engagement, and empowerment. If you are willing to do whatever it takes to connect to students to make it interesting, your class is no longer boring! Although logical, it may sound easier than it is given that we are competing with technology, social media, and social emotional learning. Making your class interesting is about changing teacher practices and not demanding that students magically become responsible and self-driven learners.

Change Us Not Them

Sometimes teachers assign too many questions for the same concept, spend too long on mastered content, or use the same activities or organizers repeatedly. Classroom practices inadvertently become stale. Students no longer find stale classrooms interesting because they lack variety and novelty. The art and science of reading an audience and having the discernment to know when to infuse variety, when to connect socially or emotionally or when students simply need a brain break is crucial to our understanding of what boredom is. This art form can be compared to Goldilocks in a "just right" approach: Too little novel engagement and there's not enough practice; too many activities and it's seen as overdone or diluted in content.

Become an Original

The art and science of teaching not only requires planning for active student engagement where students have a voice, but teachers must also plan for accommodations for students who learn at different rates. This requires intentional planning for modified work and positive interactions. One of the easiest and novel ways to engage students in their own learning is to offer choice. Whether it is a list to choose from, or a tic-tac-toe board, students engage when they are interested. The science of teaching requires teachers to select low entry tasks with a high ceiling to provide every level of learner an entry point into learning. When offering choice, teachers must provide opportunities for every student to experience continual growth. There is always more than one way to teach the same thing. This is one of the beauties of professional learning communities. When teachers effectively share what works in content or grade level PLCs, someone inevitably has a novel idea, activity, or technique to share. The value of planning for a high ceiling is that it ensures our highest kids are not only interested, but also driving their own next level learning through creation and design. Once students demonstrate mastery, allow them to move on to something different or something deeper. Drill and kill isn't necessary. Highly effective learners should not be punished with more of the same work, (or even worse–just directed to go sit down and read a book) for being quick learners and for being quick finishers. When teachers respect effective students as learners, they give them a voice and provide novel ways to engage them in real world scenarios. They will respect you more as an original.

The Stretch Zone

When teachers lack intentionality or don't fully understand differentiation, they plan instruction that falls in a comfort zone and students are not leveraged to think or grow in their stretch zone. Comfort zones are referred by students as "too easy" and boring. The sad reality is that many classrooms across our nation are flat-out unstimulating! Effective teachers and leaders can feel the mediocre energy within seconds of entering a classroom. Students may be playing with erasers in their desk, staring at the ceiling, or walking around for no reason at all. The comfort zone is boring and disengaging and shortchanges student learning. Don't ever underestimate how the psyche of the brain in students, they love to be challenged. Productive struggle is healthy. Stop planning lessons that lack effective questioning, that lack student empowerment, that lack inquiry, or that lack multiple entry points because these classrooms simply do not "fire off" energy through the neuron synapses of the brain.

To become a master stretch zone planner, teachers must first get to know their students! Know their diagnostic academic strengths, interests, emotions, skills, and personal strengths as a whole child. Observe each individual student closely and use all the data you see and hear to inform you of how best to push them into their growth zone. Data systems and protocols can help you to strategically keep up with each individual student. Find your students' potential areas of growth and co-create dreams and goals. A partnership approach between teacher, families and student is where they learn best!

When Learning is Fun

I made a pledge to my class that every single day, they will do or learn something different or new. Some have said that this was what they looked forward to most as they returned to my class each day. They came to expect a one-of-a-kind classroom. A fun classroom requires a commitment to originality! When committed teachers catch themselves lacking novelty, they immediately shift gears to break the routine of boredom. To students, when every day looks and feels the same and there is nothing exciting for students to look forward to, it's like eating the same food every day, and that would get boring, wouldn't it?

Some days, teachers feel unimaginative. Sometimes, we have a deficiency of creativity and color within our lessons and assignments. We get tired, so our innovation sometimes goes out the window. We plan things that are dull, ordinary and uninspiring. When you lose your own excitement to teach, how do you expect your students to have fun? Should it surprise you if they disengage in learning because of sheer boredom?

Integrating Art and Creativity

Simply put, try to infuse the arts in your craft. The world of artistic development is renowned for bringing out creativity. Consider adding some drama, singing, dance, or the fine arts in your respective subject area. Have students act something out, write a song, create an interpretive dance, or draw a picture to demonstrate understanding. And better yet, ask your students how they learn best and what ideas they have to infuse art into the standards and objectives. Sometimes, their ideas are more meaningful than any activity you could come up with. Infusing art through student choice and voice will ignite different strengths and passions you may not have seen before! You will be blown away at the high level of learning and engagement as students lean into their stretch zones!

Students Are Social Learners

When classrooms are socially uneventful, they are boring. In the day-to-day grind of meeting the demands of curriculum and the scope-and-sequence of standards, it is easy to forget that students are social humans. Even introverts find joy in simply observing the socialization of education. Consider the most engaging days on your school calendar: they are the days when classrooms celebrate holidays or enjoy school-wide events; these are the days rarely seen as boring days! So why is it so much fun? Why are students so engaged? It's because students have significant opportunities to socially engage with choice, novelty, and fun learning! Having fun in the classroom shouldn't only take place on special days on the calendar. Unfortunately, the system has accepted independent assignments to overtake the fun in learning perhaps because the system expectation that requires individual assessments for grading purposes is a status quo structure that binds us. Where is the socialization and fun in worksheets, assignments and assessments? So how do we *naturally* add fun? Interactivity! Allow students to work in partners or small groups. Offer the choice to collaborate to learn together. You will find they learn it quicker and more efficiently when they have an opportunity to discuss and reflect on the content with others. Two heads are better than one and this automatically makes it more fun!

Gamify

Ironically, I've caught myself saying, "I am not a video game!" Even though I am not a video game my students relate to them. I like drawing a parallel between learning and video games by asking students what is required to master a game. This always seems to get their attention. I hear students say, "You gotta know the cheats, you have to master each one of the levels first, you have to work together with the other player." Once students are energized are fired up about the topic, I then make the connection to learning: "You gotta know the cheats (phonics rules), you have to master each level first (math fact fluency) and you have to work with the other players (classmates)." Somehow this analogy works like a charm every time, like flipping a switch and the lights come on. Connecting with student interests and trends, hooks even the most reluctant learner. Tweak your lesson and routinely ask yourself, "How can I turn the learning into a game or game connection?"

Why Should I Stop the Boredom?

Education is a fast-paced ever-changing profession that impacts all of society. When teaching is our passion and purpose, the scope of our job duties extend to the future of our real world. Boring classrooms do not lead to positive community transformations. Boring classrooms do not help students reach their potentials. Start by telling your students they will do something different or learn something new every day. Make a commitment to infuse more voice and choice, fun and collaboration. This can be done by making small changes in your planning for the day. You do not have to make big changes. In many cases, it's the small changes that last longer in your practice. These are small, simple things, but will make a world of a difference for our youth. If you ask yourself the following questions, remember this chapter for these reasons:

Too unvaried? Offer choice. Plan low floor, high ceiling assignments.

Too unstimulating? Discover your student's stretch zones and push them there.

Too unoriginal? Make it novel. Commit to newness.

Too unimaginative? Infuse the arts - drama, music, dance and fine arts.

Too uneventful? Include opportunities for interactivity and collaboration.

Too unexciting? Make it fun. Add elements of a game.

If you still find kids disengaged, maybe your lessons are too long, and you've talked too much! Consider their attention span and timing. When you see glazed, inattentive eyes, stop in your tracks and change things up by acting goofy, startled, or telling a joke. They may just need a brain break that gives them opportunities to talk or involves physical movement.

Each lesson plan is an opportunity for students to be engaged and motivated to learn. Get them excited to come back to see what you have in store for them the next day. Take the challenge, and go make your teaching amazing, NOT boring! Otherwise, you run the risk of being remembered as a boring or undesired teacher. Leave "Dullsville" right now! Stop the boredom at all costs!

Livia Chan is a head teacher, blogger, writer and an ambassador and digital content editor with the Teach Better Team.

Stop Doing All of the Talking in Class
DENIS SHEERAN

I was ready for my observation. The lesson was planned. I had my notes ready. The flow was seamless. I'd begin with an example of solving a system of two equations using matrices that was clear and made sense to my students since we'd done those over the past few days. Then...WHAM! I'd hit them with a system of THREE equations to shake them up a bit. I'd demonstrate how to use matrices and Gaussian Elimination to solve the system. It would take up both side boards in my classroom as well as the board at the front of the room, but when I was done, there would be an elegant and complete roadmap for them to follow when solving similar problems as long as they wrote it all down along the way. This was going to be great! My principal walked in for the observation, and the lesson went exactly as planned. I was flying high.

Planned with One Person in Mind

The next day, I met with the principal for my conference and heard the following: "I have no idea if your students learned anything, know anything, or are interested in knowing or learning anything. You certainly know the math, but do they? Don't answer that question. You can't. You never let them talk during the lesson." My heart sank, my joy drained and reality set in. She hated the lesson that I loved. Why? Because I'd planned it with one person in mind: me.

I recently replicated that lesson, almost word for word, in the exact same way with the exact same steps and the exact same seamless flow. And as soon as I finished it, I posted the video I'd just made from my basement on our internal digital platform right where it belongs. And if delivering content to students as if they are empty receptacles waiting for my knowledge and expertise is the definition of teaching, then as soon as I finished videos for each lesson, my job would be done. I would no longer be needed. And, my school district could fire me and stop having to pay me. And if you think that delivering lectures into the waiting minds of students is the definition of teaching, I've got news for you: Someone else has already made the video and you aren't necessary. That's right. You, I, and anyone who spends our time doing all the talking in our classes, are just not necessary any longer. I don't care how good we are at storytelling; another teacher is just as good and has apps, tools and video sharing platforms. It's time to say this clearly. *Stop doing all of the talking in class.*

You may have heard the phrase, "Whoever is doing the talking is doing the learning." This phrase illustrates that when we verbalize our thinking process, a new perception pathway for analysis and reflection exists. That verbalization also connects with others nearby and fosters questions and discussions that help individuals learn from their thoughts and mistakes.

How to Keep Your Mouth Shut

Here's the bright side of things: You are professional educators and if you care about the students in front of you, then you know that being a professional educator means being a professional learner. And if you know that, then you have probably dedicated time to learning new technologies, new curriculum plans, new assessment strategies and so much more. You see, the role of the teacher has changed thanks to the internet and the information available to our students. You were once the key holder and depositor of information. You are no longer that. Now, your profession consists of learning where your students are in the conceptual pathway of learning a new topic. Knowing what question to ask them that will continue their thinking and help them further along that pathway and finding ways to listen to them and discern whether they do understand what they were intended to, or not, and then decide what to do next. This doesn't sound like a lot of talking for you to do. Instead, it's a lot of talking for your students to do and a lot of listening and decision making for you. The more your students talk, the more BOTH of you learn. They learn the topic; you learn about them.

I want to end with this: Our students DO need us. They need us to hear them, guide them, instruct them, correct them, help them reflect so they can correct themselves and support them so they stay motivated and engaged in the learning that they desire. That's why your job isn't in danger. You may no longer be in control of the classroom in a traditional sense, but you will be in control of student learning in a new and exciting way. I used to hate seeing the cliché classroom poster that some of you may have on your door or wall, which states, "You have two ears and one mouth so you can listen twice as much as you talk." I don't hate that poster anymore. What I realize is that it doesn't apply to students, but to me.

Denis Sheeran completed the Running of the Bulls in Pamplona, Spain without dying and knows almost every line from The Simpsons. He is also a math teacher, administrator, nationally recognized consultant, podcaster and author of Instant Relevance, Using Today's Experiences to Teach Tomorrow's Lessons and Hacking Mathematics: 10 Problems That Need Solving.

13

Stop Lecturing Students
RYAN READ, Ed.D.

We can go a step further when we also consider what Denis wrote about teachers doing too much of the talking. There's often too much teacher talk, but then there's too much teacher *lecturing*. Can you remember when you were in the 5th grade? Did your teacher lecture you? My 5th grade teacher was so boring that she droned nearly every topic including the most effective way to read a book. Everything was a lecture. Everything was preacher-like. I also remember my 7th grade science teacher telling me all about why grass is green and how chlorophyll absorbs blue light and reflects green. As an adult I love this type of information, but at the time I dreaded the monotone one man show. Lecturing as a primary engagement activity didn't make an impression on me, nor did it help me to fall in love with science. Fast forward a few years later as I entered high school and started taking English, math and Spanish. Once again, my content area teachers gave lectures with the mere option of taking notes. I wanted to learn, and I was a good enough student, so why didn't lectures stick with me?

The Auditory Learner

After high school, I continued to college where lecturing was the primary mode of learning. During my undergraduate studies, I learned information about how market values work and how one "should" perform on a stage in theatre and yet students were never offered the opportunity to "do" something outside of listening about it. By that time, I figured out that I wasn't an auditory learner and understanding new concepts became an even bigger challenge for me. I look back at my time as a student and wonder why the practice of lecturing as a "go-to" practice is still happening today.

Tools for Teaching author, Barbara Gross David, explains that: "Lecturing is not simply a matter of standing in front of a class and reciting what you know. The classroom lecture is a special form of communication in which voice, gesture, movement, facial expression, and eye contact can either complement or detract from the content. No matter what your topic, your delivery and manner of speaking immeasurably influences your students' attentiveness and learning." The problem with this quote is that teachers get mixed up between "special forms of communication" and telling students everything they "need" or "should do" via lecturing, instead of allowing them to explore the content and possibly even present their own consumption of new information, rather than be a receiver of information from a muse. Even lecturing can be considered *performing*.

Turn Over the Conch

Lecturing students isn't an effective classroom management strategy because it doesn't work in the long run–especially if you are holding the conch all of the time. It leads to resentment towards the teachers which leads to resentment towards a classroom, which in turn, leads to resentment towards a school. This is not *active* teaching; this is spoon feeding a lesson and hoping a student will be able to regurgitate what you said and hope they get a high grade on the homework or test.

I don't know any classroom where hearing someone lecture for the majority of the class leads to any active learning and despite the use of PLCs or student led classrooms, teachers are still lecturing—both veterans and rookies. Some believe that this is how students "must" learn and what it leads to is disengagement, disrespect, and an army of inattentive students. In an age of remote and hybrid learning, lecturing is not a model that has to continue in that forum, either, yet it does. So, what will be the end product? The teacher will be burned out, the students will resent learning and a vicious cycle will continue in our schools until the lecturing stops.

Dr. Ryan Read specializes in Instructional Technology and is a Google Level 1 and 2 Educator. He is currently a Business and Technology Teacher at Stillman Valley High School in the MCUSD #223 School District.

Stop Making Decisions without Student Input

JEFF PRICKETT, Ed.D.

Listen, I get why you might not want to take input from your students. After all, a collective fear for teachers is losing control of their classroom. Some teachers even think students aren't wise enough, don't demonstrate enough responsibility, or just balk at the sheer mention of "consequences." You may be thinking that any of these examples may be a reason why students should be sidelined from any decision-making process within the confines of your school or classroom.

An Old Schoolhouse

Take what Ryan wrote about in his chapter and now think about the "lecturing schoolhouse" depicted in *Little House on the Prairie*. Teachers implemented practices that a modern-day teacher would refer to as "old school". "Old school" teachers believe that students should sit and listen. The learning environment consisted of content controlled by the teacher in the amount of time, quantity and information delved out by the teacher. Students in an old schoolhouse were only allowed to speak if hands were raised. Differentiation was non-existent and the expectation was that all students would take the same assessment on the same day. That's just the way it was done back then. Can you imagine this level of restriction and suppression from the age of five until the day of graduation thirteen years later? Is thirteen years of asking permission and obeying commands truly enough to set a student up for success as an adult? These "old school" practices seem archaic and obtuse. Living in a tech-driven, instant gratification, social media, instantaneous Tik-Tok posting world, there is no comparison to a throwback to "old school" teaching. So why are teachers still operating this way in a post-modern augmented artificial intelligence world?

The Problem

When students graduate from high school, they are sent out into the world and asked to make adult decisions. Big decisions! Without years of independent thinking and lacking problem-solving practice in school, students are expected to live happy lives and know how to make decisions. To find a solution, we must consider student input. We must offer a process that includes students while simultaneously offering tools, strategies and experiences that will equip them to make logical, informed, real-world decisions. Students may not always make optimal decisions in their learning process, but they are more than capable of making informed decisions. Teachers can solve this problem by strategically planning lessons that include student input. The goal is to fully develop the skills needed to apply your content to the real world for every student.

While Under Our Roof

Like the "old school" approach decades ago, you will find the "under our roof" mentality in schools all over the world. For as long as I can remember, and this certainly includes the time when I, myself, was attending public school as a youngster, content was king. Teachers taught the students; students learned the content and parents raised the children. This was the community mindset and unspoken were the social expectations. These roles included understanding and adhering to the concepts of "sitting and getting" while the teacher explained, "doing as you were told" when your parent(s) asked something of you and "taking an adult at his/her word" when something was shared with you as fact. Teachers and parents, alike, expected you to do as you were told at face value while "under their roof". This "under our roof" concept was expected both at home, at school and throughout the community.

Society changed, family units changed, jobs and work changed and the "while under our roof" mindset dissipated over time. Life became fast paced and design and innovation became dependent on group work and think tanks. The 21st century student deserves 21st century strategies that incorporate collaboration, decision making, team building, creativity and social skills all driven by student input, voice and empowerment. These thriving and effective practices extend beyond home and community. Student input isn't outlined in the learning standards of our craft, however. Student input may or may not have been embedded in teacher trainings even though it is a key ingredient for real-world leadership development. The good news is that many teachers find these classroom practices worth knowing and practicing. Unfortunately, in too many places, many teachers still haven't been able to figure out where to "fit students in" to what they feel they have to do each day, as teachers.

Fitting in Student Input

Student input will not just magically happen. Student input must be intentionally planned for each unit and lesson. There lies the second problem: we say these things are important and we hear from other professional organizations how critical these skills are to be successful in the 21st Century workplace, but teachers are rarely trained on the artistic design of how to infuse student input.

I have had the distinct pleasure of being a building principal at the elementary, middle and high school levels. I have also taught 6th and 8th grades, as well as being an assistant principal and dean of students. One might think that there is a huge discrepancy between our youngest and oldest learners, but you might be surprised to hear that I have had opportunities to hear student voice at any level and intentionally seek their input on any number of decisions we were thinking of making.

These have been among some of the most rewarding experiences in my entire career and they have not simply been limited to hearing from the student council leaders regarding what they would like to see served in the cafeteria at lunchtime. These decisions have not simply revolved around whether the class should receive extra recess if everyone can manage to stay focused and complete their morning work. When we listen and act, student input becomes the magic.

When Students Weigh In

Rather, the decision making I have been involved in has resulted in some pretty serious changes to programming, planning and, ultimately, the overall culture in the school building. I remember empowering our student body to weigh in with their thoughts about a particular program we were offering at the time. The result was fascinating and not what we had in mind when we first started the project. And to think it all began with wanting to get student input. It was as simple as that: getting a couple of passionate educators who wanted to really know what the students thought, what they wanted to change and what students thought we could do to make positive change. When these student leaders were finished polling their peers, visiting every classroom, and allowing the student-body a chance to have their voices heard, the only decision we could possibly have made was to get rid of the program that was under review.

We listened to our students that year. We focused on what mattered: allowing our students to provide input and to have a seat at the decision-making table. It was just one small step, but a step in the right direction. It was an intentional step towards making decisions with student input by putting a stop to ignoring them.

Dr. Jeff Prickett is a high school principal living in Northern Illinois with his wife and kids. He earned his doctorate degree from National Louis University and is also a podcast host and writer.

Stop Making Students Feel Like they are Interrupting

ALANA STANTON

"Go sit down."

"Can't you see I'm talking to someone right now?"

"This is teacher time."

"I'm busy right now and you should be getting busy too."

Have you ever heard these words or ever used similar words when speaking to a student? I know I have. These words are often used when students interrupt our teaching, our conversations, or our lessons in the classroom. Now, I want you to think about someone you love dearly, someone who makes your heart jump for joy, someone you always have time for no matter what is going on. Would you say any of the above words to them? Would you allow them to interrupt a conversation you were having? Most likely the answer is *yes*.

When They Matter to You

Students need to know the manners of not interrupting someone, yes, but this chapter discusses something a little different: how adults might treat students terribly when they can really listen to them instead. When someone matters to you, you allow them to interrupt you and break a conversation, no matter who you were talking with at the time. You would allow them to interrupt you because that person matters to you. They matter in your life and you want to show them they do by listening to them. This is the new attitude we can adopt as educators. We can start to believe that our students are our first priority in the school day. We can stop making our students feel like they are interrupting us. Instead, we can take the time to listen to them and make them feel like we are an open door that welcomes them in with each conversation.

To ensure listening to our students is a priority, teachers must intentionally practice putting our students first. The moment our students walk through the school doors, we need to be prepared to be on their time because they are our biggest and our most precious customer. We can do this by greeting them at the door or in the classroom, using their names when they come in and making sure throughout the day, we take time to listen to their stories, input, and ideas.

Morning Time was My Time

During my first few years of teaching, I failed at this greatly. I felt that the morning time and often the students' time was my personal planning period. I believed that until the school bell rang, that getting ready for the day was my best option. My students would first come into the classroom and I would be working on some lesson for that day or grading papers. My students always had morning work and I always had my own things to do too. I had the best intentions; I really did. I was preparing great lessons for them. I had hands-on lessons with a ton of manipulatives or props. My lessons took a lot of time to prepare, so I felt I had to use some student time to get my plans exactly right. After all, these lessons were for my students and I knew they would enjoy them. It continued this way until my third year of teaching. Anna, one of my students, walked in during my morning time. She unpacked her bag like any normal school day, started her morning work, but then she came over to talk to me as I was preparing my lesson for the day. I quickly listened to Anna's first few sentences, but then I said, "Okay you need to get to work, Mrs. Stanton is getting her work done right now. You will love our lesson today."

Little did I know that I should have taken the time to listen to Anna. It was not until after lunch that she revealed that a situation was going on with another student. This situation needed to be handled immediately. It was not okay that Anna had to wait hours to talk to me about it. Here, I was thinking I was preparing the most important thing in Anna's day, yet there I was not taking the time for her that she needed. Anna needed something simple from me: for me to listen. I failed her.

The Day I Made a Vow

After arriving home, I continued to think of Anna and the situation that she was in. I felt like I broke her trust and I had trouble sleeping that night. I kept thinking about what I could have done differently. In the middle of the night, I made a vow: I would not let this happen again. I would change my routine so that my students knew that they were the most important people in my school day. I now work hard to make sure that when I leave my school, I feel that I took the time to listen to my students. No one is ignored or brushed off to later in the day, any longer.

Over time I saw that my lessons were still prepared without me doing any extra planning on student time. I found that I became more creative, and my lessons became more essential without all that tedious planning. I also found that the relationships with my students became stronger and that my students felt like I was truly there for them, always.

Listen to What Matters to Them

It is so easy to dismiss our students. It is easier to tell them to sit down or get to work than take the time to hear every story or help them with their personal problem solving. As educators, we did not sign up for this career because it was easy. Think back for a moment about why you decided to work in education. Why did you want to be an educator? Who was someone that made a difference in your life during your school years? You are called to make a difference in a student's life in your community. This can be done when we take the time to listen to our students, to truly listen to them and hear what they have to say and to hear their stories and to show them that we think they matter. They do matter.

Every child you work with, every student you work with is someone's joy. They are someone's everything. It is our job as educators to reflect on how we listen to our students. We need to stop telling our students to sit down or to get back in line or to be quiet. Instead, we need to start taking the time to listen to their needs, to their dreams and to the stories that matter to them. When we do this, when we truly take the time to show our students we know them, we love them, and we value who they are. Stop making your students feel they are interrupting you and, instead, start listening to your students so they know they are valued.

Alana Stanton is a passionate educator in Watkinsville, Georgia and creator of the "More than a Lesson" blog.

Stop Squashing Student-Generated Interest
ISAIAH STERLING

Educators maintain student engagement by generating questions and facilitating discussions. In classrooms, students at times have the floor to share formulated ideas with their peers. For what reason? No, not for a participation grade for that day. That isn't true engagement. When educators foster a learning environment where students generate their *own* discussion interests and topics, true engagement is ignited.

The Squashing of Student Generated Discussions

Student generated discussions driven by students, is an authentic engagement tactic that can be nourished in any classroom. These discussions aren't discussions that are moderated, edited, or morphed by educators but rather a collection of real and raw perspectives that naturally occur within classrooms. These discussions are a part of the infamous "by kids, for kids" education strategy.

Theresa Birk, a ninth grade English educator in Missouri, loves asking her students questions in class to keep them engaged. One day, Ms. Birk asked her students their opinion on the top issues at their school. As usual, Andrew, a star student immediately raised his hand. Ms. Birk asked him to share what he wanted to say with the class. Andrew said, "I think that a lot of students here don't comply with the rules because we are required to dress a certain way."

Moments later, Ms. Birk told Andrew and the rest of the class that they couldn't discuss anything that was out of her control, such as the dress code. Ms. Birk said, "How about we talk about why we have that dress code in place?" Silence fell upon the classroom. Andrew stopped raising his hand or interacting with others in class from that day forward. I understand the importance of remaining on topic to make sure our students learn the required objectives, but when did squashing students' discussion interests ever improve education or engagement in learning?

How might the discussion have gone if Ms. Birk had asked Andrew to, "Tell me more about that." Might she have uncovered a root cause by asking "why" or "tell me more about that" several times? By allowing this discussion, it may have uncovered a completely unrelated root cause, or it may have even just provided value for being heard. So many times, student discussion interests are being squashed by educators when legitimately, students want to be heard.

Students Have a Desire to Generate Discussions

The social aspect to learning involves informal conversations. While in high school, I was always the student who had several "controversial" discussion topics on the tip of my tongue. I attended countless school improvement student council meetings, professional development sessions and open forums. I would often say, "Students aren't being heard; that is why morale is low and absenteeism is high."

I will never forget when my high school principal was the moderator at a school improvement forum. She said, "Let's focus on the positive. Next question please." in response to my statement. My opinion was squashed. Dead in the water. My voice was halted.

Oftentimes, educators fear that they will lose control of their classroom giving students the floor to generate discussions. They also might feel that certain students generated topics are "out of their control" like Ms. Birk. In most cases, students aren't trying to generate their own discussions in classrooms because they want to distract the teacher, get off topic or waste time. It may appear to the teacher that it is a no-nonsense topic, but with just a little oral discourse and discussion, they might discover that powerful connections are being made. This is extremely hard to grasp in the classroom for some. What students have to say is what educators need to hear to go from good to great.

From my point of view as a university student and educational leadership voice, I view Ms. Birk as lacking one of the most critical of educator skills. If only she would hear what her students have to say rather than minimizing what she considers irrelevant thoughts. If she would recognize that her biggest leverage was the power of connection, she would witness student motivation and learning soar rather than curiosity silenced. Teachers must embrace every opportunity for students to be heard even if it means acknowledging the value of thought and coming back around to it at a different time or reaching out after class. When students are considered and valued as social and meaningful learners, everyone benefits.

The Effects of Squashing Student Interests

Disengagement settles in when student generated discussion interests are squashed altogether and immediately dismissed. The lack of acknowledgement of student social processing is a formal invitation for the status quo to shows up on the radar and prompt a high learning alert warning.

When educators stop students from discussing topics they are interested in, students retreat back to status quo listening and minimally listens to the content the teacher wants them to hear. When this happens, many students even turn their ears completely off. The "fake it until you make it" mentality in today's student-mindset is real. Because we are social learners, connecting student interests bridge new learning to the schema that students already possess. If you were to ask any currently enrolled student what motivates them for life-long learning, I guarantee you not one student would share that they are interested in reading a textbook and answering boring questions. If we want our students to gain knowledge that will integrate deeper with a more profound application to the real world (especially post-secondary), why not give them a chance to be engaged in a conversation they create? Yes of course there may be norms that can be set, and yes there is a foundation of learning that must be facilitated, but that process can still incorporate the integration of student interest. *When student generated discussion interests are squashed, school improvement stops.*

School improvement truly takes an invested effort from everyone. All stakeholders must be invested with aligned a mission, vision, norms and goals. As a high school student, our faculty tried to improve many exceptional teaching practices. The one teaching practice they failed to incorporate was listening to students for ideation. My high school teachers were able to make some improvements, but their efforts were capped because of one reason: students were not involved in the topics or conversations of interest that could have increased student investment. Without authentic collaborative conversations of interests from students, we cannot reach our full school improvement potential. When we place student interests on a backburner, we withhold dynamic school improvement processes could possibly take flight. *When student generated discussion interests are squashed, teacher-student relationships are disrupted.*

Let me pose one question for this section: If a student feels like their teacher will not even listen to a topic of discussion that they brought up, how do they know the educator listens to anything else? Daily learning losses are far higher and more permanent by dismissing an interest rather than taking a moment to acknowledge and discuss in the moment or pose a time to continue. When student conversations are dismissed it creates relationship damage, which leads to learning damage directly or even indirectly. *When student generated discussion interests are squashed, students stop speaking out.*

Just like the star student, Andrew, in Ms. Birks' class, he stopped speaking out after his discussion interest was squashed. This is happening in more classrooms than we realize. Why should students feel obligated to keep speaking out when everything they say is shut down? The truth is, we don't always realize how many great things could come from raw and authentic student discussion interests. Yes, it is important to stay on topic in the classroom to meet learning objectives, I get that one hundred percent. But being open to student generated discussion interests is more crucial than you may realize. Connecting authentically and providing an atmosphere of desired contributions by students, could even change your perspective and education ideology. Embracing a belief in student discussion contributions could net you the best teacher year you have had yet.

Five Ways to Promote Student Generated Interests

1. Designate allotted time in your lesson plans for authentic student-teacher discussion.
2. Allow students to create questions during the lesson and post them on digital boards. Use these questions at the end of the lesson to engage your students in topics they are interested in.
3. Host open discussions during advisory or "free" periods so students can participate in discussion interests within a forum where it is safe to speak out.

4. Allow your students to generate their discussion interests at any time they think of them.

5. Ask your students how they would like to format the lesson to ensure that they have routine opportunities to speak up.

Isaiah Sterling is a college student, author, national speaker and education consultant from Cape Girardeau, Missouri. Isaiah is focused on the implementation of student voice and has contributed to various educational books including Let Them Speak and Recovery Mode.

Stop Trying to Be Friends with Students
SILAS KNOWLES

I remember it like it was yesterday. It was my first day student teaching at Algonquin Middle School in Des Plaines, Illinois. My passion had always been history, and this was the moment that would set the course of my career. I was assigned to student teach multiple levels of a United States history class. Like every college program, I was assigned a teacher-mentor who would ultimately decide if I was qualified to graduate and continue in the profession. From the first time I ever met my mentor Mike, I just knew this was going to be a positive experience. You could tell he cared about people and that teaching mattered to him. As his student teacher, even before he got to know me, he wanted me to succeed. As time progressed, I was grateful that Mike put his full trust in my practice. To this day, I thank God for Mike because he was able to teach me the greatest lesson I would ever learn as a teacher… *after the biggest mistake I ever made in the classroom.*

The First Day Was the Scariest

On the first day of my student teaching, my first class started filing in while I was standing there shaking like a leaf. I distinctly remember Mike capturing my eyes with his look of concern and mouthing the words, "Are you OK?" Then it happened: the bell rang. In that moment, it sounded like a nuclear siren rattling my nerves. Deep down, I knew I needed to make an impact right away. I knew the impression I made in the first few minutes of class would dictate the next 16 weeks of my student teaching. As I started to speak the words began to form from my mouth as I introduced myself to this new group of students. Near the end of my introduction in a compassionate tone, I said, "I am here to be your friend and help in any way that I can."

I can't believe I said that or even thought that.

Mike took me off to the side after class and spoke with me. "You know what you did wrong, right?" Honestly, as a newbie, I had no idea at what I did wrong, so I muttered, "I'm so nervous right now, I have no clue, but I have the feeling you are going to let me know." Mike shared with me his wisdom and reasons why teachers can lose all credibility and face even more challenges when seeking a friendship with students. After talking with him, I realized that teachers have an unspoken moral obligation to stay within their role as a facilitator of knowledge, a motivator of learning and a co-problem solver, but certainly not as a "friend." Friendly, yes. Friend, no.

Set Clear Boundaries

It is ethical to keep a division between your professional and personal life with students. If you socially or emotionally need students as friends, then teaching isn't the right profession for you. There is an imbalance of power when a grown adult requires the validation of a 17-year-old to be a part of their personal life.

I had good intentions and hadn't even thought about it as a student teacher, but I sure learned this very quickly. So why haven't some veteran teachers or even rookie teachers learned this lesson yet? Why do they friend-request their students on social media? Why do their students call or text them on their personal phone off hours? As a teacher, you are an influencer, you possess power and yield authority. Because of this, your students need to understand boundaries and respect what you do as a professional. Mike taught me that effective teachers set up boundaries with their students the very first day.

Friendly Not Friends

One day of putting "my foot in my mouth" took weeks to fix. To make sure my students in that first period knew the newly established boundary that needed to be established, I had to rebrand everything. Finally realizing what I did, I adapted and made changes for my other four classes, so that this initial mistake was not repeated for the rest of my first day. I had to backtrack and reset everything. One phrase that took a few seconds to come out of my mouth cost me weeks of classroom management. It could have been easily avoided.

This year marks my eighth year in education. I teach English Language Learners for two of my history classes. In those environments, I have aides to support our Spanish speaking students. Coming into the EL program at my school, I had an open mind. However, I had an aide named Karen. She had been there for two years before I came to my current school. I stood back and watched her Snapchat with her students, braid girls' hair and text students during and after school. Eventually, I had to call a meeting with my department chair and my aide. The thing that made me do a double take was the fact that the aide thought she did nothing wrong. It was compromising my classroom management. It was not helping me maintain a high level of respect in the room, nor did it help me address students as scholars who are highly capable of entering a professional work setting or university. This adult misbehavior was blatantly wrong from my vantage point. From there, I had to do damage control to establish the understanding that I was their teacher and their aide was a professional too. Being friends with your student does not work. All it causes are mixed messages and time away from what you are there for: academic growth and developing happy thriving, problem-solving students.

I know there will be naysayers who might reject this notion. People will say, "Yeah, but it's OK to be friends with your students especially if they have no one else." What you need to understand is that everything you do will affect your classroom in some way. Those decisions might result in positive or adverse effects. There are far too many instances where friending students has turned into false accusations, teacher reprimands, or community disapproval for the educator. Most schools that I have meet have rules about personal phone numbers going out to students and strict social media policies for staff. Take it from someone who has made a mistake and recovered. Supporting and nurturing students is much different than being friends with them.

Silas Knowles is a master teacher in Chicago, Illinois and the host of the Pushing Boundaries podcast.

Stop Showing Favoritism
DEMETRIUS A. BALL

Students are always watching every move you make. They sense your tone and body language and interpret your actions and then emotionally internalize them. Even when you are not paying attention, your students are watching your every move. They are watching your forehead and the furrow in your brow. They see that scrunched up nose and crooked smirk on your face. They see your slouched shoulders or your folded arms. They also see the smiles, the high fives, and the bright-eyed expressions.

They are listening to you too. They hear every single word that you utter, the praise, the jokes, the sarcasm, and the callouts. Even the students who rarely make eye contact know what is happening. After a short time with you, your students know every single one of your gestures and favorite phrases whether you realize it or not.

They All Should be Your Favorite

Part of being a kid is testing the adults in their lives--especially their teachers. Students are always pushing the boundaries to see how far they can go. They want to know how much fun they can have in class. Can they get this teacher off topic so they don't have to learn components of a linear equation? Is this the teacher who does not tolerate students picking their own seats? They need to know how much they can get away with in class. In just a short time in your class, they know what each gesture or comment really means and they know whom you favor and whom you do not. They will see pockets and patterns of favoritism. Stop showing favoritism to students because the bottom line is that they all need to feel like they are your favorite.

Teachers Groom their Pets

Principals receive requests over the summer from parents who desire to not have their child assigned to a particular class. This is a common practice. Take Ms. Baxter, for example. Ms. Baxter is "old school." She thinks that school must be conducted in a certain way, in a particular manner, with particular non-negotiable rules. Unfortunately, Ms. Baxter's delusional view of school is that she believes it's "her way or the highway." Student choice is non-existent. Child compliance rules the roost. Ms. Baxter lectures to her students and if they get the wrong answers in her class, they get called out. When they are off task, or are having trouble grasping a concept, then the entire class is made aware. On the other hand, the students who check all the boxes and are compliant, focused and organized, gain Ms. Baxter's approval. Those students will be the first called on to respond. They are given nicknames, such as "sweetheart" and "genius." It is plain to see by students and families, that Ms. Baxter has little room within her restrictive mindset to create basic supports for students who need them. She gives the clear message that if you cannot keep up, her classroom is not for you. The impact on Ms. Baxter's students is far reaching. Not only are the students that are not in her good graces impacted, but the students who are deemed as "favorites" are isolated by their non-favored peers and called names like "teachers' pet." Students do not want that label. Then you start to see those favored students act out in class to lose their favored status and get back in with their peers. It is a silent social and emotional war; her classroom is purely a battlefield. While there are requests that students do not get Ms. Baxter, there are also those who are favored to do what she wants. Both the system and teacher perpetuate favoritism.

Focus on What Works for Each Student

Now, take a look at Mr. Jensen. Mr. Jensen won the teacher of the year award every year. He taught Advanced Placement Psychology. Everyone wanted to take his class. Though the class had as much reading as any college course, Mr. Jenson made his class one of the most fun experiences on campus. He built a community and it started before school started. He sent a letter to all his students' families as soon as he received his new class roster introducing himself and welcoming them to his class. He worked to know every student's name by the end of the first week of school and made a point to know at least one personal fact about them. Mr. Jenson made a phone call to every single family within the first month of school. If a student played a sport or performed in a group at school, Mr. Jenson attended his students' events, but never excused them from anything demanding, such as a test the next day after a game.

Do What's Right Not What's Easy

Ms. Baxter's approach is easy to take on. She wanted the middle of the road students where she could teach to the middle (and all her rules) because it is less work for her. Undoubtedly, it is easy to teach already compliant students. But is it the right thing to do? Is it the most *effective* thing to do? Becoming a teacher of the year requires a massive amount of work and relationship building in order to support all students. Maybe teachers like Ms. Baxter lack the empathy necessary to be effective? Maybe they lack the skills to teach and support all students? This teacher focused on herself and what works for her, not what was best for her students. She was oblivious to the long-term implications on her reputation and the damage that she did to her students.

Conversely, Mr. Jenson's gestures are above and beyond, but he certainly didn't see it that way. His moral compass was high, and his passion was fueled by student success. Deep down, he knew it was the right thing to do to build a strong sense of community that everyone deserved. At the end of the school year, students were united and felt individual acceptance and success because Mr. Jenson never played favorites. Every single student felt like they were his favorite. His actions will carry on in a positive way for the rest of his students' lives. Students may not remember everything that Mr. Jensen taught, but they will always remember how he made them feel.

These contrasting styles of playing favorites have long term implications. In the former case of Ms. Baxter, she may have turned students off from education for the rest of their lives while Mr. Jenson may have inspired the next generation of educators. Do not be that teacher that plays favorites unless ALL of your students feel like they are your number one reason for being there.

Demetrius A. Ball currently serves his community as a Middle School Principal in Northern California.

Stop Judging Students
KATHLEEN MCCLASKEY

Judging students is the "ugly" side that can so easily permeate into many school cultures. After 37 years in education as a teacher, K-12 administrator, graduate instructor, school board member, educational consultant, and author of two books, I developed a deep understanding of school culture, the good, the bad and the "ugly." Before I share my story, I have a favor to ask: For us to move forward with this topic, it will require an open mind and a sense of vulnerability from you. I ask that you remove all preconceived notions from the story that I am about to tell.

Back in the 1970's

I did not start my career in the education field even though I earned my bachelor's degree in education back in 1970. I lived in a generation when girls typically only had three career options: I could become a nurse, a secretary, or a teacher. Out of these three choices, I chose to become a teacher. In the 1970's, there were more teachers graduating than there were positions to be filled in schools, so I ended up entering an industry career until 1978 just before I gave birth to my first son in1979. I hadn't spent a day in a classroom as a teacher and, instead, entered a new role as a mother. I first experienced the "ugly" side of education through the eyes of a mother.

The "Ugly" Misconception

As my son entered public school in 1985, as a readiness student (one grade before entering 1st grade), he had two wonderful years in a child-centered school where he thrived. He was a curious and creative child who was gifted and had the ability to tell incredible stories, engaging kids and adults wherever he went. He loved exploring the outdoors and he was skilled at fishing by the time he was only seven. He could not wait to go to school to learn to read.

His experience as a first grader was a difficult one; his teacher used the whole language method for reading which simply didn't work for him (which we know now isn't even backed by the science of reading). He did not learn to read that year. Most of that year, he spent time sitting outside the classroom alone as punishment for distracting the class. This was painful and "ugly," but it did not stop there.

Although he was exceptional in math, this gift, along with his aspirations, talents and interests would never be recognized. Before the end of first grade, he was finally identified as LD or learning disabled rather than labeled a distracting child.

It has only been recently that I finally realized exactly what happened to my son in school. After he received the "label" of learning disabled, his teachers only viewed him through that lens. Soon even the strengths he once had were now overlooked by a disability. This is the "ugly" misconception that still exists today for so many students. He had a myriad of strengths, so why did those go right out the window the moment he received an LD label?

A Misdiagnosis

From first grade on, we would develop IEP goals with a focus on reading and writing. As a mother, I never felt like things were quite right. I knew his strengths, I knew he was smart and just because he couldn't decode words like a strong reader, something still didn't seem right after all these years. I had had enough and was determined to get an outside opinion. It was during my son's 7th grade year through an independent evaluation that we discovered he was dyslexic. He was already having a tough year because his teachers not only judged him but demoralized him in front of his peers. He wasn't able to acquire knowledge like the other kids, so she would send my son to the vice principal's office stating something to the effect of, "He was a bad kid and no one should play with him." However, my son was loved by his peers and the kids revolted against the teacher. In the same year, his math teacher stated to me in a meeting with the special education case manager that "he faked his disability." The substitute science teacher also felt compelled to announce that she refused to provide any accommodations for quizzes or tests. This was the most painful and "ugly" year for him as he had a set of teachers who made judgements and took actions that would impact him for years to come. He became another academic and social emotional victim of a school culture that is based on the "ugliness" of the deficit model.

Successful Despite School

Years later, when my son was 22 years old, we had a discussion about his experience in school and how it made him feel. Throughout all his years in school, we never really talked about school because my son was often depressed or angry. But enough time had passed, and he was happy in life, so I decided to ask him about his K-12 educational experience. His response was brief and to the point, "You know mom, I felt stupid every day of my life in school!" That statement was piercing. As a mom, I felt his emotional pain and rejection flow into my body and all I wanted to do was hug him and share his talents and strengths. That's just what I did. The beauty is that he overcame his negative school experience by cultivating his strengths and developing into a thriving successful young man. As an adult he recognized his special abilities and began a career in car sales and is doing well as a professional even though the emotional pain he experienced in school is still carried with him to this day.

Vow to Find Value

When my son started his freshman year in high school, I wanted nothing more than to return to education, so I enrolled in a master's program for computers in education and graduated from Lesley College, a major accomplishment in my life. During this time, I was a volunteer computer teacher providing technical training for teaching teachers at my local elementary school. I was most excited to teach them how to integrate computers into classroom instruction as another tool that could be used for students. It was meant to be, I guess, because I was soon hired as a Title I math teacher where I often used computers with children to help them understand math. I knew that students with learning challenges needed different modalities for learning math, so I took a multisensory approach with my lessons. I knew the science of the brain. I was familiar with computer integration and I wanted my students to springboard from their strengths. I had always vowed to find value in all students' strengths.

Rise Above the "Ugly"

It was during this first full-time job as a computer teacher in 1988 that I first experienced the "ugly" side of educators, now as a teacher, not just a mother. I remember it vividly: we were all sitting around a knee high, horseshoe table with the special education coordinator present. This was an initial meeting before the school year had even started. This SPED coordinator managed to describe the most negative side of every child who had an IEP. I was appalled at the descriptions she had of student scholars we had not even met yet. I heard judgmental phrases, such as "He is a bad kid who is confrontational." or "This boy has learning disabilities so do not expect too much from him." or "This girl has serious family problems and may act out." While she was talking, I was thinking about what the SPED case manager at my son's school would have been telling his teachers about him because he had an IEP too. I shared my son's "ugly" and true story with these teachers and explained how teachers judged my son and how it impacted his self-perception and self-worth for so many years. Back then, I decided not to judge the students in my classroom but to build relationships with them by having conversations with each and every one of them in order to discover what support they needed to learn. I kept my vow to find value and seek strengths for each one of the 220 kids I was assigned to during my first year of teaching.

This experience at my first full time job was one of the "ugliest" experiences in my educational career. Unfortunately, this experience was often extended to the teacher lunchrooms where small talk and "ugly" conversations about kids occurred more often than not. I made a decision early that year to not partake in the "ugly" that went on and often reflected on my father's advice which was to "Judge not, less you be judged."

So, if you catch yourself judging a child . . .

–Take 3 deep breaths and exhale slowly,

–Remove all negative and preconceived thoughts of this child,

–Be PRESENT and then ask yourself:

"How can I get to know this child, find value and dig for strengths as a learner?"

Stop seeing children as just "students" and start understanding and valuing them as "learners." Here is a quote that has guided my work in education for many years that I want to share with you: "Every child on the planet is a learner."

Judgment does not fit well here.

Kathleen McClaskey is CEO & Chief Learning Officer of Empower the Learner, founder of Make Learning Personal and co-author of two bestselling books, Make Learning Personal and How to Personalize Learning.

Stop Ignoring the Fact that Students Learn in Different Ways

PATRICE BROWN

I refuse to believe that any student does not *want* to learn. I refuse to believe that a child is born and immediately does not like school. I once thought I hated history. I learned it was not the subject I hated; it was the way it was taught. The lessons did not reach me. I wasn't an auditory learner, so I did not connect to the lecture and note-taking cycle. Did my teacher change anything? No, my teacher continued to stick to the lesson plan that was written without my input as a student. I often mumbled that I was bad at history which later morphed into a definitive, "I hate history." I was then labeled a poor history student. That was my crutch for many years until I met a professor who took the time to recognize that I needed to be introduced to the material in a different way to connect to it and learn it. It does not matter how many students you have in your class; they don't all learn the same way or on the same day. Stop thinking your lesson plans cannot change. Stop thinking that it's the student who must change the way they learn to conform to your way of doing things. Stop blaming the student because you were unable to teach them effectively. Your issue should not be with the student. Recognize that the ability to reach each student in their own unique way, begins with you.

We Teach the Way We Learn

It is said, "We teach the way we learn." Some students will not learn the topic you choose on any particular day because it was not planned for all students. Think back to a lesson you knew would be the best lesson ever. You truly may have thought every student would be excited and surely master the topic. Have you experienced working through a lesson and student questions start pouring in as hands are shooting up at the rate of a popcorn popper? The sheer number of questions for clarification may have caught you off guard but you trekked on with the lesson thinking about the vast amount of material you had to cover and assumed they would get it if you just repeated the process. Failure to understand learning differences is a set up for a lesson disaster. Students learn in such a wide array of learning styles and modalities which means that teachers must plan for these varying styles.

Various Learner Types

As teachers, we have all experienced professional development and coaching on different learning modalities. We have sat in many trainings and probably read books about differentiating instruction. When looking into the lives of our students we know we see differences. Yet, we still teach every student as if our learning pathways are identical. Let's analyze four completely different learner types.

Learner 1: The Novelist

Ashanti, a bright teenage student who prefers to sit close to the teacher's desk. Ashanti comes prepared to class with a pencil and notebook and hangs on to the teacher's every word. She wants to write everything. She asks questions because she cannot write as fast as the teacher talks. Her questions become annoying to both the teacher and the class because her questions stop the "flow" of the class. Often, the teacher thinks she is just not paying attention and becomes frustrated because of the constant restating and explaining needed. When Ashanti takes a test, she usually will show around a 70% proficiency associated with the grade of "C." She always seems to get partial points due to her answers being incomplete. The problem is Ashanti only recalls what she writes. She has had teachers who try and stop her from writing by supplying her with notes. However, she is not a reader, she is a writer.

Teachers: If the Novelist can't keep up with you, maybe you are talking too much.

Learner 2: The Daydreamer

Amari, a middle school student, always seems to be staring out of the window or at the walls. He comes in the class and seems prepared but after ten minutes, he's staring off into an unknown land waiting for his teacher to redirect him. Amari is extremely intelligent. He can recall several facts and does well in mathematics and science; however, he has a difficulty turning in assignments on time. Amari's teacher has changed his seat, required him to write his homework in a planner and has continually tried to use proximity control–none of which has stopped him from daydreaming, however.

Teachers: Allow the daydreamer the time to use their imagination while applying what they were taught. Continuing with a lengthy lesson with no mind stimulation or student-led application will just allow the daydreamer the time to do what they enjoy most: dream.

Learner 3: The Listener

Alexander is an honor student in Advanced Placement (AP) classes. He has always done extremely well on standardized tests, but his report card reflects a "C" average. He doesn't do much work because he doesn't feel the value in it. Alexander's favorite saying is: "The point of all 'extra' work is for me to pass the test to prove that I understand what the teacher is saying. So, if I pass the test without all the 'extra' work, then why am I expected to do the 'extra' work in the first place? Didn't I prove that I understand what the teacher is saying by passing the test? Why, then, is my grade lowered because I didn't do the 'extra' stuff? Evidently, I didn't' need it." The listener is not the writer or even the reader. The listener is just that. They can fully master a concept just by listening to an explanation. That is how they learn.

Teachers: Does every student really need homework? Does it really help every student learn? Are we just giving homework to give it and then just give credit to those who conformed?

Learner 4: The Combination

Antoni is a vibrant special needs student who is full of energy. Antoni has a short attention span and he loves to draw. He combines phrases he has learned by watching movies and television to hold appropriate short conversations with classmates and teachers. He learned to write by imitating the handwriting of his teachers. Antoni learned basic mathematic concepts by verbal repetition. When he believes enough time has been given to a task, he may get up and move to the next task. Antoni's parents were informed by a licensed psychologist that he had learned every word he would ever know and speech therapy was dropped for him at the age of thirteen years old. They were told he would probably never speak in full sentences or hold conversations with others. At the age of fifteen, a teacher took a different approach. Antoni can now use complete sentences and he can hold short conversations using appropriate language. It is because of Antoni that I truly believe teachers must stop ignoring how students learn in different ways. The truth of the matter is EVERY student can learn. EVERY student has a desire to learn.

Teachers: Realize there is not one way to teach the masses. Plan lessons that fit all.

Stop trying to make students conform to your way of learning. Stop finding fault in students for not mastering the content.

Patrice Brown is a Mathematics Resource Teacher and Mathematics Department Head in Hillsborough County, Florida. She is a wife and mother of five children and a National Springboard Trainer and Teacher Professional Development Writer and Trainer.

Stop Handing Out Worksheets & Packets
TRISTA S. LINDEN-WARREN, Ed.D.

Cease and desist immediately. Worksheets are a waste and packets are a plunder. Caution: please save the trees and step away from the copy machine. Worksheets and packets are not teaching tools. They merely provide a way to capture the regurgitation of facts. The no-nonsense reality is that worksheets and packets serve as an easy way out for you as the teacher and it only becomes an intense frustration for you and a daily battle for your students. Worksheets do NOT teach students much of anything. Worksheets and packets are busy work. Worksheets do not make thinking visible, nor do they check for understanding.

Effective Instruction is RE.AL.

Instructional practices are effective when students are Rigorously Engaged and Applying Learning. Do worksheets or packets provide for a rigorous education? Clearly not. So, if we are to rise to a high standard and implement practices that are far reaching, then teachers must keep it "RE.AL.". Let me further explain.

Rigorously Engaged

Rigor in education is defined as academically, intellectually, and personally challenging. Using search engine answers to complete a worksheet does not provide for deep thought or real-world application on any topic. Students deserve to be challenged and to think critically and worksheets do not provide for this application. Rigor in the classroom represents learning that can be applied in a myriad of educational, career related, or real world contexts.

Students should question their assumptions and think deeply about topics. Students should problem solve. A fill-in-the-blank worksheet or a multiple-choice test is not elevating the ceiling of rigor nor does it provide practice for application of knowledge. Worksheets, packets and tests of this nature demand rote memorization and information recall. Classrooms should be representative of rigorously engaged, applied learning.

"Education is not the filling of a pail, but the lighting of a fire."

–William Butler Yeats

Engagement in education refers to the degree of attention, curiosity, interest, and passion that students demonstrate when they are learning. Students must be both covertly and overtly involved in their learning. Students must own their learning. Worksheets do not support engaged learning.

Most often, when worksheets are assigned, the entire class is required to do the same worksheet or packet even though it may be too easy for some and too hard for others. Student choice is not provided as part of the worksheet process. There are many more engaging and applied ways to differentiate instruction, provide valuable practice, encourage deeper critical thinking, improve achievement, inspire creativity and most importantly, keep the learning RE.AL.

"Tell me and I forget, teach me and I may remember, involve me and I learn."

–Benjamin Franklin

Applied Learning

Application of material in education using worksheets creates two problems. First, it erases the value of formative assessment: If worksheets are meant to be used to teach students something or give them practice on skills they are learning, then why would students be penalized for making mistakes on them? Failure, with reflection, is the application of learning. Second, worksheets represent a passive process of learning. Applied learning can occur when there is a direct application of the skills taught in the classroom.

Learning by doing, a concept introduced by John Dewey, is a school of thought that was popular at the beginning of the 20th century. His research supports the belief that the best education involves learning through doing. There must be an application of what is learned to something in the real-world, not a worksheet. Students should pursue their passions through projects, solving problems and reflecting on their learning. Worksheets and packets do not provide for application. Applied education requires students to learn by doing. Classrooms should be representative of rigorously engaged, applied learning.

"Learning is more effective when it is an active rather than a passive process."

60

–Kurt Lewin

What if you could only take the driver's test one time? What if you were not allowed to practice driving before you took the test? Learning is about the mind's development and the application of skills learned. Worksheets do not authorize creativity or divergent thinking or provide for this application. Learning occurs when you think outside of what is being taught. A blank sheet of paper encourages more out-of-the box thinking and learning than a coloring book. Those lines and ideas are already determined. Classrooms should be representative of rigorously engaged, applied learning.

"Education is not the learning of facts, but the training of the mind to think."

–Albert Einstein

The RE.AL. Classroom, Explained

Students are exploring and collaborating. They are out of the classroom investigating and taking notes. They are applying their learning to the real-world situations. Students have a choice in their learning and they own it. Here is your challenge. Give the copy machine a rest. Replace the worksheets and packets with hands-on activities. Let students interview experts or professionals about the topics learned. Let students find and create their learning. Let students engage in small group discussions. Let students create their own assignments. Let students create their own learning.

Dr. Trista S. Linden-Warren is an educator and owner of Linden Warren Consulting, Inc..

Stop Ignoring Students' Personal Space
DEANNA OLIVER, Ed.D.

We all know "that person" who is a close talker. You know the person that makes it their life mission to invade your bubble zone by feeling like they need to be an inch from your face to get your complete attention. If this does not annoy you, then maybe you are an invader of personal space yourself. I am profoundly sensitive to this topic for many reasons and have more stories than I care to share. As a professional woman who towers a mere 5'2", taller adults have taken it upon themselves to hug me like a baby doll or lean on my shoulder like we are best buds–so awkward. The imaginary highlight reel in my head has me turning and punching them in the face.

If They Can Smell the Garlic on Your Breath, You are Too Close

Many teachers use proximity as a classroom management technique. Walking in the quadrant or direction of a student who may need a visual cue to settle down or regain self-control is quite acceptable. That's not what I'm talking about here. I am talking about the in-your-space-bubble closeness that may trigger or be off putting to a student. Infringing on students' personal space is taking proximity to a whole new level; it is nothing short of a power trip. Leaning in or inching closer and closer to a student only sends a message that you dominate the classroom and are far superior to students. As educators, our job is to nurture and provide security and acceptance not the contrary. It is our responsibility to establish boundaries and courtesies with students for effective and respectful communication that honors another person's space.

When a student feels overtaken in their personal space, it may trigger a negative response, such as shutting down, backing away, dropping your class, or feeling so uncomfortable that they report your behavior to their friends, parents, teachers, or administrators. Even worse, they may remain quiet and withdrawn from their experience with you leading to feelings of rejection, low self-worth, or inadequacies. More serious: you may also want to consider how you would explain this to your principal and parents when a sexual harassment complaint is filed because you made a student feel uncomfortable. If students can smell the garlic on your breath from lunch, you are way too close.

Socially Distant

If the COVID-19 pandemic taught us anything, it is that you need to be six feet away from others to avoid a respiratory virus; the same thing can be said of giving your students learning space. Can you honestly say that you are "socially distant" enough from your students to make them feel comfortable? How do you know? Did you even bother to ask them how they prefer positive reinforcement, redirection and assistance in the classroom? Student voice matters and incorporating their need for space must be honored. You should stop looking at the proximity of you and your students from your lens. When was the last time you sat in the student desk and had an adult stand next to you? Guess what part of the body your students make eye contact with first? The thought of this may help you to take a few steps back from your students.

Stop believing old advice that students will behave better if you move closer to them. This may actually work against you. Students who have experienced physical, sexual, or emotional abuse need to feel in control of their own physical space. When you do not allow proper distance between you and the student, it triggers an emotional response in their brain of "fight or flight." Flexing your control in the classroom through proximity is not normally acceptable. We need our students in the right mindset for learning; they will never get there if you strip them of the empowerment of their personal space.

Relationships, not Invasion

I have often heard teachers say, "My students are like my own children." But, they are not your children. Unless you are a homeschool parent, then do not treat your students like your own children. Your relationship and boundaries with them should be vastly different. If space is not protected, then you are violating some serious breaches of professionalism.

I Forgot My Glasses

Each author in this book selected their topic for reasons that are personal to them. I am no different. Here is just one story that I feel compelled to share. When I was in elementary school, a teacher was upset with me because I forgot my glasses. On this particular day, my optometrist dilated my eyes which caused me to not be able to see the board when I arrived to school later in the day. My teacher proceeded to stand behind me, grab me by the back of the neck and he talked closely in my ear to reinforce that it was awfully bad that I forgot my glasses. Here I am, forty years later, and I still remember the details of that incident, vividly. Actions have consequences and my teacher's aggression left a terrifying impression on me that impacted my trust of others.

Each time you approach a student, keep in mind that not all students are comfortable being touched, approached, or even near an adult. This may not be their norm. Believe it or not, some students do not need a hug, high five, or fist bump as positive reinforcement. Stop ignoring students' personal space and rethink your physical actions towards them and honor their personal space.

Dr. Deanna Oliver serves as the Assistant Superintendent for the Kane County Regional Office of Education in Geneva, Illinois. She has served as a high school teacher and administrator for 30 years.

Stop Creating Confrontations in the Classroom
ROBERT A. MARTINEZ, Ed.D.

Students deserve to be treated as people, first. When students are considered a vital part of humanity, then the focus shines on dignity, care, compassion, kindness, thoughtfulness, and love. Students of any age are not *subordinates*; they are not to be looked at as *inferior*.

Oppression Cannot Co-Exist with Dignity

Consider those closest to you in this world. How are your loved ones treated? How do you treat them? How do you feel when you loved ones are mistreated in some way? This is the same mindset we must have as educators if we are going to create dynamic and thriving classrooms of excellence. A five-star classroom will never co-exist with omission of dignity, shaming into compliance, or making students feel lesser than, in any manner, another person. Because teachers, educators, paraprofessionals, and other school staff are in a role of authority, they must wisely yield this power with students. Consistency and coaching come into play while guiding students to understand rules and boundaries, but this does not include the ridiculously extreme level of oppression, either.

Teachers have the power to place undue expectations, limits, or arbitrary measures on students or to provide a nurturing pathway that leads to the same desired outcome. When teachers flex muscles of ridiculousness, they run the risk of stripping students of their dignity and manipulating a system of authority into one of shame and control. When a teacher enforces an arbitrary set of rules in the classroom to lord over or govern students, they prevent student success. There is great fault in thinking that without enforcing authoritarian type of limits, anarchy will ensue.

Stop arguing with students about not having a pen, pencil, or crayon in their hand and work to ensure that they have access to the tools they need to advance their learning, to be engaged in your lessons, to connect with you and other students, to support other students, to produce thoughtful, innovative, personal work that will advance their personal access to new ideas, new ways of thinking, new ways of seeing information come to life so that they can make memorable connections and advance their synapses to learn more. Stop the faulty logic. Stop the personal need to control others. Stop the

64

shaming. Stop the power play to maintain your authoritarian need to be in charge!

Conflict is a Valve that Shuts Off Learning

Stop arguing with students about wanting to use the bathroom, visiting the nurse, or asking to go to the office. Instead, work hard to learn about student's needs, their personalities and connect authentically with them so that they are ensured access and opportunities that will improve not only their life at school, but their overall capacity to learn and go find the future that they deserve. All the above behaviors could be avoidance behaviors, so find out why students use these excuses to get out of your classroom because they do not want to be in your class! Be a person who cares about each student, not a person who seeks to control every aspect of the classroom. Imagine being at work and you had to raise your hand to use the restroom or were shamed when you forgot your lunch at home. It simply does not feel good, and it surely does not fix the problem.

Every time that we choose a path that leads to conflict for students, we shut off a valve of advanced learning. Every time we seek to shame a student into compliance, we add toxicity to the soil that diminishes any future opportunities for learning to occur. Every time we seek to ensure that we hold the power in the relationship, we embrace the notion that we are the most powerful person in the room and this mindset robs a student of so much.

They "Why" Behind Student Behavior

Looking a little deeper, we must seek to ensure we are understanding the "why" behind a student's behavior. Consider the following:

Could it be that by wanting to use the bathroom the student simply needs to go, and should be allowed to go? Yes, it can be that simple.

Could it be that the student simply has a medical need and might not want to share that with the entire class or you? Have you connected with and learned about all your students for that matter?

Could it be that the student has learned to self-regulate and needs to escape the classroom environment to take a breath? Don't you wish that in your lifetime you were given the grace to remove yourself from a situation, if even for a moment, to be able to return with your dignity?

Could it be that they have a positive relationship with another person on campus, such as the school secretary, and they are wanting to go see that person, if only for a moment to obtain some reassurance?

Have you worked with the entire school team to create a web of safety nets for each student to help them with their growth?

Connect with students as people first and develop trust with them. This offers you and them a greater benefit of building a stronger relationship that is more authentic than one based on authoritarian systems of shame and power.

Try This

Imagine if you had one hundred pencils, pens, crayons, or other writing instruments needed by the students in your classroom. Now, place them in an area of the room where each child who needs one could grab one when they need one. This simple strategy will alleviate the need to stop your lesson, lose engagement of all students and remove wasteful minutes from important class time.

Wasting time in arguments with students over bathroom use or visits to the nurse or office will drain both you and your students. You will find that students will learn to trust you as a person in their lives, rather than just another person out to make things tough on them if you grow relationships differently and stop thinking the worst of them. When we can lessen the load of one student through purposeful systems of care that are meaningful to that student, we improve the environment for all in our care.

Do Not Let this be You

Mrs. Steele had come to her new school with limited background information on a lot of things. Apparently, some incident occurred with her previous principal that was not shared with her new principal and she absolutely appeared to be a prickly pear. She did not engage with her colleagues, was uncommunicative with parents and somehow believed that she needed to rule this new second grade classroom with an iron fist to ensure absolute control. She was all about the rules. No talking in class. No one leaves during class time. No one may get a drink during class. No one may leave their seat. If you are not ready to work, you must just sit in silence. No one may use the bathroom. Do you get the picture? Rules ruled and none of these students were viewed as individuals by Mrs. Steele.

It wasn't more than two weeks into her tenure of being at her new school when the complaints started pouring into the principal's office. Students were completely and utterly stressed out. Students were peeing in their chairs and sitting in their wetness, sometimes for hours. Students as individuals, and as a group, had stopped learning, were regressing, and were afraid to tell their parents, friends, anyone or anything about Mrs. Steele's classroom. Students were being traumatized, daily, and had, in essence, become hostages whenever they were in her classroom. This was absurdity. Lunacy. Unfortunately, this was often the accepted way that some teachers ran their classrooms! This had to stop!

Now, this is an extreme example of the horrid abuses of one individual, but, yet, it really did occur, in a public-school setting. Pain still existed long after this person was removed from the school. However, remember, each time we fail to provide the dignity, care, compassion, kindness, thoughtfulness, and love that each of our student's need, we run the risk of adding to the trauma that too frequently impedes their potential for success.

Enough is Enough

Fights with students over piddly stuff diminishes you as a person, disengages each student from the important student/teacher relationship and demonstrates disdain for the trust that must be honed between the two. The importance of the symbiotic nature of the student/teacher relationship is so much more important than demonstrating who has control in that relationship. So, stop the argument madness!

Dr. Robert A. Martinez is the Founder of Resilience Vineyards, author, speaker and a California Superintendent of Schools. His primary goal is to create safe places for students to grow, develop and empower their resilience.

Stop Using Students to Further Adult Agendas
DANA GOODIER, Ed.D.

Learning always suffers when adult agendas drive our classroom and school-wide practices. When state and district offices dictate what we teach, how long we teach and how it will be tested, without the flexibility of teacher expertise or student needs, achievement will suffer. Relationships will diminish. Purpose will fade. The system will fail when adults use students to further their political lineup.

The Dawn of No Child Left Behind

I started teaching in the U.S. at the dawn of the NCLB in 2002. Having lived in Canada for a few years to attend graduate school following the completion of my M.A. in 2000, I was "blissfully unaware" of the policy change, partially because I was hired to be an elective course teacher, so my subject area didn't "teach to the test" or worry about a culmination exam that would rank and file my students. My first encounter with high-stakes testing occurred in the spring of 2003 when, I, along with the bulk of the staff at the high school where I taught, proctored the Colorado Student Assessment Program (CSAP). I was told that the usual proctors receive annual training, but one thing that stood out to me was the instruction I was given to not answer any students' questions that may lead to giving them the answer on a test item.

When High Stakes Testing is a Priority

Being a world languages teacher in the 2000's meant that because of high-stakes testing and the subjects that were tested on (math, science and English) received highest priority, many elective programs or choices were cut. I remember vividly the spring following my first-year teaching at a U.S. high school. It was at the time the U.S. troops were entering Afghanistan. Because the French government said they wouldn't support the U.S. invasion, suddenly the masses began to boycott everything French. Do you remember the term "Freedom Fries"? Well, in the fall of 2003, students at my high school who wanted to continue higher course offerings of French were not granted the chance, due to the decreased enrollment that spring because of the boycott of everything French–all tied to politics that are out of students' hands.

The "Rat" Race to the Top

You may remember "Race to the Top" (or RTTT). I started my principal licensure program in the fall of 2009, partially because I got fed up with the electives getting cut and wanted to be able to help make change happen at a broader level. At this time, much of the chatter was about the RTTT contest to see which state could score the highest on high-stakes tests and, thus, receive a competitive grant from the U.S. Department of Education. Of course, RTTT led us down the slippery slope of tying teacher evaluations to student test scores. I was in a cohort of practicing teachers who were aspiring administrators and I recall the discussions we had concerning evaluating teachers in this manner. My home state of Colorado actually was one of the Phrase III winners. This was largely due to several urban districts taking on a "pay for performance" approach to teacher salaries, which has since been reversed. A great deal of hostility arose among staff, because if one teacher made $10,000 more than another teacher down the hall, largely due to how her students performed on standardized tests, it became obvious that unfairness existed. Also, many administrators were asked to give only a certain number of teachers "highly effective" ratings, due to district budget restraints on how much of a yearly raise one could get. Not only did this pit teachers against each other and administrators as favoring one teacher over another, but in the local news, several stories emerged at the time of subtle ways that these "highly effective" teacher ratings were being decided on.

It turns out that after the RTTT initiative dissolved in 2015, many teachers' unions, parents and school boards were demanding for the reinstatement of the salary scales that were tied to education and experience. What a disaster the initiative RTTT was for growth in fair pay for teachers. When we don't pay teachers a salary they deserve, based on years of experience and advanced degrees, there tends to be a lot of animosity. When we judge teachers based on how students perform on a snapshot of a high-stakes test, teachers become overly stressed at test time, and tend to teach to the test. Students then experience a lack of quality instruction and the chance to dive deeper into subject areas and themes that they aren't usually tested on.

Student Needs, not Legislation

You ask about how all this affects students negatively and why it must STOP. When legislatures decide what students should learn and how they should learn it, learning will suffer. When teachers, parents, students and other school staff work together to decide how students should learn and what they should be tested on, it becomes a win-win for all. The COVID-19 pandemic forced us to reexamine how we teach and, hopefully, how we access students, both locally, state-wide and nation-wide. What transpires in the next few years in terms of how we stop using children to further the adult agenda MUST lead to positive change in terms of focusing on students' needs, not legislation. Teachers do have discussions in the hallways of their schools about everything that effects them. They are human too. But, the students are listening and we have to work hard to not pit our students against the system even if we disagree with how the system is being run. More teacher issues will be coming. I'm certain of that. Educators are never left alone. So, I leave you with this one, central question: "How are *you* going to keep your students out of your own business affairs?"

Dr. Dana Goodier has 20 years of experience in education, has taught World Languages and English and worked as a middle school administrator. She is the host of the "Out of the Trenches" podcast, which features educators who share their stories of resiliency.

Stop Doing Personal Things while Teaching or Supervising Students

SCOTT WURM

Countless times, I have walked into classrooms to see students not focused on schoolwork, engaging in off task behaviors and, generally, not getting anything out of the work they are doing. Then I look across the room and see their teacher sitting at a desk staring at their phone. Students will, unconsciously, mimic what they see. In this case, students may be subjected to a teacher who is disorganized, unprepared, and unprofessional. Every instructional minute counts. Teachers were hired to deliver engaging and informative lessons and to keep students safe. Personal things shouldn't ever get in the way of supervising students.

Despite what may be happening outside of class and in your personal life, very few things are important enough to compromise student learning and wellbeing. Families within our educational communities depend upon us to give their children a quality education and they trust us to keep their children safe. If we are on our phones, computers, or distracted in various ways, we are doing them all a disservice. We must be vigilant and make sure we know what they are doing at all times. This means putting our phones down, logging out of Facebook and focusing on the student scholars in front of us.

Students Can Smell it Too

Sharks can smell blood in the water up to ⅓ of a mile (1760 ft.) and trace it back to its source. This can lead to a feeding frenzy because once they get the smell of prey in their minds, they are singularly focused on the kill and feed off of each other's energy. Kids are the same way. They know when a teacher isn't organized, is distracted, or not paying attention to what is happening in the classroom. We all know this experience, either as a teacher, a substitute teacher, or a student, ourselves. Once the "blood" is in the water, it's very hard to bring things back under control.

Students spend more time in a weekday at school than at home. Whether you believe it or not, teachers ethically entered the profession with a societal expectation that teachers would be the ideal role model for their students. Effective teachers create a bond between the hearts and minds of their students and school community. Five-star classrooms and schools ensure that every student feels as though they are in a pleasant, safe and adaptive environment at all times. Checking your phone occasionally is fine if you need to monitor an emergency issue at home or outside of school, but we should never have the phone on and in front of us for any extended period of time. Even texting, while it may only seem like a few moments, takes your attention away from your students for a surprisingly long time. Texting, by its very nature, involves at least two separate physical/mental actions, all of which take attention away from your classroom. It requires your visual and cognitive attention. Visually, instead of watching the classroom, your eyes are looking for messages. Cognitively, your mind is no longer on your class but on manipulation of these other devices, understanding the messages and communicating to others. Texting for only four seconds is the equivalent to driving the length of a football field at a high speed with your eyes closed. Now imagine what could happen, with over 20 children who have now realized that you are not paying attention to them.

Be Prepared

We all have bad days, rough starts to days, but this is never an excuse to not be prepared. We should always have a backup plan and a backup plan to the backup plan. We need to plan for the unexpected and always give our students the feeling that we have things under control, (even if we feel things are slipping away). We must never let the class become a place where off-task and disrespectful behavior is allowed. Take control of the class. Students may become excited and may create noises. While teachers of younger students might find this difficult, it is a skill that can easily be developed. Create signals such as clapping hands, using small non-verbal signals or raising hands to keep them quiet.

Get Up and Get Moving

Teachers should be up on their feet and at the door greeting and setting the tone for the day. Yes, there are extenuating circumstances that may keep you in your seat at the beginning of class. But, remaining in the seated position throughout the class creates a lack of interest and motivation in students. Movement not only keeps students engaged and motivated, it will help you do the same. I find when I'm moving and talking to my students, I'm more motivated to see their successes and manage their emotions when they are not successful.

It's a Classroom not a Cafeteria

You'd be surprised to know how many times I've seen a teacher eating while teaching. This is not a professional practice for any level or any age. How would you feel if you hadn't eaten breakfast and were hungry and you are in line at the bank to deposit a check and the teller was sitting there distracted and eating a breakfast burrito? You would immediately be turned off by the lack of professionalism while at the same time your stomach grumbles would amplify. Over 30 million students in the United States are purchasing free or reduced meals in schools, many students and families do not have enough food to feed themselves and those that don't purchase lunch may be in a situation where they may not have enough to send in a complete lunch for their kids. When teachers eat in front of their students while teaching it has the same effect as the scenario above. It just isn't right. You might be thinking, "Well, I had a meeting during my lunch period." or "I had to call parents during my planning period, so it's OK." Shuffle your duties, then. Eat during your planning period and call parents after school. It is our ethical duty to ensure students' needs are met, not to make anyone feel uncomfortable or awkward at any time. When teachers eat in class they are not giving them our full attention. They deserve every minute of our time and attention throughout the day.

Our minds must be laser-focused on the task at hand. This means making sure every child is safe and taken care of, both mentally and physically. Every time we become distracted; we are preventing our classrooms from becoming a high quality, five-star success. We owe it to ourselves to be prepared every day, in every way to do our absolute best for our students.

Scott Wurm is a special education teacher at Hampton Bays Middle School in New York State and a technology in education guru.

Stop Pushing Your Own Political Views
QUINN ROLLINS

"The president is an idiot."

With those words, a teacher will not only lose half of their class, they may also incite a riot,. A teacher making this type of statement alienates any student that may be on the side of the president or the president's political party. Not just alienated for that day, or that discussion, but possibly for the rest of the year. Students may even have the impression that if you do not like and respect that political figure, you don't like and respect them or their family. It becomes personal. *A point of no return.*

Political Landmines

I've been in the classroom almost twenty years now, teaching social studies. The first part of my career I spent with seventh graders and then I worked at the district office as a curriculum specialist. Now I'm back in the classroom where I have always felt I belonged. As a United States history teacher, I can't remember a year more littered with political landmines than 2020-2021 has been.

As I'm writing this, we're wrapping up a presidential election season that's been a doozy. In my class, we have talked about this unique political experience and environment, almost constantly. Throughout this doozy of an election, I never once told, or even hinted to students whom I voted for. My typical response was, "I've voted for Republicans and I've voted for Democrats." and that is true. This chapter isn't "Stop Having Students Discuss Politics in the Classroom," it's "Stop Pushing Your Own Political Views." There is a big difference here.

Full Disclosure before Civic Engagement

In my course description I fully disclose the type of reading and discussions that will take place. My course disclaimer reads, "In a social studies classroom, we will sometimes talk about controversial topics, including politics, race, religion, culture and identity. Students and the teacher are expected to treat differing opinions with respect as we explore our own opinions and perspectives throughout the course."

Modeling civic engagement is the responsibility of the teacher. You can begin by just letting students know that you understand current events and that you understand what's happening in the world around you. Acknowledging that dissonance of political and current events exists may ease their minds. Whether you decide to engage in a full discussion in your classroom or not is your discretion. As a social studies teacher, I view my classroom as a laboratory where students are encouraged to actively explore these issues. Part of civic engagement is looking at multiple perspectives and developing our own opinion through researching evidence in a safe space. They should not be expected to parrot my opinions back to me or even know what my personal opinions are. Socratic seminars and philosophical chairs are both great strategies to teach students how to engage in conversations of opposing views based on facts and evidence. These practices also model when a citizen may actually change their stance or opinion based on new information. There are processes and protocols that help teach these skills directly.

There Isn't a Force-field around Your Classroom

I've talked with social studies teachers who say "Well . . ." (they always draw out the well) "it doesn't say election year, global pandemic, or Black Lives Matter on my curriculum map, so I'm not going to talk about it."

Can you imagine the first days back in school after major political controversy or turmoil and not providing students the chance to process some of those topics? What if it was war time? Are we going to sit there and ignore the reality that we are in a war? It's like avoiding the elephant in the room or placing a giant red arrow above the land mine and saying we aren't going to talk about it. You would be missing out on a once in a lifetime opportunity to model civic responsibility and to discuss the power of being an informed citizen.

Your classroom does not have a force field around it that the real world can't penetrate. Your students are already thinking about these things, they're posting about them on social media, learning about them through mainstream media and they are already developing opinions. We must metaphorically lift the force field around our brick and mortar or virtual classrooms and start showing students how to effectively and responsibly analyze primary and secondary resources to form opinions. Just remember, this, in no shape or form, requires you to assert your own political opinions in order to develop your students' own opinions. Below, you will find a few ways that I help my students explore their own political views without trying to influence them with my own:

1. Political Spectrum Activity

In the first two weeks of school, we take a simple 22-question-quiz. The questions come from the nonpartisan site, *I Side With*, and surveys from the *Pew Research Group*. The answers are all yes/no, true/false. It's anonymous and the questions include many of the topics that they'll be learning about in the upcoming year in a United States history class: immigration, taxation, voting rights, religion, government, climate change and even gun control. I emphasize that these are the simplest possible answers to incredibly complex issues and that their actual opinion on many questions is probably somewhere between "yes" and "no." They need to choose one angle, anyway. After they provide their responses, they'll put an anonymous marker (a sticker similar to everyone else's) somewhere on a number line on a long sheet of butcher paper. Only after the stickers are in place, do we look at what those numbers mean on a political spectrum from liberal (the far left end of the number line) to conservative (the far right), both extremes and everything in the middle. Without fail, the student responses end up in a classic bell curve—because they will always end up that way–students or even adults, alike.

This opens the door for a discussion about how most of American politics falls somewhere in the middle on most issues. Even though we see a lot of vocal division in society, we agree on more than we disagree on. We're able to explore the idea that even though, traditionally, a Democrat would vote on issues more towards the left of that spectrum and a Republican more to the right, that doesn't automatically make the students on either side a member of that political party. When students ask me where I am on that, I tell them "somewhere in the middle" with usually with a vague, sweeping motion that covers the entire spectrum. Students want to know you have an opinion. They should know, even early into the school year, that they are not likely to hear your opinion because you do not want to divide your students or pit them against one another.

2. Pro/Con.org

Pro/Con.org is another nonpartisan site that can be a teacher's best friend. A jumping off place for research and discussion on hundreds of controversial topics, it's a simple list of some of the most intimidating classroom discussions possible. Selecting one issue, such as "gun control," it opens a page that has fifteen arguments and ideas that would support stricter control measures and pairs them with fifteen arguments opposing those measures. Each argument is sourced. Most of the fifteen points are briefly summarized making them ideal for classroom use. In reading the opposing arguments and the reasoning behind them, students see examples of civil dialogue, building a model for classroom expression of differing opinions. Having students write a response either defending or rebutting the opinions is a safer way than having a teacher slip into their own political opinion on the matter.

3. Anonymous Conversations

The families in my current school are almost an even mix between liberal and conservative mindsets. This last spring and summer, there were demonstrations in cities across the country after the killing of George Floyd. The polarization that followed is still felt in my classroom, with the potential for conversations to "defund the police" to spin out of control. And yet, I want students to have a safe space for that conversation.

After the acquittal of the police officers in a racially-charged case, I wanted to allow students the space to process these events and to offer their opinions on them. A simple digital form with assured anonymity gave them that opportunity. I told the students, in advance, that I'd be sharing pieces of their writing with their peers, but that they would be disaggregated: 1st period's responses would be seen by 2nd period, 2nd period's by 3rd period, etc. That was Monday's assignment.

Tuesday, I selected the four best responses (two on the side of the police, two opposed) and shared them with students in other classes; those students then wrote responses to the opinions and arguments. This "anonymous conversation" was more engaging and emotional than I expected. My students got into this. They didn't know who they were writing to, but they knew what they were writing about. They knew it was students their own age, in their same community, with the same teachers. The key was me setting up the format and the security, knowing that they could share their opinion without being targeted by other students or *by me*.

4. Media Literacy

My last tip is to help students learn media literacy. Help them assess sources; help them to recognize the dangers of believing everything they read online. This year, in addition to my political spectrum activity above, I added a media bias chart from *Ad Fontes Media*. It ranks major news outlets from the most reliable (Associated Press, Reuters) to the least (National Enquirer). It also rates outlets from most partisan to least. The extreme ends of that spectrum are *Wonkette* and *InfoWars*, with Associated Press and Reuters back in the center. Funny how that works.

There are about thirty news outlets in a green box in the center of the chart, highlighting those that are both reliable and nonpartisan. I tell my students when they bring a news story to class, it needs to be from a source within that green box. We're not going to discuss conspiracy theories, we're going to assess *actual events in as nonpartisan a way as much as possible*.

As a citizen, I definitely have my own ideological leanings and beliefs. I consume media from various sites and channels and sometimes end up in my own echo chamber. Consuming the bias chart is something I need to remind myself of as a teacher. Outside the classroom, I can pursue conspiracy theories all I want; they don't have a place in my classroom, however. Coming from a reliable and centered place will model responsible citizenship; coming from a pulpit of my own beliefs only pits and divides others. Ultimately, my vote is to equip my students, not infuriate them. Our future depends on it.

Quinn Rollins is a high school history teacher in Salt Lake City and teaches at the University of Utah. He is the author of Teach Like a Pirate: Engage Students with Toys, Games and Comics and has made it his mission to make education more engaging for the students and the teachers.

Stop Telling Students about Your Own Problems

LAURA STEINBRINK

Stop telling your students about your own problems unless there is a reason. I have been there, trust me. I have been totally guilty of warning students to tread lightly because of a headache that I had or because have come to school sick or because I am just, generally, having a bad day. Well, please stop. I have stopped this destructive behavior, myself, and here's why.

My Trauma Should Not Become Your Trauma

During my daughter's senior year of high school, she had a bad experience with a boyfriend who turned out to be abusive. Throughout her experience and my total cluelessness, while it was going on, I began to learn everything I could about social-emotional learning. Around the same time, my school provided training in trauma-informed practices so that we could become a trauma-informed school. During this learning process, the lightbulb suddenly exploded in my head. Students who are dealing with trauma, anxiety, panic attacks, PTSD and more are already overloaded with emotions and situations they are struggling to handle. In our efforts to create safe spaces inside our classrooms, why in the world would we add one more thing to their plate of emotional turmoil?

In my "Train Like a Navy SEAL" conference sessions, I explain why we must stop telling our students to be on their best behavior just because we happen to be experiencing a problem of our own. Students who are suffering trauma, in whatever form, are already on hyper-alert for things that might present a danger. Students of trauma have a sixth sense and can smell more trauma from a mile away and they don't need your burdens on their shoulders, either.

My Time is Your Time

Can you name all of your students who show up to school early? Do you get annoyed that they are already at school before they are *supposed* to be? I have been that teacher, coveting that alone time before the madness of my day starts. We need to check ourselves here. The moment students set foot in our classroom, the timeclock is punched, and we are on the clock working for them.

Our students deserve a teacher who is prepared each day to bring the "it" factor, that which possesses that magical combination of high energy and fabulous lesson design–which will hook them and make them feel like they matter. When we are on the clock, we must help each of them learn the content and then be able to apply that knowledge in new and creative ways. We must remember, first and foremost, that we are there for the students. Students don't work for us. We work for them and they deserve five-star customer service. It is always all about THEM.

Trauma, Drama & Emotional Roller Coasters

Students come to us with all sorts of trauma, drama and all things in between each day. You may never know that the top student in your class is starving most of the time because of his or her poor home life. You may not ever know that the kindergartener who showed up without his or her backpack, despite the timely lecture you gave the class the day before on coming to school prepared, was shoved out of the home that morning by their drugged-up parents. You won't know that the kid pounded on the door crying while the bus waited, begging for his or her backpack, only to be ignored by those who are supposed to love them the most. You may be surprised to find out that the 6 foot 4, 280 pound junior shows up at school when you do, 7 a.m., because he is already tired of his dad yelling at him. Are these extreme examples? Sure, but they happen every single day.

Students are also on emotional roller coasters when they fight with friends and break up with significant others. Believe me, I get that adults view high school (and younger) breakups with eye rolls and shoulder shrugs. We view those young relationships skeptically, knowing that these types of temporary relationships, for the majority, come to an inevitable end. We think we know about how students should feel. This is part of why we feel it is OK to load our problems on top of students, as well. We fall victim to the thinking that our adult problems take priority and are the only real problems. We like to unconsciously or openly judge student emotions. We decide for ourselves who is faking emotional distress and who isn't. We get involved and overstep our boundaries. We need to remove judgment from part of our daily work with students and give them our very best, period.

Make it a Dump Free Zone

We've all heard the phrase, "Fake it till ya make it." I once had an administrator who commented that a teacher had requested not to be evaluated that day because she was sick, but still came to school, anyway. If teachers come to school, they should be there for teaching and everything that goes with it. We do not get to ease through our days. If teachers don't feel well enough to fake it, then a sick day would be in order. I know that I have been guilty of this too. We all have at one time or another. I am

78

guilty of coming to school even when I feel less than 100%, so I was all ears when this principal talked about this conversation. Students deserve our best, so if we are at school, we need to bring it. I am not going to bring stress into the lives of my students by dumping my health, emotional, financial, or relationship problems onto their shoulders. If I am at school and not 100%, I fake it. I take deep breaths, dive in and make it through first period, then second period, third period, until I have a break. I do what I need to do during break to take care of myself, and then I dive back in. My goal is to give all students what they need without them knowing that I am feeling less. Relationship building suffers when I dump on them. So, join me. Make your classroom a *dump-on-students-no-more* zone.

Laura Steinbrink is a high school teacher, tech integration coach, national presenter and the author of www.rockntheboat.com, a Feedspot Top 200 blog in Education. She has published articles for Matt Miller, ISTE, Kahoot and other education-related companies.

28

Stop Feeling that You are Running Out of Time to Cover Content
DENISE GRANDITS, Ph.D.

What an educator does in teaching is to make it possible for the students to become themselves.
–Paulo Freire, from *Pedagogy of the Oppressed*

The weeks leading up to state standardized assessments increase my anxiety level. My mind won't shut off as I keep asking myself so many questions. Have I taught students everything I possibly could? Have I covered all the standards? Did I teach them every trick possible, so they could be successful on that state assessment? Then, just two months later, the panic sets in again as final exams roll around. Don't even get me started about the worry I feel as I send my precious students off to the next grade level. As a middle school ELA teacher, I fully understand and internalize how much pressure there is to get through all the content no matter what subject you teach. Every year, I experience time slipping away as state tests near. All teachers want their students to be successful and, as a result, they feel obligated to get every piece of content and knowledge into our students before the end of a year. We care about their future selves and want to ensure students are prepared and successful.

Rushing Through isn't Going Deep

Since I will not pretend to know what it means to be a teacher in different subject areas, I will focus my discussion on my experiences as an ELA teacher (which many will think is a free flowing course, unlike math, science or social studies). Yet, I routinely plan out a unit on a novel with a surgeon's precision. I figure how many days each chapter will take us to read, close read, analyze and discuss. I sprinkle in some days for assessments and writing. Voila! The unit is perfect. Until it's not.

Take, for example, my experiences each time I choose one particular piece of Holocaust literature, such as *Daniel's Story*, by Carol Matos. The story is factual to the degree that it is based on the collective experiences of the victims during such an atrocious time in history. The author weaves a masterful story that is powerful enough to engage young readers in thoughtful reflection without overwhelming them with the daily horrors of the Holocaust. It is certainly a manageable text in both content and length. It is a mere 136 pages. Certainly, it should fit perfectly in the time frame I allot for the novel. I could "plow through" the text so that I finish the novel in the designated time frame. But in turn, I would deny my students the tremendous opportunity to explore topics and ideas that their reading and scholarly, collegial discussions evoke. I am not willing to jeopardize that in favor of rushing through my time frame. *So, I choose to go deeper.*

Learning Gets Sidetracked

What is a teacher to do? How many times have we heard a colleague say (or have uttered ourselves) that "we have to get through this today"? The burning question is this: if the point of an education is to inspire and awaken young minds to new ideas, should we "get through" the content or should we savor the numerous teachable moments that spring organically from a rich tapestry of learning experiences? Or, is the full measure of an education the degree to which students embrace ideas and apply those understandings to their lived experiences? Even when I am tempted to "just get through," I am reminded that the best learning is often not those experiences a teacher plans for in the beautifully crafted lesson plans. The best learning happens when students are immersed in a powerful, rich, authentic learning environment where their natural curiosity sparks the *real* learning.

Take my example of what happens every year when we study *Daniel's Story*. Certainly, I focus on a myriad of Next Generation Learning Standards in guiding my students' understanding of the text on both the literal and figurative levels. That part is easy to a degree. However, every year, our learning gets sidetracked as students ask questions that are relevant to them. I do not think there is a teacher on the planet who would tell students to seek out those answers alone in favor of "getting through the book" within the teacher's planned time on a curriculum map. *Remember, maps are documents that are meant to breathe.* Because I focus much less on "getting through" than I do on nurturing a rich environment for students to learn and apply what they are learning to their lives, it is not uncommon for this short novel to take upwards of eight weeks to finish.

My 7th grade students delve into social justice issues such as racism and anti-Semitism. They explore issues surrounding being a bystander or an upstander and connect these ideas to their experiences with bullying and normal adolescent drama. They research topics brought up by the author in passing descriptions in the novel. For example, they read extensively about the Nuremberg Laws and I deliberately discuss Jim Crow Laws so they understand that this kind of oppression was not only used by the Nazis decades ago. They live by the mantra that they "will remember" and they truly begin to develop an understanding that the evils of the world cannot go unchecked for fear of repeating history.

Authentic Learning isn't Regulated Learning

Educational psychologist, Lev Vygotsky, uses the term "appropriation" to mean the act by which children take what they have learned and apply it to their lived experiences. This is the stage when what they have learned becomes a part of who they are. Their learning is not relegated to just the classroom.

For the past three years, at least one of my students has been honored with a writing award from our local Holocaust Resource Center. Students are enthusiastic to submit their writing to the annual contest and are committed to making sure our community knows they will never forget the lessons they learned by studying the Holocaust. The classroom learning becomes a part of the larger community.

For me, the ultimate goal of education is to provide students with knowledge, skills, critical thinking, and, I would argue for the ELA curriculum especially, empathy, so that they can develop into a better version of themselves and apply what they have learned in our rather sterile learning environments to their complex lives. I contend, based on my observations, that the pressure to "get through the material" may be counterproductive to the true purpose of education. We must consider whether a rushed glaze over all the content is what we should pursue or should we build learning opportunities with some wiggle room to encourage students to explore ideas that are meaningful to them so that they can, one day, have an impact on our world.

Kindle the Fire

Don't get me wrong. I get it. There are tests and there is a curriculum to follow. Allowing students the space to explore does not mean we are abandoning the curriculum or the standards. It means recognizing that there is much more to an education than merely preparing students to pass a test or to consume all of a grade level's content. There is a famous quote that speaks to me so profoundly that it has become the foundation for my work as a teacher: "Education is not the filling of a bucket but the lighting of a fire." Educators are charged with providing the kindling for the fire. Stop fretting about getting through the content and start focusing on giving students powerful, meaningful learning experiences that change their understanding and perception of their worlds.

Dr. Denise Grandits is an ELA teacher in the Kenmore-Town of Tonawanda Union Free School District in Western New York. She also teaches a variety of college courses designed to prepare future teachers for the profession. She is a proud mother of three sons and a passionate Buffalo Bills fan.

Stop Using the Same Lesson Plans Each Year
LISA BLANK

"The less routine, the more life."
–Amos Bronson Alcott

Our students come to us as unique individuals, formed from varied experiences. They may have come from different regions. They may have had different teachers. They each have special interests and talents. Our students are not the same each year. It does not make sense for our lessons to be a repeated routine year after year. In addition to our students changing, the world is continuously changing, obviously.

Following my first year of teaching in Minnesota, my husband's career provided an opportunity for our family to move to New Hampshire. As a new teacher to the profession, I was fortunate to work in a district that had been recognized with the Presidential Award for Excellence. This was a badge of honor that an exemplary school system with deeply committed teachers and administrators received. Our leaders had us working in teams which provided outstanding opportunities for professional growth. As a new teacher being part of such a high standard and expectation, I experienced times when I felt disorganized and maybe a tad inadequate as an educator. Since then, I have always put undue pressure on myself to become more organized with to-do lists like my five-star colleagues.

Recently, I felt a sense of relief just reading the title of a story on the LinkedIn Daily Post, entitled "Why To-Do Lists Kill Productivity." It might seem strange that such a title would bring a sense of relief, but the truth is that I have always believed that I should be more organized and include more to-do lists in my life. I had constructed my own myth that Presidential Award teachers must have to-do lists. In my early years of teaching, I thought I should do better, be better and be more organized. I struggled with an unrealistic expectation of whom I should be—perhaps, an organized educator with a more effective to-do list?

The Hyper-Organized Educator

A former colleague of mine was the most organized educator I have ever known. She made copies of all lesson plan handouts in July and December like clockwork. She did this for years. She knew, well in advance, exactly what she was teaching, what her students would be doing and had the timing down so she could repeat it over and over, year after year, with only minor adjustments. Suggestions of adjustments during the year caused great stress to her and were generally avoided. Modifications to the plans were for summer curriculum work. Teachers working with this teacher generally avoided changes because it caused the hyper-organized teacher much distress. After all, she had everything planned out and ready to go. Changing plans would result in wasted time and resources. This teacher was so organized that she was able to leave school as soon as the contractual day ended. By nature, most educators are hyper-organized with color coded bins and systems for just about everything that happens in the classroom.

The Curriculum Train

The curriculum train is an analogy I like to use to describe the rapid speed and unrealistic expectations we face as teaches to "cover" the curriculum. I once worked with a department in which four or five teachers would teach the same curriculum that had been developed previously by a team of teachers from the department. The expectation was for teachers to cover the same topic on the *same day* with the exact same *pacing*. The department wanted consistency. In other words, they wanted all students to receive identical tests and quizzes on identical schedules. If a teacher was sick, the substitute would need to cover the content adequately. There was no time to catch up. The train had a lot of ground to cover and it was moving at a rapid pace! If you weren't able to keep up and were not ready at the stop, you would be left in the dust–and a consequence of "missing that train" was that you would be ostracized by your colleagues.

After several years in New Hampshire, another move was in order, planting my family in New York. This state's long-running history that is firmly rooted in high school graduation based upon successful completion of what is known as "Regents Examinations," I further experienced these effects on my colleagues.

High-Stakes Assessments as the End Goal

Where in life is a single performance the end goal? This may make sense for the Olympics. How does it make sense in education?

Discussions have arisen surrounding thoughts of dropping Regents Examinations in some subject areas. The very thought of this, with assessments being such a strong driver of the work of New York educators, leave educators concerned to this day. Teachers have expressed fear that their colleagues wouldn't know what to teach and that students will suffer, as a result.

This was incredibly troubling to me! Educators, if you have had these thoughts, please stop and think about all the training we have had, the professional development we have participated in and the curriculum work we have done. Then, think of all the students we have taught. Would the removal of a high-stakes end-of-the-year-assessment stop all of that?

The truth is that in far too many cases, assessments have driven the curriculum. They have driven teachers into routines that place them firmly on the curriculum train. This vehicle prioritizes paths, stops and a destination that many hold firmly in their practices with or without assessments.

Overscheduling

Given the schedules of teachers in most schools, where is time allotted for professional reflection and collaboration? How do we ensure that data is gathered and used in a timely manner applying a cycle of continuous improvement to our activities?

Educators struggle with schedules. They generally are scheduled so tightly and not in a manner that fosters reflection, collaboration and continuous improvement. This prevents teachers from engaging in deep thinking about their practices, their connections with students and how they might most effectively help students learn. The debacle of overscheduling is another factor that keeps too many educators in regimented routines, limiting opportunities for creative though.

Value for the Individual vs. Value for the Routine

My teaching career officially began in Red Wing, Minnesota. A few weeks prior to the start of school, all teachers new to the district met with our superintendent. He went over basic policies, personally provided the group with sound financial advice, arranged a luncheon with the entire school board and we left that day with our first paycheck. He knew we had expenses that might weigh heavily upon us as recent college graduates who were new teachers. He visited our classrooms throughout the year, making a point to know each of us personally. It was clear that each of us, as individuals, were truly valued.

I also had the benefit of learning from my mother who was also a teacher. She began her career in a one-room schoolhouse in rural Wisconsin and retired as a reading specialist and first grade teacher. I fondly recall her sharing concerns about the children she taught–each coming from different homes with different values, expectations, and vastly different emphases on educating young children. She was always thinking of ways to better reach her students and how to engage and excite them about learning. I am very thankful for what I learned from her. She was my greatest influencer—helping to form my basic views of teaching and learning from an exceedingly early age.

My experiences left me equipped with great models of teaching, models that focused on the value of the individual. This stuck with me through the years. While I have certainly felt anxiety over such things as not having all plans laid out well in advance and never feeling I had found my seat on the curriculum train, I have learned that I was on the right path all along. I have often made modifications to my lessons, sometimes in short order before instruction began.

Value for the individual and concern for the unique learning needs of each student should drive our efforts. Truly, student-centered approaches to learning have been challenging in the era of standardization. A one-size-fits-all model that funnels our students through standardized tests does not prioritize the needs of individual learners. I even developed an aversion to the term "data-driven," but am recovering from that since I learned that it doesn't always have to be tied to assessment data. Data is powerful. It can prove helpful or harmful to us depending on its use.

Pursue new tools and resources that improve student engagement and understanding. Using the same lesson plans year after year equates to being stuck in a past that no longer exists.

Always think forward. Try new things. Make personal connections with each individual learner and remember that it is OK not to operate from a to-do list! When we become too focused on completing tasks, we are prone to lose sight of making connections, a critical component of our own teaching and learning.

Lisa Blank serves as the Director of STEM Programs for Watertown City School District in Northern New York and is a Lead STEM Fellow and Advisory Council Member with STEM Learning Ecosystems.

Stop Running End-of-the-Year & Holiday Countdowns
JACIE MASLYK, Ed.D.

As a family or community member, imagine the first sight on the first day of school being the school secretary sporting a neon green t-shirt with purple lettering that reads, "Is it June yet?" This just happened to be my secretary. She sometimes wore it during the first week of school or right before long breaks! I get it. It's a joke. But this joke is telling everyone that you see that you are already looking ahead for this school year to end. This is the first impression of the school or the face of the school building that people see, first. She was often the first person who greeted familiar faces and welcomed new visitors into the school. Whether you truly mean it or not, when you convey this type of messaging on a poster, cup, or hat, you are signaling that you are ready for the year to be done. You are ready to stop working, stop serving kids, and move on to your summer vacation. Why would we want to tell our students and families that?

Only 35 More Days until Christmas Break

As an elementary principal of a K-6 school for ten years, we boasted strong academics and a supportive school community. I loved being a principal and I loved our school community. Our school was located in an amazing neighborhood with bright students and engaged families. Our staff was incredible: dedicated teachers, caring support staff, friendly cafeteria workers and hard-working custodians. We also had a superstar secretary. She was quick to anticipate needs, understanding and accommodating students and parents and responsive to teachers and staff. She knew everyone by name and knew their cousins and neighbors too. She was exactly what you would want in a school secretary, except for that one flaw: The "can't wait for this to be over" t-shirt, countdown mentality.

I remember walking in the office early one morning in November. We were heading into the second nine weeks of school and things were getting busy. The main office had a small "work area" where our teacher had their mailboxes as well as a whiteboard where we would often display messages. This helped with communication and updates and teachers would see these messages immediately as they were signing in each morning and grabbing their mail. Typically, this whole area and bulletin board inspired, informed, and united us as a staff.

One morning in November in beautiful block handwriting centered on the bulletin message board, in my secretary's handwriting was: "Only 35 more days until Christmas!" What? We just got done trick-or-treating. It's one thing if you want to alert me to the number of shopping days left, but that was not the intent. This was meant to be a countdown to the holiday break. Sure, we all need a rest, but the message digs deeper to some.

Messaging Matters

Why do we do this in schools? Is it so bad that we need to start anticipating the 7-10 days off for the holidays? Are we so exhausted that we need to start the hype 35 days prior? I understand culture, community, and the power of a positive social dynamic. This does not negate integrating holiday joy and infusing personal social and emotional connections to holidays. But, it does send a message that your personal life is more important than your students' learning. Unfortunately, some people do function this way and possess this toxic mindset, but as a school leader, I take issue with this.

Do we realize the message this is sending? As educators, we must focus on the positive and create an awe-inspiring vision for teaching and learning. Yet, teachers encounter bad days and stressful situations, but we must keep positivism as our main focus. What we put out there is what others see, hear and feel. What do you want people to feel about your school?

Let me be clear. I do not believe the secretary wearing her, "Is it June yet?" t-shirt intended to be negative, nor did she mean to offend anyone. I had to live by my moral compass and muster up the words to essentially let her know this was unacceptable. I reminded her that our school was a positive place because of the people who filled our hallways and classroom. We were special because we had incredible individuals that made it that way. I assured her that this practice did not align with our mission, vision or core beliefs and moving forward this approach to holidays or summer vacation was prohibited. And. It. Should. Not. Happen. Again.

It does not matter who you are or what your role is, but what we share about our schools' matters. From the bus drivers to the secretaries to counselors, principals, or central office staff, we are all stewards of our schools. If we act like we dread going to work each day, then what do you think our students are going to feel? If we wear shirts saying that we cannot wait for the year to end, what motivation does a reluctant learner have when considering coming to school each day or not?

Invest in Inspiration

Our perspective influences others. If the message you see in the main office of your school is reminding you when it's Friday or how many days until spring vacation, then that is likely what you are going to focus on. We cannot allow these messages to permeate our school buildings. Do not spend another minute counting the number of days until school is over. How about doing everything you can to make sure that each one of those days' counts? I sound like a stick-in-the-mud for fun, but messaging can import so many feelings about the messenger. What if students were not looking forward to not coming to school because of an abusive parent or because they have no food in the house?

Dr. Jacie Maslyk is an educator in Pittsburg, Pennsylvania; a speaker, author of five books and a Solution Tree Associate.

Stop Teaching Only the Topics that You Enjoy
ROMAN NOWAK

Infusing our passions, interests and vulnerability in life lessons are ingredients to five-star classrooms. Culture begs teachers to emit joy in our teaching and share the things in life that we love. Communicating the things that make us happy is an effective model of being a connected community member. This isn't what I am talking about; I'd like to go deeper. It is high added value when teachers incorporate their passions in the classroom, yes. When our passionate permeates a classroom or lesson, students can feel our positive energy and connection to the learning. But, when your interests and topics are the ONLY basis for lecturing, thematic learning, providing assignments and classroom activities, students run the risk of disengaging and, even worse, halt long-term learning, as well.

Something that intrigues and interests you may not interest or inspire all of your students. Teaching through passion is crucial; selecting all topics of learning and dominating learning through your perspective, ONLY, is not. As educators attempt to grapple with ever-changing teaching delivery methods due to the COVID-19 global pandemic, we must also realize the power we possess in our classrooms both in person and virtually.

Hobbies and Talents

Your hobbies and talents are assets. These things make you unique as a teacher and delivers synergy and offers a perspective into your life experiences. Yes, it is important to teach or utilize our own passions in the classroom, but if we like penguins and spend months teaching about penguins in a science classroom, penguins are going to drive everyone crazy at some point!

Consider a teacher who possesses a talent in music: this teacher may infuse soundtracks, sounds, or create catchy songs and jingles in the classroom to hook students in a lesson. If a teacher is a seasoned traveler, they may share rich stories of exotic, historic or international trips that include pictures and video footage or artifacts. This real-world perspective of using a passport and international travel may open a whole new world of possibility for students that may never have had the opportunity to travel. This is the good stuff. Since I happen to enjoy hockey, I may create arena themed activities, have jersey days, or divide my class into three periods. Another teacher may enjoy basketball and use the inspiration of March Madness to create brackets, to have daily competitions or go through hoops with three-point question challenges. Although all these methods can create engaging activities, they should only be used periodically. The real magic comes when teachers utilize both their own hobbies and talents and include students' passions, perspective, and interests in the classroom.

Amplify Student Interests Too

Teachers cannot forget that some kids are neglected at home. There are students who have little attention at home or little time is spent with them. Students of poverty and neglect often are lacking life experiences, hobbies, or the ability to identify their own talents. Students may lack a variety of hobbies and talents due to various reasons: the need to work, other family obligations, generational poverty, abuse, neglect, and trauma or in extreme circumstances, a total lack of love. The bottom line is our students do not have the same background knowledge or variety of experiences that most educators have. When the good-natured educator ONLY chooses their own passion and dismisses students' passions, this lack of intentionality can be detrimental. If a student does not feel seen at home and this same feeling is amplified or repeated at school, their self-worth and love will be called into question. We must seek strength building and interest-rich situations as much as possible.

Some teachers are talented athletes and thrive on competition. Students, who participate in many community sports and even competitive teams, love adding the thrill of competition to the classroom. Although, this may motivate the teacher and some students, in many cases, they speak directly to the extraverted students. For other students, it becomes a moment of dread and worry. When a student who has been the target of bullying, name calling or is isolated by other classmates, stumbles across something in which they are not "good at," this situation may beat down their self-esteem. If a student is used to not being included or is chosen last all the time, having that competitive element may have adverse effects. For a student who is not an athlete, who simply wants to learn, because they are not comfortable with scenes of attention, such scenarios become instigators of anxiety. Student may be asking themselves: "What if I get it wrong?" or "What will teammates say if I take too long?" These are all legitimate questions and worries that students have on a regular basis and will often not feel comfortable voicing to the teacher. The focus, therefore, needs to go from the topics we enjoy to the topics that we need to be talking and learning about. When classroom teachers are not teaching about equity, social justice movements, anti-racism, or how to question things or social media, teachers are missing valuable skills.

Provide Purpose and Validity

Students often find work in the classroom as long, tedious, boring, and even useless. It is our job to help students create those links and be more explicit about how school can prepare them for future challenges and give them the necessary tools to succeed in life. Yes, it is an important skill for students to learn how to deal with or use what is being taught in the classroom, even if they do not enjoy it. We live in a hyper-stimulated world where graphics, sounds and messages are bombarded at students on a constant basis. If there is a hint of boredom at any point, we might choose to go on social media or download a new app to find a way to fill their missing stimulation. Our students need to learn how to deal with situations that are not always high impact, where they do not necessarily ENJOY every single second–I get that. However, if we do not give purpose to our learning or explain the validity, then *why* are we doing *what* we are doing?

Ensuring that every student is seen, heard and valued are pivotal components of a five-star classroom. Teacher joy should permeate and student joys and passions should find their niche there too. We live in a time of high accountability, societal trauma and teachers are in a high rinse cycle within a stressful system. Regardless of these obstacles and challenges, we must capitalize on the opportunity to impact every student. Put forth a vision for teaching, learning and leading. This is our moment. Will you join in and move past the penguins?

Roman Nowak is a master educator in Clarence-Rockland, Ontario; the founder of the #BuildHopeEDU chat and an educational author.

Stop Focusing Only on At-Risk Students
TODD STANLEY

Most classrooms use the "hospital approach" to education. The philosophy in hospitals is to treat the most severe cases or at-risk patients, first, and to put off patients with minor ailments until the severe ones can be dealt with. This is known as *triaging*. This makes sense for a hospital because there are only so many doctors and staff, so if you do not give your full attention to your most severe patients, they die. The person who has a broken arm or comes in with the sniffles is going to survive no matter how long they wait or even if they leave without any treatment. They just aren't going to get better as quickly or not at all, but it is not *life-threatening*.

Triage Treatment

Sometimes, classrooms adopt the emergency room mentality and only treat the "code red" bleeders or broken-bone visitors. This idea of triage in the classroom happens when attention is given to students who are most at-risk. What do I mean by at-risk in this case? At-risk refers to any student who is non-typical, which can mean a variety of things. It could be a student who is struggling in class because of a learning disability. It could be a student who does not show any motivation. It could be a student who does not turn in any of their homework. It could be a student who is a chronic discipline problem. It could be a student who is often absent and is always playing catch up with their work. It could be a gifted student with emotional issues whose anxiety distracts him from his classwork. It could be a second language learner or refugee that just fled their country. Any of these factors could warrant a need for additional supports and gap-closing techniques.

No matter the cause, non-typical students tend to require more attention from the teacher. Since the

91

teacher only has so much attention to give, what happens to the compliant or high performing students? Because so much attention is given to the at-risk students, these students are stuck in the waiting room, waiting and waiting and waiting and waiting for the teacher to pose a high interest real world challenge so that they can reach their potential. Sometimes this does not come to light and many teachers are OK with this because their philosophy is that the high students will be alright. They are bright and capable of making it on their own with truly little teacher intervention. While this might be true, they do not need as much attention or motivation as the at-risk students, they do deserve customization and individualized learning. Without a five-star teacher mindset these students leave school having an adequate education. They deserve more. High achieving students deserve to move forward on a learning continuum and to gain a deep understanding of the standards applied. We must equalize our attention on all students rather than triaging the at-risk students.

Coach Them Instead

What if we used a coaching philosophy in our classrooms? The coaching philosophy is remarkably simple but effective. You have athletes who are the most athletic on the team. You have others who are not as skilled or who are not as willing to put in the work to be that elite athlete. The coach does not spend all their time with these at-risk athletes who are not working to their potential. The coach develops the talents of the best athletes while, at the same time, develops the skills of the less skilled athletes. Coaching looks different for each teammate because the players possess such varied strengths. If all teammates were coached the same way, no one would be working on the skills that would accelerate their game performance.

Could you imagine parents allowing their elite athletes to be ignored to the point that they become stagnant because the coach is giving most of their attention to athletes who are not able to match this potential? This would be unacceptable, and parents would demand customized training or their money back. Imagine a football coach saying to his star quarterback, "Hey, I'm not going to be able to work with you today because the 4th string quarterback is really struggling with learning the playbook. Just go over there and throw some passes." That coach would be ineffective because his top athletes would not be performing to their potential. But that's exactly what some teachers do in their classroom. The at-risk student is given the accommodations, the interventions or the one-on-one time. The students who are high performing and can work independently are left to quietly work by themselves because they will get it done without much support needed.

As a tennis coach of almost two decades, I understand the value of coaching individual skills. What if during practice, I only worked with the at-risk players, feeding them balls and giving them instruction, and I just had my top player work on a court by himself? That high octane player was never going to get any better. In fact, they might regress in their skills. I could apply this same concept to my classroom. I knew the conversation I was having with my gifted student was going to be different than the student who was reading two grades below level, but I had that conversation with both of them. I did not just work with the at-risk students and ignore the needs of students who didn't need as much of a push, but still needed some sort of a push, nonetheless.

Equity Not Equal

Differentiation requires you to personalize the learning for each student and instead of addressing them as an entire class, having individual conversations with each student is crucial. Do these conversations need to be equal in length? Absolutely not. You might have to have a longer conversation with the at-risk student while the high performing student might only need a nudge. That nudge will make a difference in the level of learning that student has. It will make them a better student.

What if we stop focusing on only the at-risk students and, instead, focus on all of them? Schools can embrace the coaching philosophy and figure out what each student needs and then provide that to the best of their ability.

Todd Stanley has 25 years of experience as a classroom teacher and coordinator for gifted education. He is also the author of various books for educators including Project-Based Learning in the Gifted Classroom and When Smart Kids Underachieve in School.

Stop Taking Everything Seriously
MELISSA CHOUINARD

"Sometimes originality needs perfect maintenance not modifications."
--Sonal Takalkar

We are organisms, science defines. But, as beings, we are electricity, signals, and functionality. There is a circuitry highway on which our emotions travel. Synapses charged with exhaustion, frustration and passion. We see the landscape of these facets, whooshing by us, as we traverse the curves and inclines of our profession, of this passion we call education.

Traveling a Highway of Emotion

Consider the last road trip that you were on. Billboards attract your attention. Scenery lulls you at times into a groove. You arrive at your next stop without even remembering how you got there. Other times, the traffic beside your lane is so blaring and obnoxious that it stirs our anger with the rev of an engine. Some points on your road trip may be relaxing and fulfilling and, at times, downright stressful. We have very little time to pull over at a rest stop or roadside diner. We see them in our rearview mirror. Often saddened, we did not take the time for a respite. After all, a milkshake and fries can be comforting on a long journey.

Classroom Road Trip

We often find ourselves on these daily, weekly and yearly road trips with a backseat full of students asking, "Are we there yet?" The driver (teachers) are trying their best just to keep their eyes on the highway while entertaining their riders (students). In addition to following the rules of the road, teachers are also trying to keep their passengers safe, entertained and happy. This may require tuning the dial to the local radio station, monitoring the temperature, and constantly checking their peripheral for other traffic. Teachers are like road trippers feeling hyper-aware of the yellow lines down the middle of the road, each whizzing by in rapid succession or feeling the dread and road tripping misery of the never-ending asphalt. Teachers are road warriors on a multilane superhighway while driving a double decker bus in the rain. At least, that is how it can feel some days. Like a driver, teachers sometimes feel that if they are not entertaining the troops. If their attention is not always centered on the backseat, they are not doing their jobs–becoming the driver of the mobile learning machine.

When the Check Engine Light Comes On

As the driver of a mobile classroom learning machine, there are times when the check engine light suddenly lights up the entire dashboard. Before you know it, the warning light begins blinking. Road tripping requires regular maintenance and routine regulation. As teacher drivers, we must stop every once in a while, at those rest stops just to breathe some fresh air and stretch our legs. Regulation may require pulling into the roadside diner to partake in a frothy malt or basket of cheesy potatoes. We need sustenance to keep going. We need to stretch our muscles and stop to notice how far we have come. These are the moments we often miss because we are set on arriving 'there,' wherever that place is, before dark.

Our vehicles, engines and interiors need upkeep and nurturing. The engines of our mobile learning machines are only going to sustain us for so long before our educational conveyance forces us off the road with a flat tire or an overheated engine block. We cannot take everything so seriously. We are important, yes. We are essential, yes. But we are also human. Our engines need more than an occasional trip to the mechanic.

Things Happen

Engines sputter, stall and seize even in the most luxurious cars. There are so many moving parts, connections, and branches in an engine: some pieces stretching with the heat, others fastening and binding. The frame of the car, being the visual aspect of our journey, becomes tarnished over time, nicks and dings showing that it has traveled far and wide because it has welcomed the roadway and accepted the inevitable wear and tear lifestyle.

It is the craftsmanship that prevents a misfire or trouble the longest. But no matter the brilliance of ingenuity and construction, all engines need maintenance. All hoods need to be looked under, occasionally, or the entire machine will fail. Some vehicles need a new paint job while others only call for simple touch-ups. But, even the most traveled vehicle has spirit. No matter the gloss or shine, every vehicle has potential and style.

The so-called "lemons," those vehicles assembled in haste and happenstance–the ones that are in the shop once a month–they just need some love and care. With a little patience and compassion these can become reliable, hopeful, and graceful forms of transportation. We just need to not take everything so seriously. We must understand that no matter our mechanism, no matter our agent, our engines are strong. Our engines are well oiled and roaring.

How can we not take everything seriously? We take our lessons seriously, our student relationships seriously, our parent communication seriously and our colleagues seriously. But seriously does not mean inflexible. We should learn to enjoy setbacks and view the detour as a pathway to growth. Nothing is perfect.

During these tumultuous times, a rock may have flown up and cracked the windshield. A fracture may be spreading before you. Strong teachers stay the course because they understand that things happen.

Detoured Not Deterred

How do we stay the course? When the rest of the world is hunkering down, we are leaning in. How do we continue to stay focused on the progress, not the perils? We have learned through experience, through miles of travel, how not to take ourselves seriously. We have learned to steer away from the potholes yet brace for impact when they surprise us. We are navigators and sightseers. We are locals and tourists. We are mindful, courageous travelers. When we share our stories of acceptance and endurance, we encourage others to do the same. We spark compassion and interest in a field once neglected. We are the positive voices in a sea of dissidence and doubt.

By not taking everything seriously, we see our reflection in the windshield on a sunny day. We no longer focus on where our journey began, but where our road trip will take us. We are educators and in our engine is a connection, a network of resiliency, forgiveness and well-deserved maintenance. We understand that we need help, and we pause for the advice and guidance.

Routine Maintenance

If you need a nudge, a reminder, I hope this has resurfaced your roadway and removed some of the gravel off your highway. I hope you notice the yellow and orange vests around you and welcome their repairs. There will be more impairments and disturbances on our journey. But if we continue to read the signposts, look up from time to time, and appreciate view on the horizon, you will find peace and enjoyment in the journey. Just remember to exit and enjoy a creamy, ice cold milkshake or another food every now and then; check under the hood frequently and buff up your paint job if that is important to you–knowing that another scrape or scratch is on the horizon.

Stop taking everything seriously and believe that the road trip is the memory, not a perfect exterior. Then settle in for the ride of your life. For the hazards are not abating, but our foresight is improving. Our endurance is heightening. Our camaraderie is strengthening, and our passion is marking our path. All we must do now is *buckle up*.

Melissa Chouinard is a 7th grade science educator in Katy, Texas. She is also the well-known blogger of iteacherimother and practicalrebellion, along with moderating the weekly #teachmindful chat.

Stop Expecting Respect Just Because You are a Teacher

DENNIS GRIFFIN, JR

"R-E-S-P-E-C-T, find out what it means to me." Undoubtedly, when you began reading the melody, the iconic Aretha Franklin began to fill your head and you continued mouthing and humming the rest of the song. I know I did. To really deconstruct this concept and meaning of the word *respect* especially in the context of our classrooms and schools, consider these next five questions.

1. What does respect mean to you at school and how did you come to this ideology?
2. Does your vision of respect resonate and is it practiced by every member of the school?
3. Do all students come to school with clear expectations regarding respect?
4. Do you believe that in your school, respect is not given but earned?
5. Do you believe that the definition of respect would be altered if you used the word society instead of school?

If you had an unfavorable answer to either question 2 or 3 and if you answered yes to either question 4 or 5, you are guilty, and this chapter is for you! Stop expecting students to walk into a classroom and respect you immediately!

Respect or Compliance

In many schools, respect usually comes up when an educator makes a statement, such as "Students are disrespectful." When asked, "What did the student do that was disrespectful?" answers vary. You may get responses, such as "The student did not listen to me when I asked him to do something. The student questioned me in front of her peers. The student rolled his eyes at me. The students were loud and this is a quiet area."

How does our functional definition of respect apply here? How do the questions I asked at the beginning of this chapter apply to this? Ask yourself, was it really respect that you were looking for or compliance? One of the reasons why I am emphasizing that educators must stop expecting students to just respect teachers because of their title is because most of the time we are seeking compliance. I am big; you are small. I am the teacher; you are the student, so just do what I say. Stop expecting students to respect you when all you ever wanted was to continue the tradition of compliance. Think of it this way, just because a student rolled her eyes at you does not mean she does not have a deep admiration of your abilities, qualities, or achievements. It simply means that in that moment, she is non-compliant.

Say it to My Face

When we refer to students as "low-ability" behind their backs, where is our admiration for those students? Respect in the classroom is giving second, third and even fourth chances for our students because they need us as support systems. Respect is establishing reflective routines, emotional regulation tools and classroom expectations cuing. Respect is co-creating a social contract and establishing norms for how to treat one another. Respect is helping every student believe they are the brightest, funniest, and most creative scholar in the room. This is how respect is earned as a teacher. Stop expecting students to respect you when you display behaviors that demonstrate that you do not fully believe in them. We are the adults and can rise to the greater challenge.

Let's go a little further, and believe me, this one will touch a nerve. How can you demonstrate respect for all students in your school if you stand by and watch from afar as students are disrespected by other teachers? Would you want your own child in a classroom of disrespect? This mindset of disrespect for students and staff means inadvertently dimming the light on opportunities and advancements that we can provide. We did not respect the sanctity of our educational institution when we choose not to advocate for our students. Stop expecting students to respect you if you are not willing to advocate for them and respect staff and students enough to do something about it.

Absence of Trust is an Absence of a Relationship

Do you trust your students? As reflective practitioners, when was the last time that you answered this question? Far too often, we tell our students that we need them to trust us without trusting them. Trust is not a one-way street in the same way that respect must be a two-way avenue. Trust is the only increment of control that our students have. Most times, they did not choose the school that they attend. They did not choose you for a teacher. The absence of trust leads to the absence of a relationship. If I must tell my students to trust me, what has created the mistrust? Was the mistrust created by me or was it created because I sat idly on the sidelines when they were powerless and needed me the most? Stop expecting students to respect you if you do not have a trusting relationship with them. When you think about it, students who break the code of respect do it after a fall out of something that we created. Until we can begin to model our admiration for others' abilities, qualities and achievement that drive respect, let us stop automatically expecting it from our students.

Dennis Griffin Jr. is a principal and national presenter. He is also one of a very small handful of Edugladiators and author of the heartomakeyouthink blog.

Stop Making Excuses for Poor Teaching
PAUL SOLARZ

It is true that there are barriers to our autonomy as teachers. It's true that teaching outside the box can lead to pushback and possibly worse. But it is time to stop worrying about what MIGHT happen to us and start realizing that much of what we do as teachers does not work! If your instructional practices aren't evidence-based and backed by the art and science of teaching, then your classroom is most likely experiencing poor teaching. When classroom environments do not net positive relationships and high achievement, then poor teaching exists. Undeniably, our students arrive with deficiencies and challenges, but that is no excuse either. Five-star teachers produce thriving, high achieving successful students despite any obstacle. Stop making excuses for poor teaching.

Excuse #1: "I'm not allowed to..."

As a classroom teacher of twenty years, I get it. We can't do everything we want to do in our classrooms. We cannot do everything we believe is right when it comes to teaching. We do not have permission from our principals and district administrators to do what we might want to do. We don't have time to add in project-based learning or passion projects. We continue to spoon feed our students with information through lecture, video and reading in an age where students know they can look up anything with a smartphone in hand. Students do not see the point in memorizing historical facts and mathematical formulas. If it's not fun or interesting to them, they don't believe it's worth their effort to study for tests or try their hardest on projects because most don't have the intrinsic motivation and work ethic to show pride in the work that they accomplish in school.

In my experience, teachers who try new things in the classroom and teach "beyond the curriculum" are referred to as "rogue teachers," by some. Since rogue teachers aren't following the script given to them and aren't on exactly the same lesson as their peers, many times aren't considered "team players." This perspective must stop. Every teacher has attended a workshop or webinar that was recommended or required by their school district where the presenter has asked teachers to take more risks in the classroom, stop teaching in traditional ways and be open to finding better solutions. But as soon as we are back in the classroom, we are given programs to use which are not always that effective and then we complain about everything.

Administrators talk about how important it is to get everyone on the same page and have everyone follow their direction. "Consistency across all grade levels" is a common demand that I hear all of the time. But the real question is, "Should everyone be on the same page?" I know that everyone needs the same scope and sequence of skills and concepts to both avoid repeating things year after year and avoid missing vital components. I know I'm responsible for ensuring my students' success on the standards, objectives and themes that are required for my grade level. Should someone be upset if I find a more enjoyable way for my students to learn this information than completing the worksheets that came with our program? Should someone be upset if I integrate subjects, if I teach media literacy while they learn, or if I have them demonstrate their learning on an electronic portfolio?

I challenge you to look at the pros and cons of moving education forward vs. blindly following orders. Challenging the status quo vs. accepting directives regardless of the consequences. It can be rejuvenating. Trying something new in the classroom vs. doing what has always been done is refreshing. Sure, there are arguments for both sides of each of these debates, but what might be better in the long run for our students? I believe that we need to be pushing boundaries, trying new things based on valid reasoning and always having our students' best interests in mind.

I know that it's not easy to lead the way. I know that if what you try doesn't work out, people might not love your decisions, but you can back it all up by saying, "I took a chance. I wanted to help my students find more success. I thought this might be better."

I know that I'm not a perfect teacher. I know that I get crabby sometimes, overreact to minor misbehaviors, or demand too much of my students, but I also know that I'm making a difference in the lives of each of my students. I hope they remember all the curriculum that I taught them during their fourth or fifth grade year, but I know they will remember how unique our class was and how fun learning was. They will know how much of a voice they had in their classroom and how much their teacher cared about them. Make a difference in the lives of your students. Do not make excuses for why you can't do what you know you should do. Take chances. Try new things. Ask for forgiveness rather than permission. Be the teacher you have always wanted to be. Your students will be better served because of it.

Excuse #2: "I don't have the time to..."

We should be encouraged to eliminate the least important things in our curriculum and replace it with more meaningful learning. This might include opportunities for students to research and learn independently or collaboratively, according to guidelines set forth by the teacher. This might include inserting more engaging and fun activities into the instruction so students discover a love for learning. This might include teaching students the skills necessary to be better learners, stronger workers, or more independent thinkers. The bottom line is that the world is adjusting to some new expectations and colleges and businesses will accept the fact that some students never learned about "The Alamo" or how waves travel through a liquid. But they might not be as happy learning that employees have no work ethic or can't get along with others.

We need to make the time for teaching the things that we value and believe in so that we help to guide capable and caring citizens of the world. We need to stop saying the phrase, "I don't have the time to..." and start saying, "If it's important enough, I'll make the time." Pressure from parents, administrators, state officials and placement test companies should NEVER be prioritized over what is best for our students. We were hired to teach our students because someone felt that we have the ability to impact on our youth. If we believe in our talents, we must make decisions that are ours to make.

There will never be enough time to do everything, and that's why we need to take time to plan out our year before the school year starts, ensuring that we get to everything that we value most and if there's extra time, we can revisit areas that we skipped over. We need to review our year-long plan every month or more often to see if we are still on schedule or if changes to the long-term plan need to be made. We need to integrate subjects when possible and merge units that have similar themes. We need to get rid of favorite lessons that don't have much value, like Ryan wrote about in his chapter regarding penguins in the curriculum and replace them with lessons that meet a need that we know our students have.

Excuse #3: "My students can't (or won't)..."

One of the biggest barriers preventing teachers from trying new things in their classroom is the belief that their students won't be able to handle it or will misbehave so much that it ruins it for everyone else. Now I cannot claim to know your students as well as you do, but I sincerely hope that you give each student a chance, rather than making such an assumption before even meeting them. Every student should be afforded the right to start fresh each year and should be allowed opportunities to make mistakes and redeem themselves before their teacher decides that they are not going to be able to handle something.

As much as I might make excuses for why my chores are not done at home or why my bills are not always paid on time, I never make excuses that prevent me from doing what is best for my students. Students deserve the right to be able to make mistakes and learn from them with my guidance. They should not be forced to spend hours upon hours learning things that they do not value. Students deserve our absolute best each day, even when it is hard for us. Let us stop making excuses and start doing what's best for our students, no matter what.

Paul Solarz has taught 4th and 5th grade students for over twenty years. He is the author of Learn Like a Pirate and has earned several awards for his work in education, including being named a Top 50 Global Teacher Prize candidate in 2016 and the Illinois Technology Educator of the Year Award in 2015.

Stop Creating Homework Inequities

HEATHER L. KEAL

How many teachers out there feel that giving homework is a best practice for teaching and learning? How many of you assign homework regularly, rely on it for grades and assign the entire class the same work? How many of you have issued consequences when homework is not completed?

Equity Issues

Major equity issues arise when homework is assigned. It is imperative that we address this issue if we want to see our students succeed. Our adult behaviors NEED to change. Here are some reasons why:

Inequity of Student Ability

When all students receive the same assignment, individual abilities are not considered. Many of our students with disabilities have been identified for a singular academic reason or deficit. They may have a lower IQ, are unable to complete grade level work, or need differentiated assignments or assessments. Requiring students with deficiencies to complete homework that is not individualized for their independent level, is unethical (and unlawful depending on the wording of their IEP).

Inequity of Home Resources

Resources are not equally available at home. Some students do not have access to the internet. Other students do not have a quiet workspace that is dedicated to completing their work (chaos may swirl around them when they walk in the door). Some students do not have an adult to answer questions or provide examples when they struggle with a skill or an assignment (this leads to frustration and work being done incorrectly). When any of these children come to school without homework completed and are denied an opportunity to do it in the classroom, equity was not considered. If you are not going to give thought to the potential lack of resources in students' homes, then do not assign homework.

Inequity in After-School Activities

Often, students after school responsibilities are not taken into account. Many students are involved in sports, have after-school jobs, or babysit younger siblings. Extra hours of homework are not realistic for them due to these responsibilities. When homework needs to be given, teachers should consider giving assignments that require minimal or flexible time spent on them.

Inequity of Stamina

When students dedicate focused hours at school to learning they may not have the stamina to continue with hours more, at home. Most students go to school for eight hours each day with little downtime because every instructional minute counts. Assigning more work to complete at home can do more harm than good. How many times have you heard a student say, "Yay... I have more schoolwork to do when I get home tonight!" The reality is students dread having to sit down and do *more* work. If teachers feel the need to give an assignment outside of school hours, then it should be fun, engaging and at their independent level. If students enjoy an activity, then they are more apt to do it.

Inequity of Skill

Grades are not accurate placeholders of achievement and true mastery of skills cannot be determined from homework grades. Issuing grades for assignments that are done outside of school can be extremely problematic. Scores can be skewed (both higher and lower) and a true understanding of standards is not offered for most assignments. Teachers should avoid collecting homework for grades because daily homework usually does not provide rubric guidance and it can be very subjective in nature.

Punishing Students for Inequity

Students often receive a punishment for not completing work. Many times, students receive double consequences for not completing homework– a grade of zero AND detention, AND loss of recess, AND a note or phone call home etc. Is it necessary to penalize students' multiple times for one assignment? Teachers need to stop the double jeopardy and consider the value of assigning homework in the first place. When considering the topic of homework, teachers need to ask themselves if the assignment is worth it. What is the GOAL of homework? Why do students need to complete it away from the school setting? Is the teacher able to ensure that all these inequities will not become potential issues? If teachers genuinely want to see students succeed, then we must consider inequity before assigning homework. We can do better than our past practices. Much, much better.

Heather Keal is a wife, mom and proud principal of Mayfield Elementary in Middletown, Ohio. She is passionate about urban education, equity-centered leadership and championing for the students that we serve each day.

Stop Assigning Projects Over Long Weekends & Holidays
ERIK YOUNGMAN, Ed.D.

In a day and age when society is seeking balance and emotional regulation, it sure seems harsh to assign work when students should be rejuvenating and recharging. Since you have a district day off or a vacation from school, shouldn't students too? Compassion and preservation of school and life balance matters. At a minimum, teachers must consider abolishing the wrongheaded practice of assigning projects over long weekends or holidays. Take into consideration the inequities of homework written by Heather from the previous chapter and stop assigning any homework, project, or studying over any weekend. Ever.

Holidays and Weekends are for Memories

Rigor does not equal more homework on long weekends. As I say in my book, *12 Characteristics of Deliberate Homework*, "holidays and vacations are for memories, not homework," and, "The amount of time needed to complete homework should be reasonable so as not to prevent students from participating in extracurricular activities, interacting with family and getting adequate sleep." As my fifth-grade daughter, Fiona, recently acknowledged (when we were discussing this topic of homework on weekends), "Enjoying the weekend, especially a longer weekend, is sometimes a major motivator for working hard in school during the week." Her words matter and student perspective matters. Let's motivate students to work hard during school and let them recharge, unwind and connect with passions and families over long weekends.

Students who are not overwhelmed with weekend homework may also have more time to read books that align with their own interests. This extra time allows students to enhance their passion for reading or gain hands-on experiences, such as cooking, gardening, designing a website or video game or even playing sports. Free time does not guarantee students will read, but they may be building background knowledge and life experiences that help them to later connect with future learning or just arrive in our classrooms balanced and refreshed. When students desire to learn more about topics they are interested in, our hope is that it will inspire them to learn and make connections to their dreams.

Community Involvement Cultivates Happiness

When projects are assigned over long weekends/holidays, the primary negative impacts on students relate to missing out on fun opportunities. When students are working on homework projects, they must make decisions to decrease their involvement with happiness-driven activities with families, friends, and community members. Events with family and friends are typically positive experiences that include celebrations for holidays and could include travel time to and from all types of events. Students work hard during the week; shouldn't they have a day off too?

Another negative impact of homework projects over long weekends/holidays is that it produces stress about the homework they have yet to complete. Students who do not finish their homework on Friday night, usually do other activities and delay completion of projects. However, in the back of their mind there is stress as they worry about not completing their homework rather than relaxing and having

105

fun. Assigning homework projects over long weekends/holidays extends stress for students as it nags at them and prevents them from thoroughly relaxing and engaging in enjoyable things. This stress compounds even more when a student has homework from other classes, as well.

The Ripple Effects on Families

Assigning projects over long weekends prolongs stress for the student and has a ripple effect regarding negative emotions and interactions between a student and their parents. Families may expect their child to complete a different task, such as a chore or the parent may be trying successfully or unsuccessfully to help with the homework. There are numerous negative interactions and outcomes that may occur until homework is complete. It becomes a battle and a checklist for what could have been a bonding, balanced, joy filled weekend. Proactively, educators should not put students into scenarios where they must choose between family traditions or homework projects over long weekends/holidays. It is not emotionally healthy.

Reflect about how you or others you know are impacted by stress. Now think about the benefits of students having a few days of a break from school and learning. Those benefits are magnified for students that have anxiety, attention issues, depression, learning or socialization challenges, or are simply over scheduled or overwhelmed.

Consider changes you can make so students are not overburdened with homework over weekends. Allowing multiple days to complete homework assignments and projects empowers flexibility, but if we are avoiding homework on weekends, different strategies must be used.

If not a group project (which is another complex topic), make sure students can complete the project independently. Ensure students understand routines and self-help strategies before assigning concise homework. Provide scaffolded supports and multiple check-in interactions to empower independence and confidence while completing long term projects.

Hypocrisy in teaching could very well be applied to a teacher who assigns lots of homework and projects over the weekend or during holiday recess while they, themselves, relax, party or do not do much of anything for their classroom or students.

Dr. Erik Youngman is an educational leader who is passionate about topics such as homework, growth mindset, grading and leadership. He is the author of 12 Characteristics of Deliberate Homework.

Stop Using Grades as Punishment

KATELYNN GIORDANO

"A grade is just a punishment for not understanding something yet."

That quote came directly from the mouth of one of my sixth graders. Even at the age of twelve, my student had internalized the idea that grades were punitive measures, set in stone and not to reward, but to punish for mistakes and misunderstandings. Not only are these words profound, but they should hit us squarely between the eyes and stop us right in our tracks. Clearly, schools have participated in malpractice if this is the message that we are sending. How can we, as educators who are dedicated to student growth, buy into such a practice?

The Outdated Traditional Grading System

Grading has positively, rapidly evolved in the past decade, which is a good thing. Grading practices have been through a massive overhaul; there have been awareness and reformation discussions and practices in place that steer away from a punitive approach to a standards-based philosophy. Many of these changes are newly recognized practices that have yet to become common practice. We are living in a great divide as five-star teachers question efficacy and alter practices to meet the needs of students, while old school practitioners adhere to traditional practices.

Prior to educating myself on the topic, I was staunchly opposed to *any* type of grading reform. I craved the "concreteness" of points and percentages within a traditional grading system.

I was wrong.

Looking back, I cringe at my prior opinions about grading and how loudly I proclaimed them. This transformation in reporting academic proficiency is one that has been wholly personal for me and has profoundly changed my approach as a teacher.

The big turning point for me was when I began considering the purpose of assigning a grade. A grade should communicate academic proficiency (i.e., how well a student understands a given academic skill

107

or standard). My question to you is, do points, percentages and letters demonstrate that? Truthfully, I do not see how they can. When a student takes a test and earns or is "issued" a 15/20 points, a 75% or a "C", do they know what they do and don't understand about the information on the test? Do they know how well they mastered a particular skill? Do they know how deeply they understand the content standards? Do their parents have any idea? Probably not. They know they received a "C" and their overall grade for the course went up or down depending on weight, total points, or extra credit opportunities. Many times student focus is on finding a way to "win" the most points and, certainly, not on learning.

I can say this with confidence because I was that student: My goal in school was to get the required number of points to earn the grade that I wanted, and I became particularly good at it. I knew what I needed to do, depending on the teacher that I had, to get enough points to earn an "A."

In many of my classes, I wasn't learning much of anything. I was making my way through the game of school, memorizing what I needed for my assessments, gathering points for my assignment and earning enough for the grade. There came a time, however, when I had some teachers who really challenged me. Their idea of assessment was different and/or unfamiliar to me. *I was forced to learn instead of earn.* I remember sitting in a biology class, knowing my teacher would curve the grades and freaking out because the test sitting in front of me had a 67% on it. I knew how the human immune system worked and could explain it to anyone who asked me, but I didn't earn the correct number of points, so it really didn't matter to me that I had learned anything at all.

I never, ever want my students to think that way. It can be damaging, or even destructive, to their educational lives. When students align their ability and worth, to a letter grade, we've lost them. School should not come across to our students as an "earning" mentality. Students attend school to build a future, make connections, develop new skills and master learning key concepts.

Standards-Based Proficiency

Contrary to a letter grade or assigned percentage, standards-based grading shifts the focus from one and done assignments to mastering content standards or learning targets, learner behaviors and focusing on learner progression. This includes do-overs, replacement grades and multiple attempts over time to demonstrate learning. Students are no longer locked into an average of grades. Think of it in terms of a continuum of learning. This new lens requires a pedagogical shift in thinking.

Moving to a proficiency-based grading system is a lot of work and there's discomfort to be experienced along the way, as to be expected when trying anything new. This requires thinking deeply about why and how we assess students' learning. Understanding standards-based proficiency requires delving deep into the purpose of education, the systems that exist and the harm that grading can perpetuate. We must be willing to do the heavy lifting to dismantle the "earning points mentality" to shift to a mastery of learning mindset. Shifting your pedagogical paradigm and approach of the systems to grading is challenging, especially in the beginning stages, but it is so worth the learning outcome.

When we shift towards standards-based proficiency to learning, the positive impact on our students becomes student driven. Some of our most stressed-out students are more comfortable knowing they are not defined by a onetime grade in class, but in fact, can demonstrate the key learning through multiple attempts. Students thrive and become self-directed when they have a system for focusing on the progress they've made since the beginning. Facilitating targeted, productive conversations about what students are learning is a cornerstone of success. When students learn to talk knowledgeably about what they understand and what they don't, referring to specific feedback they've received on formative assessments, ownership happens. The greatest reward is that students come to class and learn, not earn. When students work hard, put forth their best effort and ask questions knowing that their focus is solely on making progress toward their goals, purpose compounds. When students know they will not be punished for not knowing or taking longer to get to their arrival point in understanding a concept, joy in learning is present. When students' grades are replaced based on a retake or a new demonstration of mastery of a standard, shifts happen. Shifts in effort. Shifts in motivation. Shifts in collaboration. Shifts in goal setting. Shifts in community. Shifts in happiness. Shifts in possibilities.

The Toxicity of Grading "Additives"

A student's ability to turn in homework assignments on time is a behavior that is completely unrelated to their writing skills. In a toxic additive learning environment, student's attendance or participation is often a root cause of a low or high grade. When a teacher has taken off points from an assignment for lateness, the grade is no longer telling that student how capable he or she is at the given learning target, demonstrated behavior(s), or progression in learning. Toxic additives within archaic grading systems, send mixed messages as to the value and purpose of school.

Another toxic additive is subjectivity. Rubrics are at the heart of standards-based proficiency, but when they aren't focused on standards, behaviors and progression, they too can become toxic . The subjective system for grading, for communicating and reporting student proficiency, can include factors that are completely unrelated to academic skill, which then makes grading highly subjective. When we use an archaic system of grading, are we truly using it because it is good for student learning? It seems to me that the answer is "no." Many of us fall back on the argument that this system worked for us and we turned out successful. However, when we think about the learning we did, the skills we mastered, I'm not sure our grades really reflected that.

I believe that the system, as it still stands now, encourages students to "play the game" and learn to be good at school. It seems that the grades earned in our current system show how well a student meets the requirements on the good student checklist and not how much progress was made. This system encourages students to be compliant and to figure out what they need to do for each teacher so they can earn the maximum number of points in a class.

Recalibrate

It is time to recalibrate. We might not feel that we have control over a system that is set up to assign grades, but here is what we DO have control over:

- Reflecting on our own attitudes about grading.
- Utilizing rubrics that are standards based for grading.
- Carrying out "do-overs," retakes and replacement grades.
- Re-teaching and intervening with learning gaps.
- Providing systems for interventions and enrichment for individualized gains.
- Motivating students to learn not earn.
- Facilitating a strengths-based approach.
- Advocating to those who hold policy control–locally, regionally and nationally.
- Communicating progress.
- Trying new methods of assessment and reporting with an open mind.

We have the opportunity, as experienced professionals, to weigh in on the conversation surrounding grading practices. We can make enough effective changes within the scope of our classrooms that we can outsmart the systems that we do not feel in control of each day. When we do this, we ensure the focus is on learning and not on compliance.

We must affect change in grading and move toward a mindset that mastery does not happen on the same day in the same way. And, when students master a standard, it is our obligation to adjust their grade to reflect their current proficiency, not their grade in a past point and time all averaged together.

This can only happen when we stop using a punitive system that makes grades a punishment.

Katelynn Giordano is a renowned middle level educator in Illinois and the Director of Curriculum and Instruction for the Teach Better Team.

Stop Accepting Low Quality Student Work
KATIE MCNAMARA

Every teacher has experienced grading a stack of work that, in retrospect, seemed like a waste of time. You go to grab the assignment out of the tray to discover that the stack feels noticeably light. A quick flip through the stack makes you initially wonder what went wrong. As you look closely at each assignment, you start to question if your directions were clear. Halfway through, you wonder if you simply daydreamed your instruction inclusive of modeling with an exemplar, rather than actually having done it. Flipping through the rest of the stack, you notice minimal one word responses and the first thought that pops into your head is, "Is it worth it to continue grading?" Clearly something went wrong. I had a mentor once tell me, "You must inspect what you expect." In this case, it was evident that I must not have expected very much because that is exactly what my students delivered. Ninety-five percent of the work turned in that day was incomplete. It was time for me to reflect and examine my own classroom practices and figure out how to motivate students to produce high quality five-star work.

Low Quality Still Counts as Incomplete

It turns out there is an easy fix to the low-quality work madness. When teachers make this one shift, student work quality skyrockets. When teachers stop accepting incomplete work, the expectation rises. Really. Low quality is often a synonym for incomplete. Every teacher has experienced a student who is fully capable, but when the standard is lowered, they revert back to one-word answers, sloppy handwriting and very little proof of metacognitive thought. Why send the message that your assignment doesn't matter? Therefore, we must have norms, exemplars and a high-quality learning community expectations.

Sure, there are times when teachers differentiate and provide options of completing just a cross-section of an assignment or a choice board. That is not what I'm talking about. I am talking about when teachers provide clear modeling, directions and communicated expectations AND still accept low quality work. When the majority of students turn in incomplete and low-quality work, my instructional practices and expectations need to be reviewed. Even if I facilitated the best instructional lesson with stellar questioning and high student engagement, when it came time for students to produce work to make their thinking visible, I must inspect what I expect throughout the process. It is my job to provide high-quality instruction and monitor student progress, while they are working, in order to give feedback that will ensure high-quality work.

Beware

Beware of the first time you have students turn in an assignment. The first time you give points. The first time you grade an assignment could be the first assignment you give a student permission to not complete. The first time you simply checkmark a response without providing specific feedback, you are sending a message to your students.

In my personal quest to stop accepting low quality work, I began to implement a single point rubric. If a student completed a task, I maintained records that it was filled in at first glance. This did not take into account quality, but really when we grade quality, what are we looking at? Quality as compared to what? If the goal is for each student to improve, the quality of one assignment is different from every single other student's assignment in that class (unless they copied another student's work). If students are completing everything, their quality will improve.

The power of a single rubric, based on completion, tells students that I believe in them while simultaneously eliminating their worry of not doing well enough. Students know their grade before they turn in the assignment. What if most of it is done? Don't take it. Just don't. Stop accepting incomplete work. Do not let yourself feel bad. Don't allow them the comfort of partial credit. Just don't. Send it back, just like you would a steak not cooked the way you ordered it. Letting students do half the work and squeaking by with a minimal grade does not serve the purpose of mastering learning. I don't want to be in a world when people do things "halfway." Halfway stops at a red light, halfway sutures after surgery, halfway cooked chickens, or…This may be tough at first, but students will learn that there is an expectation as well as a belief that they are capable of more than mediocrity.

Set the Bar, They will Deliver

Set the bar at "they can." Don't embrace the "It's OK if you kind-of, sort-of" mentality. If the assignment is meaningful, it needs to be done. It needs to be completed. It deserves your inspection and feedback. If completing the assignment in full doesn't matter, rethink the assignment. If your assignment is full of frivolous time sucking elements read the other chapters in this collaborative book which earlier discusses this. Once you have set the bar that completion is necessary, they will deliver.

Showing you their complete work further cements the importance of doing all the pieces of a task. But now, end the "game over" concept. A turned in assignment does not mean it is done; it does not mean that it is acceptable. Embrace revision. Embrace a mastery of standards mindset. Eliminate the "I turned it in; therefore, I'm done." Re-doing work isn't a penalty and it isn't something a student should have to beg for to ensure mastery of standards, growth in behaviors and learning progress. Revision needs to become part of your five-star culture. If I make a batch of cookies that don't turn out right, I don't declare that I am a failure and will never, ever bake cookies again. Instead, this is a time for reflection of what worked and what didn't and then try again.

Learning is improving. Learning is ideation. Learning is the design cycle of improvement on a path to mastery. Revision needs to be placed at center stage.

Make this one shift and watch the sub-par work vanish. Create a culture of pride in your students' work. When students experience a culture of high expectations and they meet those expectations, their intrinsic reward and value of growth becomes greater than any extrinsic reward you could ever offer.

Katie McNamara is a teacher-librarian in Bako, California and the CSLA President.

Stop Lowering Expectations
BASIL MARIN, Ph.D.

You are on the operating table, barely surviving a five-car crash on the interstate. As you lay there being prepped for surgery, you overhear one physician ask the lead physician, "Hey, is it OK if this surgery does not go well?" As you lay there with your life in the balance, you realize that expectations are the driving force for individuals and leaders within any organization to perform well and to meet the needs of their targeted customers.

Give "Ganas"

In no profession is it acceptable to lower expectations in order to see a greater outcome--not on the Apollo stage, not in a national car show, not on a life-saving operating table, or at a Super Bowl. However, as educators why are we okay with lowering expectations for students and why are we okay with, historically marginalized students, not performing at the same level as their affluent counterparts?

One of my favorite inspirational movies of all time is *Stand and Deliver*, based on the true story of a high school math teacher, Jaime Escalante. Mr. Escalante was given the worst classroom in the school building; he had students who could not have cared less about school. Yet, he believed in his students and raised the level of expectations for his students. One of the greatest quotes from Mr. Escalante was, "The only thing I ask from you is 'ganas' or desire. If you don't have the 'ganas,' I will give it to you because I'm an expert." Our students deserve educators who will champion for them and see their full potential regardless of any deficits or shortcomings the student possesses now. Katie's chapter on low expectations and receiving low-quality student work aligns itself with this chapter and the foundation of "ganas."

Gatekeepers of High Expectations

The Brown v. Board of Education of Topeka Kansas (1954) taught us how the U.S. Supreme Court ruled that separate but equal schools were unconstitutional. Six years later, Ruby Bridges and five other African American students were given an assessment to see if they could compete at a high level of academics at an all-white school. Even as a student, Ruby was ostracized at her elementary school and other parents pulled their children from classes with her and sent them to other schools. Ruby was taught by one teacher, Barbara Henry, who was loving and supportive of Bridges. Ms. Henry was invested in not only teaching her but helping her to withstand the hatred and negativity she experienced every day coming to school. Ms. Henry was impressed by the academic growth that Ruby exhibited and, as a teacher, she raised her level of expectations for Ruby and made sure that she received a quality education even though she was her only student for an entire school year. The interesting part of this history is that it only took place sixty years ago and this event changed the narrative for so many students of color.

I often think back to Ruby Bridges and the bravery she exhibited each day as she was escorted to William Frantz Elementary School by her mother and federal marshals. Ruby marched to school through large crowds of people gathered in front of the school entrance as they yelled curse words and threw objects at her. There were barricades set up and policemen worked to secure the area. Would we be where we are in education today if students like Ruby did not take the step to fight against a system that refused to change and believed an integrated school was a disadvantage to white students? The racism that Ruby Bridges felt walking to school still exists today; it is just shown in more subtle ways. Teachers, counselors and administrators are "gatekeepers" and control students' access to higher levels of education; they can keep students in a box they feel is appropriate for that student.

It is imperative to note that lowering expectations stems from our own expectations for failure. It is easy for educators to lower expectations for schools that have low socio-economic students, a high percentage of students with disabilities, or linguistically diverse student populations. Students are tracked from a young age and that tracking is tied to ability and expectations. If a student is perceived as an average student, they will be scheduled for average classes unless they have someone to advocate for them. Who will advocate for special education students, ELL students, or at-risk students? These students may come from families that do not understand the school system or they may not know how to advocate for their child. Education is power and it is rooted in having access to knowledge and understanding the educational system. The system is often not set up for every student to succeed, especially students of color.

Value and Honor Differences

As educators, it is important to honor and value our students' differences as our national educational landscape is ever changing and growing as a multicultural melting pot. All educators must work to understand their students' cultures, academic interests and family values in education. Often, we continue educational transitions that we were taught years ago. You must ask yourself, are we holding back our students and do the instilled traditions lower expectations for certain groups of students and maintain expectations for other students? If the answer to either of those questions is "yes," then we must be change agents until we can truthfully answer with a resounding "no!"

As a former alternative school student, myself, I was often told that I would be lucky to not become a statistic like so many males of color do with our judicial system. I was told that I would be even luckier if I could graduate high school. Year after year, my teachers would lower their expectations for my success, except for one teacher: my ninth-grade teacher saw something in me and she worked hard to remind me each day that I mattered. She was intentional in telling me that I could turn my life around if I would just change my mindset about life and use my gifts for good. This was the first time I can remember a teacher holding me to higher expectations than I may have even had for myself. These raised expectations completely changed my trajectory in school and life. I did become a statistic, but not one to be ashamed of. Not only did I graduate high school, I became among the 4% of all adults who possess a doctoral degree. When we lower expectations for students, especially historically marginalized students, we are killing their dreams and ambitions. We must raise our expectations for the benefit of our students, society, and future generations! Stop saying that we can't and stop acting like we shouldn't.

Dr. Basil Marin is an educator in Atlanta, Georgia. He was also a 2017 ASCD Emerging Leader and currently serves as President of ELASCD. You will often find him presenting at conferences speaking about equity in education, social-emotional learning, whole-child approaches to education and disrupting the status quo.

Stop Babying and Coddling Students
SCOTT MCLEOD, J.D., Ph.D.

Coddling is for babies who are helpless at birth. They depend on their parents and need nourishment to live until they can feed themselves. *Your students can feed themselves.*

Regurgitated Lessons

Let's analyze the dynamics within a controlled compliance-based classroom. The teacher transmits information to the student. The textbook transmits information to the student. The online tutorial or learning software or YouTube video transmits information to the student. The student's role is to be the recipient of what is transmitted. The student's role is to regurgitate what was transmitted with enough fidelity that the teacher or software system can check off that the student knows it. The student's role is to be obedient and compliant, not to demonstrate a deep understanding nor to make their thinking visible and applicable to the real world. When students are expected to transmit or regurgitate lessons, they may become noncompliant, disengaged, bored and even flat-out resistant. A response to this disobedience may result in a lower grade or discipline referral. Not only is this ineffective, but it is also the type of practice that coddles with low expectations rather than teaching for growth and application.

As the previous chapters in this book discussed grading and the pitfalls of grading systems, we have been brainwashed to participate in a transmission cycle of teaching that is in play just long enough for students to regurgitate a true/false answer or multiple choice answer just to produce a grade. A box for teachers to check off. This malpractice is like throwing a plate of spaghetti on the wall and hoping it sticks. Babying and coddling students is not the students' fault. The fault lies in us. Students deserve to be engaged, motivated and connected to their learning so that they can apply it to new situations and transfer their learning and skills. We must stop the malpractice.

Disenfranchisement of Our Youth

The biggest indictment of our schools is not their failure to raise test scores above some politically determined line of "proficiency," it is the day-in-and-day-out practices we routinely ignore when our students are bored, disengaged and disempowered. The disenfranchisement of our youth continues to happen in the very institutions that are allegedly preparing them to be lifelong learners. When students are bored out of their minds and we ignore, waste, or deprive them of engaging learning opportunities, we deprive human potential that could lead to new inventions, medical breakthroughs, or solving the world's greatest problems.

You Can Do This

Do you believe that your students can do more without your help? How can you create opportunities that foster critical thinking and deeper learning? How will you facilitate chances for students to address real world challenges in real world contexts? How can you alter your learning environment to one that is high in student agency and ownership? Teachers must lift the transmission and regurgitation cycle by using digital learning tools to foster robust student communication and collaboration with outside partners. Five-star classrooms are focused on student meaning-making and difference-making than curriculum coverage and when teachers focus on curriculum, coddling takes over.

Find an Entry Point

Improving the student experience in a classroom may seem daunting. The key is to find an entry point. Here are a few ways to pull back on feeling as if you are babying your students.

Entry Point #1: Follow Organizations

There are so many organizations that showcase high expectations: the Big Learning network showcases, the New Tech Network, EL Education, EdVisions, High Tech High and New Visions for Public Schools networks, not to forget Envision Education, the Independent Curriculum Group, the New York Performance Assessment Consortium, ConnectEd California, PBL Works, ISTE, and the Internationals Network for Public Schools. This list could go on and on. The idea, here, is that coddling is indirectly addressed by these high-octane organizations through what they do with students. The "doing" is your masterful project for "weening" your students from a reliance on you and these organizations will provide endless resources to get your classroom to function on its own.

Entry Point #2: Follow Five-Star Schools

Thousands of individual inquiry-based and problem-based learning schools are exemplars and models for effective classrooms. You may want to look up Blue Ribbon Schools or state level school award winners. Exploring schools with out-of-the-box practices beyond your traditional public school deserve our attention--not because they are recognized for high test scores, but because they do not coddle their students. Much can be learned from Montessori, Waldorf and Reggio Emilia schools. Network. Observe. Learn.

Entry Point #3: Read & Connect

Hop online and see what's trending in the educational world. The organizations above feature new practices in the form of articles, blogs and books. Jump on social media channels and connect with other educators who are looking to grow. Ask for recommendations from them. Read a book or two. Join an online learning community. One of your most valuable assets is your professional learning network. Connect with educators in your cooperative or geographical region through conferences and trainings. The bottom line is that effective teachers gather allies and learn together how not to coddle. That is, after all, how all the authors in this book gathered together to carry out a non-coddling mission for teachers. If you start tomorrow with a commitment to weening, your students will rise to the occasion.

Dr. Scott McLeod is an Associate Professor of Educational Leadership at the University of Colorado, Denver and the Founding Director of the UCEA Center for the Advanced Study of Technology Leadership in Education (CASTLE). Scott has authored four books and is the co-creator of the 4 Shifts Protocol for instructional redesign for deeper learning and student engagement.

Stop Believing that High-Stakes-Tests Prevent Creativity

MELISSA DRUMMOND

Think back to when you had the opportunity to attend a quality professional development workshop--but, not just any workshop, one that had you and your colleagues learning about and practicing hands on or higher-level thinking activities that were designed to improve student learning and engagement. You likely found yourself having some fun completing tasks that you could see your students enjoying as well. Most likely, you were highly engaged, highly creative and socially connected with your colleagues through activity design.

The dynamic of this level of training has purpose. Yes, the trainers fill the time that is available to them on a respective Superintendent's Conference Day, but they are also typically aligned to the district and building goals that have been outlined for the year. Your leaders also participate in order to learn more about evidence-based instructional practices and how to best support students.

At the conclusion of many of these workshops, participants are asked to provide feedback. The feedback is usually genuinely positive. Participants appreciate the time to collaborate and to learn something new. When trainings are viewed as high quality, teachers can see the logic behind the strategies given and the value of refining instruction. Reflective and growing teachers are willing to design and implement these newly learned strategies and skills in order to add creativity and engagement to their lesson.

Comma, But . . .

In a perfect world, we know that not every participant leaves their professional development ready to revitalize their lessons. I have heard teachers say things to me, such as:

- "These are great ideas, but I teach a course that has a state assessment attached to it."
- "This stuff is fun, but my job is to prepare those kids for the test."
- "I'm sure students would like this, but there isn't enough time for fun."

These educators know their content. They have attended content specific training and, in some cases,

119

created and scored countless exams. They know their exam frontwards and backwards whether it is the typical set of multiple-choice questions, how the essay will be presented, or what to expect on the short answer questions. It is evident that these teachers have worked hard to ensure that they are preparing their students for the final exams at the end of their courses. My professional rebuttal to the "Comma, but . . ." reservations go something like this:

- "Why doesn't the same pedagogy apply to your course?"
- "Why can't learning be creative and prepare students for deeply applied learning?"
- "Can students be set up to recognize the skills being tested without testing skills each day?"

I find it difficult to believe that all instructional experts and their evidence-based research can only be applied to non-tested classrooms. Effective pedagogical practices are founded in student engagement and improve overall student comprehension and retention of knowledge. This mindset seems ironic because the exam focused teacher strongly advocates for the importance of building the skills that enable students to retrieve prior knowledge and apply this knowledge to new learning yet believes creative engagement should be excluded.

Five-star educators utilize higher order thinking skills in discussions and apply motivating and creative practices that engage students. So why do some teachers view creativity as an obstacle and timewaster and then revert to their primary strategy of recall level questions in class? It seems counterintuitive when classroom goals focus on extrapolating information from resources and developing analytical compositions, but they do not design creative learning opportunities for their classroom activities which provide practice opportunities for these skills.

When Teachers Struggle to Implement New Practices

According to Elena Aguilar's adult learning theory, "Mind the Gap," there are identifiable reasons why we may struggle to apply what we have learned as teachers struggle to go from their own learning to application in the classroom.

1. Lack of Skill: You need to practice creating these lessons and ask for feedback from coaches/peers.
2. Lack of Time: Creating a creative lesson takes a great deal of time and effort. Locating and gathering all the necessary resources can sometimes be difficult and very time consuming.
3. Lack of Desire: If your passion for creativity is lacking, collaborate with those that can reignite and inspire you.

Recognizing your own excuses will give you the liberation of unclutching your test-driven classroom.

What about the Joy of Learning?

Will Peterson had been teaching Social Studies for seventeen years. In that time, he taught nearly every course that the department offered. He loved everything about history and no one could deny his passion for his content. His students joked about his over-the-top exuberance when he introduced a new unit because of his incredible ability to tell a great story. Mr. Peterson also prided himself on the success his students accomplished on the state and national exams.

Recently, his district decided that there should not be any limitations placed on students who wanted to take advanced courses. This increased the number of students enrolling in these courses, and the "types" of learners became more diverse as a result of such energetic change. When Mr. Peterson reviewed his most recent test scores, he had mixed feelings. When he was asked about designing with more creativity in his lessons, he just did not see the point and asserted the following "Comma, buts":

- "Most of my students do great on the exam. Why would I teach it any differently?"
- "I tried a 'fun' project a couple of years ago. The students had 'fun' but then did terribly on the unit test."
- "Some kids just don't get this stuff and probably shouldn't be in these advanced courses anyway."

If you happen to find yourself relating to Mr. Peterson, I can only imagine your frustration. There is a great deal of pressure to help your students be successful on their exams. Stop using the exam as an excuse for changing your instructional practices. Trying something new, with no guarantee that it will be successful; putting time and effort into creating new materials and activities, when the way you have already taught it is quick, easy and done; feeling uninspired with a lack of personal motivation are all real feelings. But remember the purpose for making the effort to be creative is not about you, your past results, or your willingness to change. It is about engaging your students in the joy of learning.

Melissa Drummond has been an ELA teacher, principal, and professional developer throughout her career. In each of her roles, Melissa's greatest joy is to see engaged learners who are inspired to ask the questions that drive their own learning.

Stop Telling Students that hey Have to Go to College

ELIJAH CARBAJAL

"Go to college," they said. "It'll be fun," they said. Those were the thoughts of my 21-year-old self as I walked to my car in the snow that day. My last class had just ended at 6:15 pm, and I had been there since around 7:00 am. To be there at 7:00 am, I had to leave by 6:00 am. To be ready to go at 6:00am, I was up by 5:30 am. I wouldn't be home until at least 7:30. I was cold, tired, hungry and frustrated. That's when the words came out of my mouth: *"I hate college."*

The College Trap

Hate is probably too strong of a word, but it still felt freeing to admit it. I didn't enjoy going to college. I felt trapped. Oh, sure I had good classes and I was able to take classes with friends or at least make some new friends while I was there. I was the world's most "okay-est" student (C's get degrees, right?). I had some good moments, but all in all, I couldn't stand it. I hated driving back and forth to class because I didn't live on campus. I hated walking across the humongous campus. The homework, which seemed endless at the time, always kept me up late. And, of course, I accrued enormous debt.

Honestly, the only reason I went to school is because I wanted to be a teacher. I knew that much. I knew I wanted to teach and inspire. I had to attend college to get my degree. I had no choice. If I wanted to do what I was feeling called to do, I needed to put my head down and just suck it up and go to college. Still, as I write this chapter, the lyrics to Relient K's, "College Kids" are echoing in my head. College really was not for me, though.

College for Some, not All

I don't mean that only some are fit for college and others aren't. I'm saying that there are some people, like me, who will have to go to college in order to work in the profession of their choice. If you want to be a doctor, you have to go to college. Lawyer? College. You want to be a professor? You are required go to college. Some jobs will require that extra bit of education. People, like me, who aren't excited about college, well, we just grin and bear it.

College is not for everyone. I say this because not every profession requires a college education. This does not make the people in these professions a lesser person than those who go to college. In fact, a lot of the professions listed below that don't require college (perhaps, some require trade school or other training, however) are essential and vital to our society:

Military, law enforcement, firefighters, construction workers (roads, houses, etc.), mechanics/automotive technicians, farmers, paraprofessionals (educational assistants), janitors, drone operators, plumbers, electricians, welders, professional umpires/referees, postal workers, truck drivers, hair stylists/barbers, realtors, caregivers, grocers, transportation inspectors, park rangers, oilfield workers, air traffic controllers, bankers and ranchers.

I'm sure that you can list some more professions. There's a lot of different jobs/professions that are some of the most essential jobs ever. A recent study conducted by the Georgetown University Center on the Education and Workforce presented some intriguing data. The key findings from the study state that there will be an estimated 55 million job openings in the economy through 2020-2021. They predict that 35% of those jobs will require a bachelor's degree or higher. That's right. Only 35%. Which means that of those 55 million jobs, 65% will not require a bachelor's degree or higher.

Weighing the Debt/No Debt Debacle

Imagine you teach 100 seniors in high school. You tell all of them all that they should go to college so that they can get a degree and have a great career. Now imagine that all of them do as you say. They graduate with degrees. Some enjoyed college and others were miserable. But, at least they all get jobs they went to school for, right? Not according to the study from Georgetown University. According to this study, only 35 of your students will get jobs that they went to school for. This means 65 of your students will have to find work in an area that they did not study for. This is okay in the long run, because work is work, right? But it also means they spent money or owe money they can't get back, they gave four or more years of time that they can't get back, are you content with that outcome?

So why do so many teachers put so much emphasis on going to college? I once heard a teacher tell her fourth grade students that the whole reason for coming to school was to graduate from high school and, eventually, go to college. Is that really why we tell kids to go to school? Just so they can get a piece of paper that says you took enough classes and did well enough on exams to earn a piece of paper? And what does that piece of paper really mean?

Student loans are financially crippling graduates after college. A friend reported to me that he will be over $100,000 in debt after he graduates. Sure, he was going into a profession that paid close to that amount per year after graduation (if he gets hired), but there's no easy way of paying that off. It's absurd that we encourage students to go to college knowing the insane amount of debt they could potentially wrack up without a true sense of knowing that they will love the job that they think they want to pursue.

I'm not discouraging anyone from going to college. Some may be required to go for their career path, like mine and they might also enjoy the full experience. Lots of people do and if that's what they want to do, I encourage this. However, I think there is a problem with the way teachers talk about kids' futures in a blanket fashion. Why do we encourage college when so many professions that do not require college education are just waiting to be occupied by someone willing to work and do a great job?

My father was a proud member of the United States Air Force and served in the Air National Guard for thirty-two years. There was a saying around their shop: "Someone with a Ph.D. designs the fighter jets. Someone with a Master's degree builds the fighter jet. Someone with a Bachelor's degree flies the fighter jet. But, it's someone with no college education who keeps the fighter jet up in the air."

Stop telling kids they have to prepare for college. We need incredible workers to keep the "fighter jets" in the sky.

Elijah Carbajal is a teacher in Albuquerque, New Mexico and the founder of the "Shut Up and Teach" movement.

Stop Holding Grudges for Misbehavior
RICK RAMIREZ

Holding a grudge against someone gets you nowhere, especially when a teacher holds a grudge against a student. Students will test you because they are kids. As tough as teaching is, some students are more challenging, but educators worsen these problems by the way they react to situations. Instead of grading behavior and holding grudges, we need to learn to not take misbehavior personally. As the adults in the building, we are more in control of our emotions and our reactions than students are. Students are still finding their way and still learning how to navigate their way through life. The best thing we can do, as educators, is to teach students valuable life lessons, not by what we say, but by what we model.

Every Day is a Fresh Start

I had to learn this humbling lesson the hard way from Rob, one of my 8th grade students. I truly enjoy teaching and, for the most part, I am fairly successful at establishing positive relationships with most of my students. I say most, because a few students have confessed that they did not like me, nor did they like my class, and that's OK! Early in my teaching career, I had no idea how to handle students who don't care or what some call the tough students. Rob was one of those adolescents whom I mistakenly assumed didn't care. Being the novice teacher that I was at that time, I naturally grew frustrated and made the mistake of allowing Rob's misbehavior to determine how I interacted with him. After reflecting, I realized that I was, indeed, holding a grudge against him. Holding a grudge against this student got me absolutely nowhere; all it did was ruin my mood each day.

I noticed that my teacher neighbor, Mr. Green, had a positive relationship with Rob. Rob would greet Mr. Green and appeared to like his class a lot. During our planning period, I vented to Mr. Green and told him that I was struggling with Rob due to his bad attitude in my class and I desperately needed help or advice in working with him. Mr. Green gave me some simple advice that I never forgot. He was brutally honest with me and said it was obvious that I was holding a grudge against this student. Then, he told me that every student deserves a fresh new start every single day; it doesn't matter what the student did the day before, they need to know that we are happy to see them each and every day that they walk into our classrooms.

Sadly, my immediate reaction was to go against this advice. I thought out loud, "Why should I give Rob a fresh new start? He's disrespectful and doesn't turn in any assignments; he doesn't deserve a fresh new start until he changes." Mr. Green recommended that I give his advice a try and attempt to build a relationship with Rob. I reluctantly agreed, but was open to being more positive. Rob really turned things around in my class. Had I held on to my grudge, I would have missed out on witnessing Rob's true potential as a student and as a person. Not all of these stories end the way my story about Rob ends. Some students will never come around even if you try to get them to. Not everyone connects with everyone and that's just life. But, the fact that you can change your mindset, and give every student a fresh start everyday, is what matters most.

Misbehavior is a Form of Communication

Our actions and how we respond to undesirable situations far outweigh our words and educational jargon. Teachers provide a disservice to students when they hold grudges against them or grade their behavior. It is OK to become upset or frustrated but it's not OK to label a student by his or her misbehavior. When students misbehave, I believe they're actually letting us know that something is wrong, and they need our help in dealing with their problem. I have learned that taking a humble approach, reflecting and giving students a fresh new start is what students deserve.

As adults, we are not perfect, and we must stop expecting perfection from our students. This leads to the question of "how?" How can educators stop holding grudges against students? Understandably, this work can be challenging at times, but we must learn to let go of the bad moments and grow from them. Asking ourselves reflective questions can be painful, but they can drive helpful growth at the same time. Teachers will be surprised to learn that sometimes, they are the problem. I've learned that a lack of communication often leads to more problems and misunderstandings. When a student misbehaves, I have a calm conversation with the student to let them know his behavior is unacceptable and that I know they can do better. I also tell her that I hope her day gets better, and that I can't wait to see her tomorrow because tomorrow is a brand-new day with a fresh start! Hell, sometimes, I just point-blank ask my students, "What's your beef with me because I feel like a failure because I can't get you rolling in here? What am I doing wrong and how can I help you?"

We may never know what issues students are living through that may lead to them acting out. This is why we must be their ally, not their enemy. By holding a grudge, we are sending a message that we are better than them. When educators hold grudges against students, they are missing out on who that student really is. Educators must do better in this area because our students are human beings with feelings. This is why I always tell teachers to "reach them before you teach them." What if all your former teachers held grudges against you for all of your flaws along the way?

Rick Ramirez is a former U.S. Marine and boxing champion and is currently a national presenter and award winning educator from El Paso, Texas.

Stop Escalating Student Misbehavior

CARRIE LABARGE

My grandmother always said, "Little pictures have big ears." Students hear so much, regardless of whether we are aware of it or not. They pick up on so many comments and gestures, facial expressions and sights. Their brains are always thinking, making connections and remembering everything–especially when it comes to how we make them feel. The impact that teachers have when dealing with behaviors is crucial to creating relationships, future encounters and in my opinion, how students grow into adults and perceive others throughout the rest of their lives. Think about Ricky's previous chapter where his student, named Rob, was probably thinking the worst of him. Escalating or deescalating behavior will make or break a student's day, month, year, even a lifetime (and future educational experiences). If you think back to your educational experience as a student, you may recall an encounter with a teacher, whether your teacher escalated or de-escalated the behavior, whether it was you or someone else. You do remember, don't you?

Three Strikes and You're Out

Picture this scenario, Kyle, a fourth grader, has already had a difficult morning. When he was dropped off at school, his entire lunchbox spilled all over the sidewalk and his mother hollered at him while driving away. An adult helps him, tells him to get it together and he goes off to class. As Kyle settles into his classroom, he realizes that his lunchbox is leaking and his teacher is less than thrilled. She proceeds to make sure that the entire class knows that she is annoyed. This is strike number one.

Kyle is not prepared for his spelling test, either and again, his teacher has a less than comforting comment. That's strike number two. Kyle then manages to get through his test and it is now lunchtime--enter the leaking lunchbox. The teacher reminds Kyle what he already knows: that up until this point, he has had a miserable day. Kyle gets to lunch, finds his sandwich soggy and undesirable.

The cafeteria workers inform him he cannot get lunch because he has no money on his account. That's strike three. Kyle is not only miserable, but also very hungry. The teacher picks the class up from lunch. The class, as a whole, was not well behaved in the cafeteria and you guessed it, Kyle has gotten lumped into that whole mess too. On the walk back from class, a teacher comments on the still dripping lunchbox and Kyle's teacher makes a snide remark about how Kyle is always having a problem and the whole class was not behaved in the cafeteria. Is Kyle really always having a problem, or is it just today? Dealing with absolutes is difficult for children and let's face it: it's tough for adults, as well.

More than three adults in the span of four hours have not only failed to connect with Kyle, but have added fuel to what will become an inferno. This is an escalation that will be remembered by each and everyone in the class.

Finally, back in the classroom, students are asked to take out their projects from their backpacks. Kyle's backpack is tossed across the room because it was still dripping wet. Picture a red-faced child, who is crying out of anger, and the stunned teacher screams, "Pick that up, right now!" The battle ensues, Kyle gets louder, his teacher gets louder, the principal is called and Kyle is disciplined. Escalation. Unnecessary escalation.

Keith, a presenter at one of our professional development sessions, had a bottle of soda and started shaking it in front of the audience. He was shaking it once for each of the things that were bugging him that day. Keith then handed the bottle to someone else and asked them to do the same. The bottle went all the way around the room. Keith then took the well shaken bottle and placed it on the table in the front of the room. He asked if anyone wanted to open it and as you might guess, no one volunteered. Keith reminded us, "You never know how many times someone has been shaken up before they get to you; be sure you are not the one that pops their top!"

Task Avoidance is Not Misbehavior

Monica Green, a kindergarten teacher at a private charter school in Florida, was preparing her students to go to the technology center to work on a computer-based reading program that was focused on closing achievement gaps. The task for the day was to complete a benchmark test and the results would be discussed at an upcoming grade level meeting with administration. Most of the students were focused and moving along with completing the test as expected, but then Natalie was incredibly fidgety. Natalie was making noises and playing with her shoelaces. Miss Green approached her, but Natalie did not comply with her request to focus and the wires on her headphones became much more appealing than her own initially distracting shoelaces. Miss Green exclaimed, "Get busy and focus, Natalie! Your other teachers and your parents want you to do well on this task, so get moving!" Natalie began crying, escaped under her chair and started banging the back of her head on the metal computer table. Natalie's meltdown escalated because of the public humiliation which simply resulted after a child just did not want to do something. Could Miss Green have handled this differently? Of course.

One of my most favorite quotes is by Urie Bronfenbrenner: "Every child needs at least one adult who is irrationally crazy about him or her!" You can be that adult, an encourager who knows how to de-escalate behavior. Stand up for a student when a colleague is escalating a situation.

Carrie LaBarge is an Early Learning Program Facilitator in Hernando County, Florida and an educator and mother.

Stop Embarrassing Students in Front of Others
NICOLE BISCOTTI

My eighty-five-year-old grandmother often tells a story of what happened towards the end of her education in elementary school. She grew up in poverty in New York City with parents who could not always afford to feed her and her four siblings. When things got tight, she and one of her brothers were sometimes sent to an orphanage or to live with relatives. Since my grandmother did not always receive much love and encouragement at home she wanted to be accepted and do well in school. *Like all children, before she could focus on her academic performance, she needed love and acceptance.*

She was all too aware that the other girls in school had prettier dresses. Most of them even wore slips with lace borders that you could just barely see when they walked. One day she found a slip in a dumpster near her house and took it home and washed it. When she proudly wore the slip to school, she wanted it to show so that when she moved, people would know that she, indeed, owned a pretty slip. She admits that she probably exaggerated how much of her slip was showing, but she was so proud of it and, truthfully, it was also too large for her. Imagine her shame when her teacher accused her of lewd behavior and dressing promiscuously in front of the class. My grandmother's teacher continued her rant and accused my grandmother that her motive was to get the boys' attention. The other students in class giggled. When the teacher shamed my grandmother that day, she validated her fear that she did not belong in school.

Then and Now

The experience of being a student has changed dramatically since my grandmother went to school. Slips went out of fashion a long time ago. However, one thing that hasn't changed is that our students possess the very same need for acceptance and love. Like my grandmother showing off her slip, our students have a need to show off in a modern-day way. Perhaps, students of today are even more vulnerable because someone would have likely recorded the showoff and shared it on social media. Can you imagine how utterly powerless a child must feel when their shame is posted on social media?

While our circumstances may change over time, some things about human nature never change. In today's classrooms, we have students with invisible disabilities, such as ADHD. Many more of our students have disabilities waiting to be identified, making our support all the more critical. The youth of today desperately wants to be accepted for who they are and on their own terms. Some of them are struggling to understand their own gender and sexuality. Others come from diverse cultural backgrounds. The common theme is that *everyone* wants to not only be accepted but welcomed in our classrooms. Students NEED to feel that they are wanted, needed, brilliant and loved.

All Students Belong

Children today are shamed in countless ways and that needs to stop immediately. In the last chapter, Carrie writes about how shaming can take place through escalating a situation. Some of this is so embedded in our experience of education that we have become unaware of the harm we are doing. Students are not always able to control if they have school supplies, get to school on time, or are prepared for class. Not everyone has access to a quiet space to do homework or to even find the time to do it. Some students are required to help at home or work to help their families. Their difficulty focusing or reading may be a sign of a disability and a student who is possibly in need of support. We must stop shaming kids over these issues. We can never forget how much our words mean. Our words can establish a sense of belonging or rejection.

Students Create their Own Truths

Maybe my grandmother said it more succinctly when she shared that the assumptions that her teacher made about her that day established the idea in her mind that she did not belong in school. Everything else in her world outside of school supported her belief of not belonging: no one in her family had an education, she lived in poverty and she was told that she was wasting time studying rather than working. This cemented my grandmother's truth and perception about school. She wanted more than anything for her teacher to make her feel that she belonged at school. But instead, her teacher made my grandmother believe she did not belong.

Shame is Born Out of Assumptions

When we shame a student, we are making an assumption about the motives for their behavior. In that assumption, we then miss a critical opportunity to provide our students the support they need. As an educator, I am confronted with my own biases and presumptions. To continue to be effective with children, I must be willing to look at my preconceived ideas, gaps of knowledge and personal opinions about everything. Our perceived attitudes towards a child can affect their self-esteem, beliefs about themselves and their ability to be successful at school. We have an opportunity to reassure students that they belong at school and that they are loved and appreciated. But first we must stop shaming any student for any reason. We don't want to live with the memory that we have ruined someone, possibly forever. That is how powerful the teaching profession is. We cannot design the truths of our students from our negative interactions with them.

Nicole Biscotti is an educator from Yuma, Arizona and the author of I Can Learn When I'm Moving: Going to School with ADHD which is about her nine-year-old son. She empowers parents and teachers to provide game changing support for children with ADHD in school with kid approved, researched-based strategies.

Stop Punishing Students without Listening to their Side of the Story
VICKI WILSON

"Take a time out."
"Go to the office."
"You've lost your recess."
"No, I'm not interested in your side of the story."

Behavior Feedback in Real Time

Stop feeling like you need to "show face" in front of your class. What harm does it bring to listen to and to show respect for a disrespectful (or misbehaving, or non-compliant) student?

Misbehavior is a cry for communication, like Ricky suggests in his earlier chapter. Behavior is real-time feedback sending information to the teacher regarding any level of engagement, student happiness agency or understanding. Behavior is communication—always–100% of the time. It is the in-your-face reality of teaching. We need to look under, over and around the behavior and we need to look in the mirror regarding how we address it. When a problem behavior is present, no one knows more than that student. They know the rest of the story, the untold story and it may be very different from your first glance interpretation.

Rock Tag

Matthew, a third-grade student near Detroit, Michigan had a negative reputation at his elementary school. A child with a long list of adverse childhood experiences (ACES), Matthew was always under scrutiny and under the watchful eye of staff–and he knew it! He may not have been able to define every teacher movement, but he could feel it and he could see it painted on the scowls and disappointments of his teachers' faces. Matthew became conditioned to negative perceptions to the point that he believed he was a failure or a mistake just like Nicole wrote about her grandmother in the last chapter. Matthew was no stranger to being in trouble in school and he was rarely given the opportunity to tell his side of the story. His anger would often escalate quickly when punishments were doled out.

On one sunny spring day, Matthew was playing with his two closest friends–the same two friends he always played with and sat with at lunch with every day, Mia and Zack. After about ten minutes of outdoor play, Matthew was seen throwing a rock at Mia. The rock hit her in the head and Mia had a bump on her head. Thankfully, she was okay. Matthew was immediately directed to the principal to be disciplined. The discipline referral stated that he assaulted Mia by intentionally throwing a rock at her head. The report also stated that Matthew regularly bullied Mia and would not leave her alone at recess. Matthew ate his lunch alone on the bench outside the office waiting for the principal to call him in.

Matthew was visibly angry and frustrated when he was finally called into the principal's office. He sat down and watched the principal read the report while waiting to hear what his punishment would be this time. Typically he would be shamed and given a punishment followed by a call home. Matthew's eyes shot up from the floor in shock when he heard the words, "What happened?" Matthew was hesitant and surprised. It caught him off guard because this wasn't the normal speech that he received in the principal's office. He lifted his head, peered through the curtain of his long bangs and softly spoke.

"We went out for recess . . . me, Mia and Zack. We started playing a game we have played before. We call it Rock Tag. First, Mia had the rocks. Me and Zack ran back and forth in a straight line and tried not to get hit by the rock. Mia was 'it,' so she had the rocks and threw them at us while we ran. Mia's rock hit me on the chest so then I was 'it'. Zack and Mia were running back and forth and I threw rocks to tag them. My rock hit Mia in the head. I felt really bad. I told her I was sorry. She said she was okay."

"What were you thinking while you were playing Rock Tag?"

"That it was fun."

"What do you think now?"

"I like Rock Tag but I am sad that Mia got hurt when I threw the rock at her. I didn't mean for it to hit her in the head."

The principal called Mia and Zack into the office and listened to each student tell their story one at a time. Their stories matched Matthew's story. The three children sat down together with the principal to talk about recess rules and safety and the four of them concluded that Rock Tag was not a safe and appropriate game for recess. Together, they came up with a safe version of tag that they could play the next day.

Opportunities to Gain Perspective & Change Perception

An adult who is willing to ask questions, listen, empathize, negotiate and be respectful (even when it is hard) is the one that will make the greatest difference in the life of children. Whether it is the child who is hard to love in the moment or the twenty-seven other children watching you model kindness, empathy and care during a time of difficulty, they will all come out better in the end if you stop and remember to get all of the facts of every matter.

Punishing students without listening to their side of the story first, will result in a substandard classroom community that is absent of trust and strong teacher-student relationships. Without a trusting relationship, your students will disengage from learning, have increased feelings of anger and frustration and fail to show you mutual respect. No one wins in that kind of class.

Vicki Wilson is an elementary principal in Wyandotte, Michigan and the author of Lead with Instructional Rounds. She is passionate about education and collaborative professional learning.

Stop Ignoring Possible Signs of Trauma, Abuse & Neglect

KRISTINA MACBURY

Nearly one third of United States youth, ages 12-17, have experienced two or more traumatic experiences in their lives. Traumatic experiences in youth are also referred to as Adverse Childhood Experiences (ACES). Events do not affect all children in the same way. When an event inflicts fear and negative reactions, it can be traumatic. But sometimes, the warning signs are difficult to spot or are subtle in nature. Because trauma, abuse and neglect are not obvious we must become more attune to the signs and symptoms of ACES.

Do Something about Pollution

Statistics show that one-fifth of children will develop a mental health disorder in their lives. Eighty percent of these mental health disorders will reach one's onset prior to the age of 24. During the 2015–2016 school year, 88% of Caucasian students graduated from high school. In comparison, only 76% of African Americans, 72% of American Indians and 79% of Hispanics graduated. This is important information to note, not just in terms of inequitable economic opportunity, but also in terms of health and stability. Adults with a college degree live longer and have lower rates of chronic disease than those who do not graduate from college. I would dare say that based on this conservative representation of such data, that ignoring these data points is like ignoring pollution in the city. Just like pollution, most people know mental illness is all around us and many times no longer realize it is there. Like pollution, mental illness affects us all in different ways: we smell it, feel it, contribute to it and have the power to improve it. We have the power to advocate and make it better or can continue adding to the landfills and oceanic garbage patch.

The Myth of "Our Plates are Full"

I do not think that most educators set out to ignore signs of trauma or mental health challenges. Teachers have a lot going on. Many educators feel grossly inadequate or ill prepared to deal with mental illness issues. Understanding the signs, symptoms and actions of trauma, abuse and neglect is one more thing on our plates. It is not easy to address because these signs and symptoms are not always overtly presented to us; serving students of trauma, abuse and neglect is hard, messy and uncomfortable for many. That does not give us permission to dismiss this arena of supporting students just because we do not like to discuss, because we feel inadequate or ill prepared to address it, or because we are too busy teaching. Teachers must step in to help students at all costs, especially when your gut tells you something is wrong.

Why Rock the Boat?

Alexia is the youngest of six children and naturally talented in so many ways. She is a genuine, kind, sarcastic and a spunky twelve-year-old who loves to make people laugh. Her parents divorced when she was three. Her father abused her mother and one of her older sisters was adjudicated for drug abuse and theft. Alexia had always done well in school and got along well with her peers. Entering 7th grade, she seemed to be much less interested in school, but she still maintained a decent academic average. She started to become off task by not completing assignments. She performed well on her tests, which kept her grades hovering at a high "C" average. It was reported throughout 7th grade from several of Alexia's teachers that she would often doodle and daydream and made-up excuses to make a long trek to the nurse each day. The nurse did not find any illness, ailment or physical injury. At the end of the year in a grade level meeting, Alexia's teachers made comments such as, "She works when push comes to shove." or "Her grades are OK so why rock the boat?" They would dismiss Alexia's behaviors as typical for a preteen.

By the time Alexia was in 9th grade, her schoolwork and grades declined. After being called into the principal's office for cutting school, her mother reported that Alexia frequently came home "high" after school and she exhibited self-harming behaviors, such as cutting herself. I know that teachers should not be alarmists at every junction of student behavior, but what if Alexia's 7th grade teachers looked at things differently back then? What if her teachers had high expectations for learning by implementing proficiency-based grading and high-quality work? What if they ensured student voice, choice and input? Would they have been able to notice this decline much earlier?

Recognizing the signs and symptoms of trauma (externalized and internalized) can be difficult. Although all signs are not always in our face, ignoring any signs, especially over long periods of time, can have a devastating impact on our student's overall health. Instead, look for some of these types of warning signs that should never be ignored:

- Loss of hope, purpose or direction
- Dramatic change in behavior
- Feeling trapped or micromanaged
- Increased use of drugs/alcohol
- Withdrawal from family, friends or society
- Giving away prized possessions
- Sleeping all the time or not at all
- Acting extremely recklessly
- Increased anxiety or anxiousness
- Moodiness
- Fluctuations in grades or on-task behaviors
- Fatigue or disinterest in much of anything

We must educate and train our school community about the signs of crisis, mental health challenges and what to do when we see these signs, symptoms and risk factors that can contribute to crisis. These are all critical components in connecting our youth with help networks. We must do our best to recognize such signs, even the smallest red flag, so that more drastic outcomes, such as suicide, do not happen.

Stop being afraid to ask direct questions of your students because you don't want to make matters worse. We must rock the boat in order to save lives.

Kristina MacBury is a co-mom of 11, an award winning principal in the tristate Philadelphia Area, NASSP Digital Principal, author of Principal Pro: An Authentic Leadership Playbook for Managing Crisis, Building Teams and Maximizing Resources and co-founder of Educate4Hope. She is a fierce mental health advocate for education and a die-hard Phillies fan.

49

Stop Suspending Students for Minor Infractions
JOSHUA STAMPER

I received a call on the radio that a teacher needed an administrator immediately. It was the start of the class period and I assumed the worst. I rushed to the classroom door to find the teacher standing in the doorway looking at their class. Every student was in their seat silently looking at their teacher.

Confused by the scene, I asked, "Is everything alright?"

The teacher whipped around yelling, "No! Everything is not alright! I have two boys who have stolen this girl's lipstick."

"Ok, you saw them take the lipstick from the girl?"

The teacher looked annoyed by my question. "No, I didn't see them take it. I was doing hall duty and when I came in, the lipstick was gone. They were fighting and this young lady told me the boys took it."

"Oh, OK. Well, as soon as class is over, I'll investigate and make sure we find the lipstick."

"No! I want these boys out now!"

Shocked by the demand, I replied, "Excuse me? Based on what evidence?"

"Do you want to teach this class? Either these boys are out of my class now or you can teach this class. I refuse to have them in my class. I know they stole that lipstick!"

I could feel the temperature rise in my face. I yelled, "Boys, you're with me! Let's go."

The two young men grabbed their things and one of the boys said, "Man, this is stupid."

Ignition of Change

We walked to my office and I was livid. As soon as we got in my office, I slammed my door with frustration, looked at the two boys and said, "You're not in trouble. Just give me a minute." I knew a shift was needed in the way the student behavior was both perceived and addressed by this teacher and our entire campus, but I was not quite sure how to ignite that change.

I was a brand-new administrator and at the time, students were frequently being sent out of class for minor infractions. I was suspending kids left and right. Our In School Suspension (ISS) room was full every day. As a campus, we punished every student mistake to try to change the behavior of our students. Instead of things improving, we found the students' behaviors continued or became worse.

Compounding the problem, after a consequence was provided by an administrator, the student would come back to class to a fractured relationship between student and teacher. I often heard from students before they re-entered the learning environment, "That teacher doesn't like me." or "I'm not going back to that class." or "He doesn't even want me in there." It was obvious that by sending the student out for minor infractions, the students felt unwelcomed and rejected by the teacher. These feelings didn't go away. As much as both the teacher and student tried to ignore what occurred previously, the relationship was never the same.

By the end of the school year, I gathered the discipline data and divided the behaviors into three categories based on the severity of the infraction. A level one infraction was categorized as a minor behavior, such as sleeping in class, perceived disrespect, disruptions, or being unprepared. Level two and three infractions were more severe, such as inappropriate language towards a teacher to physical altercations between students.

Once the referrals were categorized, I added up the amount of time students missed from class. I was shocked to see the total number of instructional time lost over the course of the school year. It was no wonder there was so much frustration with the student grades. Students were barely in class to learn from their teachers! Instead, they were sitting in the hall, in the front office, or in the ISS room. *I realized we had to stop suspending students for minor infractions.*

The following school year, my focus was on finding alternative discipline practices to allow both students and teachers to learn positive behavior strategies, restore fractured relationships and keep students in the classroom. To rectify the problems from the previous year, we transitioned to using new practices, such as de-escalation practices, restorative practices and push-in support. The new initiatives would allow level one and most level two infractions to be handled within the classroom by the teacher with administrative support.

De-escalation Strategies

The largest referred behavior in our discipline records was "student disrespect." With each investigation, there were several components that were similar in each escalated interaction. We began to teach our teachers to be a "window" not a "mirror." If a student became upset or their tone of voice was negative, instead of replicating the behavior and escalating the situation, the teachers modeled the appropriate communication skills. With this small change, the teachers were able to calm the student down and provide the redirection needed to get the student back on track. Our referrals decreased dramatically from this one change in the classroom.

Restorative Practices

Instead of sending students to detention or ISS, we focused on using restorative practices to teach the appropriate behavior, allow students to take ownership of their actions, identify who was harmed by their decisions and how they were going to rectify the harm caused. Instead of the teacher sending a student to the office, the teacher was able to teach the appropriate behavior, allow the student to reflect on their harmful actions and take ownership of the solution to rectify the situation. We started utilizing restorative circles and reflection sheets to provide students an opportunity to learn and practice appropriate conflict resolution and communication.

Push-Ins

Another common practice that occurred in the classroom was teachers asking students to fix their behavior in front of the entire class. The student then felt as though the teacher was calling them out and embarrassing them in front of their peers. Instead of redirecting and correcting the student in front of everyone or sending the student to the office, we devised a plan to allow the teacher to have a private conversation with the student. If a teacher needed to speak to a student, the teacher would call the front office. An administrator, counselor or behavior specialist was sent to cover the classroom while the teacher and student went for a walk. On the walk, the teacher would ask a few questions to coach the student through the situation. Instead of sending the student away and fracturing the relationship, we allowed the teacher an opportunity to spend more time investing in the student. This practice has been extremely beneficial for all stakeholders and we have seen the behaviors of our students improve drastically, thus allowing them to stay inside the learning environment, not be thrown out like criminals.

As we work with student behavior, we cannot keep sending students away and assuming the behavior will change as they are isolated in an alternative location. We have to find a way to keep the relationship intact while teaching the appropriate behavior, modelling proper communications, and repairing the harm that was caused. Too many students are missing important classroom minutes for minor infractions and in the process, they are losing their motivation to learn and connect with others. We must stop our own harmful practices and focus on the most important part of the student: their hearts.

Joshua Stamper is an administrator, author, speaker, Teach Better Team Podcast Network Manager and host of "Aspire: The Leadership Development Podcast.

STOP Doing These Things at Your School

This Nonsense Blocks Synergistic School Culture

Stop Complaining about Your Salary and Everything Else

ALLISON K. KREISS

As the old adage about teaching goes, "You didn't get into this profession for the money; you got into it to make a difference." The trouble is, sometimes, that doesn't exactly pay the bills. What's left to do when you're having trouble making ends meet and your yearly increment written into your contract barely bumps up your earnings by $20 per paycheck? Well, for one thing: you just cannot complain.

It's Not about the Money

Teachers are some of the hardest working professionals in the world. They make solar systems out of Styrofoam, have students journeying to far-off places without ever leaving their seats and provide them with life-long skills. What do teachers do when their salaries aren't up to snuff? They go out and get a second or even a third job. They take on after school programs, such as clubs and sports, in order to try and supplement their income. They work during the summer. They even pick up a bus route before and after school. They do all of this because their commitment to teaching is not about the salary, it is about making an impact on students.

Now, do not get me wrong. Having some money in the bank is awesome, not that I've ever really known what that feels like. I've almost always lived paycheck to paycheck. It could be because I have never been really good at saving money or, perhaps, I've got a slight (okay, larger than that) spending problem. But the truth is, I've felt the best about who I am as a person when I make a difference with students. I've felt as though I've really made a difference when I spent my last $50 to clear a lunch bill so a student could eat. I wake up each morning at 5:00 a.m., not because I want to, but because the urge to get up and go to work is stronger than the one to go back to bed and be a sloth for the rest of the day. I enjoy my job and most teachers do too.

If you are complaining about your salary, consider doing one of the two following things: reconsider your profession (maybe the job just isn't fun enough for you to forget that you're broke) or do something about it. You can become a union representative or a member of your union negotiating team for the next contract that's due for renewal. Maybe you are residing in one of the lower paying counties of your state and it's time to find a job elsewhere. The bottom line is that you are wasting your time complaining about something that you might not be willing to change. Your efforts would be much better spent lobbying for change instead of whining about your profession.

Prevent Fires

What do you do when you are surrounded by negativity and an endless stream of naysayers? I recently joined my town's volunteer fire department and with that commitment came a five month long, three night a week training camp at fire school. In the fire service training, Firefighter 1 is the course where they teach you just enough to kill yourself. They have things like "Near Miss" Reports where they document any "Oops that could've turned out horribly wrong if it had gone just a bit differently." It's these "Near Miss" Reports, firefighters are reminded of policies and guidelines that are set to help them stay alive and safe on the fire ground. We have similar policies and guidelines in education for several reasons. The reason I mention these reports is that the fire service is notorious for altering policies AFTER something bad happens. They are rarely on the proactive side of policy making. I'm guessing that's mostly because you can't really anticipate everything that could possibly happen on the fire ground, so you trust that firefighters and their officers have read their standard operating procedures, adhere to them and exercise good judgment. But even then, mistakes can happen where fire is involved.

As a teacher and parent, I have felt as though I need to be just as proactive in my teaching career as I am in firefighting. Constantly thinking at least two steps ahead of a student or problem before it comes to fruition is crucial to successful teaching. I do that mostly because, as a special education teacher, I want to try and alleviate any stress or reason for a student to struggle with an assignment before that struggle ensues. If I don't, there's a very high chance that I'll be spending my time trying to convince the kid to do the work and not really getting anything else done. But, even with these types of challenges, I do not complain.

Elevate and Celebrate Exceptional Teaching

I'm not typically a "glass is half empty" kind of person. I'm more of a "the glass is half full of something" kind of person. A few years ago, I was very much one of those people who felt like I had no will to go on in the teaching profession. I felt defeated, deflated and out of energy to do what I loved, and it was only September! I am not an overly emotional person, but I was ready to cry and that's saying a lot.

143

Luckily for me, I had the great honor and opportunity to attend and co-present a keynote at Elevating and Celebrating Exceptional Teaching and Teachers in New Jersey and Pennsylvania (ECET2NJPA) that same year. I was privileged to meet and learn with people across the region, some of whom I remain in contact with both personally and professionally today. Other than the nerves that come along with presenting to a room of 200 people, I found it hard to get excited about learning that weekend. The negativity had clouded my mind so much that I couldn't find anything in my heart except anxiety.

While participating in the conference, I attended a session held by an educational consultant, LaVonna Roth. The idea behind her session was to really come to grips with the positive influence you've had on others as a teacher, how to lift up your colleagues and focus on the good happening in any given day. In my mind, I had tried to sabotage the possibility of acceptance before LaVonna even started. But, right away, I found myself listening intently, absorbed and participating in the session, much to my surprise. LaVonna was one of the most genuine individuals whom I have ever met. To give you an idea of what kind of person she is, I was scheduled to present at a conference in Texas well after ECET2NJPA. LaVonna would have missed my presentation because she wasn't scheduled to fly in until later, but she changed her flight and surprised me by being in the audience. I'll never forget that.

In LaVonna's session, she was able to get all of the participants up and moving, cheering on people we'd never met while she tested us with memory games and challenged us to see how the brain science plays a huge role in what we do, how we feel and how we exist in our own little worlds. I felt rejuvenated after her session, but struggled to be the positive person she rallied us to be.

I had enough resolve to get myself to go back to the conference the following year. Going back made me excited to see the people I had met and connected with, but I also was able to reconnect with LaVonna. When we all sat down and started talking together, I seriously felt like I was part of a huge family dinner. There was such a sense of togetherness and camaraderie. It was like feeling as if you had been underwater, but then came up for a breath of fresh air. The drowning sensation had abated and I felt good about myself and my mission as an educator once again.

Reconnect

I was ready to tackle what remained of my school year and nothing was going to knock me down. I had made friends with those who would remain with me long after the conference was over and I also established a professional relationship with some people who have ultimately been the springboard for my entrance into presenting at conferences and becoming an educational consultant. These friends, including LaVonna, have been there to listen, help, visit and provide support whenever I needed it. I couldn't be happier that I was able to attend this conference twice and make the connections that are still strong today.

I can't say that I'm completely cured of all negativity. I do tend to indulge from time to time as I am far from perfect. But I am a firm believer that complaining and sitting idly by while someone else fights for you is not my cup of tea. I'm a fighter and a problem solver. When I feel as though the walls of negativity are closing in, I call, text, or DM my friends who always manage to pick me up. I wouldn't be the educator I am today without all of them and I always hold onto what LaVonna said that one bad thing in your day does not make the entire day bad. I've learned to embrace the positive, try to support those around me and remain constant in my beliefs and actions. I fight fires, with whatever tactics and strategies I have in my arsenal, whether it be at work during the day or on the fire ground at night.

Stop complaining about all of the things we have to do for the state and our school districts. Stop focusing on those things that bring your mood and attitude so low that no one wants to be around you. Stop dwelling on all of the negative things that are going on in your building, in your district, or even in your life. Focus on the positive. Just because one negative thing happens in a day, doesn't mean that your entire day has gone to Hell.

Allison Kreiss is a teacher leader, aspiring administrator, national presenter and passionate advocate of student voice and choice. She is also a contributor for DisruptED TV magazine and The Education Question.

Stop Skipping Steps in Your School's Chain of Command
MATT CHRISTISON, Ed.D.

Please understand this message is for all of us, including me. As a very outspoken, experienced, long time high school principal, I, too, want to be seen and heard by others. I want to matter to others, to be heeded, to have my ideas, opinions, and "this is how things should be done" advice put into practice. But there is a process for getting things done and the chain of command should not be ignored.

Stick to the Chain of Command, Always

Eventually, everyone you work with leaves or you leave, first. People have children, go to school, transfer, get another job, resign, retire or pass away. During the time you are working together, the personal relationship you have with others can be positive, negative, mixed or non-existent. The professional relationship can have these same qualifiers, yet it is essential for you and your school to stick to the steps in the school's chain of command–even if those steps seem ineffective.

First

The steps exist as part of a process for addressing concerns, issues and problems. The steps do not exist to suit you or your desire to be recognized, heard or feel important. The steps, however, should not make you feel unrecognized, muted blunted or unimportant. Yet, skipping steps is narcissistic and self-indulgent. None of us is so important that all others and all processes should focus solely upon what an individual sees as paramount and of utmost importance.

Second

Issues and concerns, as well as actions sought, occur in the context of a whole school or system, rather than the smaller daily interactions of any one of us. What is pressing and demanding for you is ultimately a small piece in a complex, complicated multi-faceted universe. Doing what I want or what you want so badly while intentionally skipping steps negates everyone else and their own small piece.

Third

Distracting from the process draws away time and energy within the system, further undermining both the process and the people involved. The steps in any process require the attention of individuals or a group that directs their work. None of us in education are lacking in demands on our time and imposing more on others undermines the process and the people in that systems-based process. Simply follow the steps to get resolve.

You are a teacher and with that role comes the responsibility to be bigger than the "self," together working to make things better for the entire system. What if parents took every complaint that they had about you to the school board?

Dr. Matt Christison is a high school principal, author and instructor. He is dedicated to public education, evidence-based decision making and the pragmatic development of human beings in our ever-changing world.

Stop Recruiting Board Members to Be on Your Side
EDWARD J. PALMISANO

"Associate yourself with people of good quality, for it is better to be alone than in bad company." –Booker T. Washington

Like the seasons, school board members come, and school board members go. There is nothing more precarious for a superintendent than dealing with the dreaded 4-3 split. "The big majority 4," as some locals will call it (when having a 7-seat board) usually work as a team to push through an agenda, which inevitably includes personnel issues. The temptation for a school employee is to make good friends with those in charge. It makes sense, then, to go straight to the top, right? That is the type of thinking that many teachers and employees have. This *political* type of thinking is often made at their own peril because every two years, some board members may change. When the 3 minority members feel shut out, they will go out of their way to drum up support and just wait for their chance to make a comeback in the next school board election. When they do, woe to those who previously crossed them. During a 4-3 or 5-2 split board, feelings are often hurt and the parties can take things personally.

It's Not Worth it

Administrators and teachers who try to snuggle up with a small section of board members will appear to feel safe and protected, but they also lose the respect of the quiet staff members who are flying under the radar. You may be feared, but you are not respected. Does it seem like people like you? I hate to tell you, but if you are playing the game of siding up with those in power just to feel safe, chances are that others who seem friendly to you are just trying not to get on your good side just to avoid problems. If a board turns and the 4-3 becomes 3-4, you not only lose job security, but also your "friends."

147

A bad board member who is all about personal ego and power will love your attention. That member might also recognize your motives and know he or she can manipulate you, as well. A good board member will see through your insincerity and likely smile and nod as you cozy up, but even an altruistic board member will have a memory about how you act at all times. Don't think you are making friends with a board member just because they appear to be friendly; if something comes up where you need defending, your motives have already been noted and you can expect they will let others know about your disingenuous style in an executive session. Plus, they might just be trying to get information out of you. Remember, a school board is an elected board and with elections come politics.

If you really want to make a problem for yourself, skip the entire chain of command and go right to the school board—in the same way that Matt posed a question to you at the end of his chapter. That one will really get you in trouble. You might get a board member to take your side and put pressure on your supervisor, but your supervisor will be the one you have to deal with every day and they will not take kindly to being bypassed. Expect to be shut out of future conversations and growth opportunities. It won't be worth it. To those who are watching—and people are always watching—you will be viewed as a troublemaker.

Crossfires and Casualties

Whether you are an administrator or a faculty member, risks remain in the pecking order of the chain of command. If you are a 1st or 2nd year teacher or an administrator, remember that you have ZERO protection, professionally. No union contract will save you and you can be fired without just cause. If someone doesn't like you, too bad. Nobody is immune to crossfires and casualties, and I, for one, have experienced both ends of the school board bone. I could write this chapter from the point of view of a staff member or from the perspective of a board member. I have been in both seats and part of the crossfire and casualties of war in education.

I have seen superintendents and principals become contractually "non-renewed" because they stood up for the students and did not tolerate corrupt boards. I have also seen boards and superintendents work hand in hand with corruption and personal agendas and who have found ways to stack up against staff that they feel challenge the status quo and attract too much attention to the district. I have even heard a superintendent and business manager tell us in a meeting that if we wanted to get rid of someone we could "manipulate the rubric" and there were always ways to get rid of an employee.

Students Lose When Adults Misbehave

A board does not always look out for what is best for children and staff, I'm sad to say. Adults often have exceptionally large egos. Adults seeking political positions such as a school board seat, often have even larger egos. Particularly, as a special educator or administrator when I see parents or students being taken advantage of, I feel it is my moral duty to stand up for them and I have stayed true to that personal ideal. I may believe I have acted justly, but that doesn't mean I couldn't have been more prudent in how I did that, however. It has been a career of living and learning, but I always make sure I can still sleep at night.

Don't Play Games You Can't Win

So, how do we do manage survival within a system that has some crooks and sneaky politicians? How do we play these political games that, sometimes, have no winners? As the WOPR Computer in the 1983 movie *Wargames* lamented, "A strange game. The only winning move is not to play." Stay below the crossfire but never stop moving forward. Stop looking at the board as either your greatest enemy or your best friend. Stay out of it. Focus on the students. That is it. Do what you can today with what you have and do the work just as the motivational author and speaker Jon Gordon suggests:

If they praise you, show up and do the work.

If they criticize you, show up and do the work.

If no one even notices you, just show up and do the work.

Just keep showing up, doing the work and leading the way.

Do not play games you cannot win. Stop recruiting people to be on your side. You might get wounded and maybe even taken out of the game, but you will maintain the respect of others. At the end of the day, you only need to be able to look at yourself in the mirror and know that you did the right thing.

Edward Palmisano has been an educator for over 25 years and has served as a school board member, special education coordinator and school psychologist in both Illinois and Indiana. Ed loves to assist local parents as an advocate as they attempt to navigate legal issues in special education. He has also been a dedicated test prep tutor for over a decade. Ed lives with his wife, two incredible teenagers, and eight parakeets in Beecher, Illinois.

Stop Using the "I'm in a Union" or "I Have Tenure" Slogans

TRACEY TAYLOR

No excuses. No justifications. No character witnesses. No protection.

Just you and what you do . . .

If your school, district or state partnered with your union organization or tenure committee and required a peer review process of your professional practice, would a panel of your academic colleagues and peers deem you fit for educational service?

Some of our K-12 readers might have some insight into my question as they may have participated in this type of behavior. Some of our higher education professors might be able to enlighten us. But let's entertain the hypothetical, shall we? Reflect if you need to and then answer these questions for yourself: "Could you provide evidentiary proof that you are an effective and efficient educator and deserve the honor of serving in the education or academic field?" Without any protection or justification, would your practice and craft stand up to the scrutiny and standards of other teachers?" Would you and what you do in the classroom pass that test?

Cut Your Own Crap

It has taken me many years to get to where I am as an educator and, often failing in my own eyes or in the eyes of others. It could be said that this message is a dose of medicine in my personal growth. Others will tell you that I have earned this message the hard way. I am downright grateful for being able to learn from my own mistakes, but it took me having to look at my own crap and then cutting it.

One of the heaviest criticisms of educational reformers is that our unions and tenure systems are protecting all teachers, good and bad. It has been said that one cannot fire bad teachers or anyone for that matter. Additionally, our unions are the largest funded political action group that lobbies and influences policy while demanding better wages and benefits that many in the public do not feel we deserve. And while our critics are not outright incorrect, they are not, altogether, correct, either.

That being said, your acquisition of tenure or union membership status is not a "get out of jail for free" card with sole purpose in excusing malpractice, malfeasance, or misfeasance in an academic/education professional setting. This is my elegant way of letting you know that, like me, you need to examine your effectiveness and ineffectiveness as a teacher and then cut your own "crap" in order to get started.

Setting the Record Straight

Let's set the record straight with some historically accurate myth busting. The original tenets of tenure were constructed over a period in the early half of the 1900s with the intent to protect those working in the academic profession. At the time, protections were needed to ensure equality for gender, religion, race, as well as the protection of knowledge, discovery and invention. Guaranteeing First Amendment rights for academic professionals whose research, science, discovery and invention might put them in a position of keeping their findings from the public or being published was a survival mode feeling.

Removing the threat of termination or censorship for those who are engaging and exploring with ideas in arenas of discourse considered controversial or adding to the transcendental knowledge that benefits humankind keeps the power of all that is to be gained from their work in the hands of academia where it cannot be weaponized or silenced, but to be applied for the common good. Now, included in these protections of tenure, which still stand today, is the maintenance of due process. The basic tenets of tenure indicate that yes, indeed, you can be fired. The due process proceedings are in place to ensure that any termination is justified and supported with evidence and with just cause.

Teachers' unions are no different than the origin of other labor unions, emerging from the need to protect teachers from terrible working conditions, nepotism in hiring, political backlash and advocacy for intellectual freedom. The purpose of teachers' unions is generally considered to be a unified advocacy for teachers with special interest in the overall education system, as well as protecting the due process procedures outlined by tenure. Through the use of collective bargaining, teachers and unions can work together on issues that affect all workers. Union support during bargaining gives teachers more strength than if the teachers tried to negotiate individually. Teachers' unions are considered a public sector union, which is typically more controversial in nature than private sector unions primarily due to the fact that negotiations regarding wages and benefits impact taxpayer dollars.

Both the American Federation of Teachers (AFT) and the National Education Association (NEA), the two largest teacher unions, focus their efforts around collective bargaining for teacher unions including wages and benefits, teaching load and the conditions for employment and termination, although these vary from local to state regions in accordance with both state and federal law.

Supporters of teacher unions most often reference an increase and overall equity regarding salaries, wages and benefits; professionalization of the profession; the ease of attracting new teachers of high quality into the career; and the cessation of discriminatory policies and/or procedures as a result of collective bargaining. Criticism aimed at teacher unions typically maintains that as a result of collective bargaining it becomes too time consuming and expensive to engage in the due process procedures in order to dismiss incompetent teachers and it prevents flexible staffing arrangements, along with insulating teachers from accountability measures.

Now, Letting the Record Set You Straight

In my experience, our unions have actively blocked education and school reform measures which then aggravates and makes the disparities of the education system worse.

The benefit of tenure and our teacher unions are actually set up to sustain our profession and protect knowledge and labor from those who wish to own it and use it for their own personal gain such as big business, big industry, big government and even big education. This is about the greater good. Stop testing the limits of your tenure and union membership if you are not a good teacher.

The problem is that some teachers are not reflective or they think that they are incredible teachers when they really are not. When we reflect on our practice, can we be so bold as to look into the mirror and ask the following questions?

- Would you survive a peer review board?
- Do you need a fresh check up on your policies and procedures of governance?
- Do you know and use the collective bargaining agreements for good?
- Do you need to sit down with a union leader and have a conversation or ask questions?
- Do you keep ending up regretting who you hired?
- Do you need a better vetting practice for hiring new employees?
- Do you need a better interviewing process?
- Are you using growth plans just to terminate teachers or do you want them to succeed and get better?

- Have you become unwilling or are unable to grow, support and educate your faculty and staff on how to be better?
- Have you become such good friends with your staff that you cannot discipline them for wrongdoing?
- Do you need professional development for your own role?
- Do you need a professional learning community for administrators where you can get encouragement and support and development ideas that will energize you?
- Do you need support from your faculty and staff through distributive leadership practices?
- Do you need a different role or job?
- Do you need change?
- Do you need to stop hiding behind your union or tenure?

We must self-reflect before we can answer the difficult professional questions about our own work.

Tracey Taylor is a well-known educator and artist in Aztec, New Mexico.

Stop Obeying Orders when Something Just isn't Right

HANS APPEL

"It is the first responsibility of every citizen to question authority."
–Benjamin Franklin

The history of civilization is rooted in a unified belief that effective societies operate best from a shared set of values, core beliefs and morals. These agreed upon ideals offer citizen's guidance and structure to avoid anticipated chaos and negativity from creeping into a group of people's way of life. However, what happens if the law and order isn't accurate, just, or a fair representation of its people?

What's Expected or what is Right?

As our tightly held beliefs transform into rules, laws and procedures, individuals often find themselves at a dichotomous precipice of examining what's expected vs. what's right. A person's internal struggle to obey yet follow their mind, heart and soul can result in a cognitive dissonance that challenges one's own character. This type of situation tugs at your moral compass because rule followers don't want to break the rule, yet the rule itself is broken. There is no synergy in this state of mind.

Lisa Bick warns that "obeying orders just to obey is the mark of a person who has ceased to think." Indeed, history is filled with people who followed orders while letting others suffer. Hitler's reign of terror brainwashed a group of ordinary Germans to commit horrible crimes against humanity through an expectation of following Nazi order. Indeed, the United States has a disheartening comfortability in oppression or omission of equity based on gender, sex, race, religion, mental and physical disability, income, age, ethnicity and more. We know we can all do better.

> *"Just as it is the duty of all men to obey just laws, so it is the duty of all men to disobey unjust laws."* –
> Martin Luther King Jr.

Challenge the Status Quo

Civil rights leaders have heroically fought against unjust racism to reshape policy, while expanding our collective societal view of what it means to be human. There is no Title IX without brave individuals willing to challenge the status quo.

Education, as a microcosm of our greater society, is certainly not immune to such antiquated inflexible thinking to the detriment of our learners. And while fully inclusive education, free from bias, injustice, and inequity still feels like a distant pursuit, generational progress occurs through a grassroots movement of teachers questioning the way we've always done things.

Combat Complacency

School culture and climate deteriorates as we fail to build systems where educational leaders are committed to exploring perspectives outside of themselves. We avoid capitalizing on others' expertise assuming that a person in authority has all of the answers. Teachers are unhappy, disconnected and disillusioned in this type of archaic top-down school system that thrives on authoritarian rule. Learners suffer as the best and brightest ideas, innovations and creations are simply left on the shelf in favor of mandates, benchmarks and demands. Trust is eroded in this culture devoid of belief in one another. Educator ownership devolves into indifference as the school community feels a lack of responsibility toward serving the greater good.

"The disappearance of a sense of responsibility is the most far-reaching consequence of submission to authority." --Stanley Migram

Responsibility ensures an inherent leadership quality to combat complacency. The antithesis to questioning authority is compliance. In our schools, compliance is mutually exclusive from creativity, innovation, critical thinking and complex problem solving; all of which are skills school systems claim to be striving toward. If we truly want to foster a culture that's filled with deep thinking future driven learners then we must empower, celebrate and expect teacher-led risk-taking. This is no different for adults and students—which the authors in Part I of this book wrote about when they defined what five-star schools look like.

A few years ago, I made a bold proclamation to the educational world that we'd be starting a cutting edge, student led leadership podcast. I wrote about its wild success to "forever shatter the ceiling on student voice" in my book, *Award Winning Culture*. But, many readers may not know how we were hit with overwhelming barriers and opposition to seeing our culture building project come into focus.

When things don't seem right, skepticism dominates over clear thinking. Here are what some skeptics thought about our podcast goal centered in student voice:

- "There's no money for equipment."
- "Students shouldn't have a voice in school."
- "There's no budget for a stipend."
- "Students aren't mature enough or talented enough to pull it off."
- "Parents won't sign off on permission."
- "The district won't approve the activity."
- "There's no space to record."
- "No one will listen."
- "You won't be able to book anyone good to interview."

How did we sidestep toxic negativity, orders and restrictions to create such a beautiful model to amplify student voice with an authentic platform driven to shape our culture? With each new question, demand or challenge thrown our way, we simply said, "Ok. Thank You." and then unapologetically moved slowly forward across the perceived "you-can't-do-this imaginary line."

"You are remembered for the rules you break." –Douglas MacArthur

155

Be Brave

In the end, each educator must find bravery to speak and live their truth by aligning their why with their own daily actions. Fast tracking a student podcast might be far less impactful than leading a historic march; however, every small decision to stand up for our learners holds a promise of hope that creates generational ripples of positive educational change. Teachers can and must be the leaders against any tyranny of complacency by standing up and questioning, challenging and overcoming orders that fail students.

Honestly, I wasn't afraid of being told "no." I wasn't afraid of being yelled at. I wasn't afraid of hearing "I told you so." I wasn't afraid to experience judgement or pity filled smirks over our possible podcast failure. Instead, I was afraid of losing powerful student experiences, learning and joy that would exist if I didn't do something about my passions. Not doing what's right for my learners terrifies the hell out of me!

I believe that education, at its highest level, is about inspiring others to discover and develop their JOY. Questioning orders that I know eliminate the pipeline to JOY will always be the right thing for me to do. But, now what about you?

"You must never be fearful about what you are doing when it is right." –Rosa Parks

Hans Appel is an educator, speaker and writer deeply committed to inspiring the whole learner. He is the author of Award Winning Culture: Building School-Wide Intentionality and Action through Character, Excellence, and Community and the Director of Culture for the Teach Better Team.

Stop Ignoring Professional Deadlines & Job Responsibilities
ANN HLABANGANA-CLAY

This chapter might hurt your feelings. Not because that's my intention, but rather because what I'm about to write will hopefully make you reflect on your actions and/or inactions. There will be times when you'll wince and maybe even say "ouch." Sadly, I can't apologize because facts are facts, what's right is right and when it comes to our students, I must write about what is best for students and NOT necessarily what's easiest for adults.

Take Care of Business

There. I pushed the elephant out of the room. Now, let me unpack this a little further. When we stepped into the educational profession, we were supposed to leave the capitalized "ME" at the door. The chapter title helps to remind us of our responsibilities. We are to act like a PROFESSIONAL at all times. In order to do what's best for children, your school or district has decided and has provided you with guidelines, expectations, protocols and procedures for you to read and to implement. You know that email attachment that you said you would read later or that PowerPoint presentation you nodded off on? That's the one. I know. You thought that document was supposed to be used as a coaster for your iced coffee. Believe it or not, that is not its purpose. It's time to act responsibly and *take care of business*–the business of professionalism.

Where Teachers Get Hung Up

There are two areas that educators can get hung up on that I would like to address here: communication and planning your lessons.

Communication

Have you ever heard that communication is a two-way street? This is not a cliché; it really is the truth. Effective communication is a tool for moving ideas and concepts, from thought to expression, from one person to another. When there is a broken line of communication, the ideas and concepts get lost or are perceived as lost. Playwright George Bernard Shaw reminds us that, "The single biggest problem in communication is the illusion that it has taken place."

Consider the story of Brenda who is a third-grade teacher in Middletown, Delaware. In her second year of teaching, she was an excellent teacher and Brenda reflected on what she did each day. She began her career as a rule follower. She had read her procedures and protocols binder from front to back. She clearly read and reread that she was expected to check her emails in a timely manner. Brenda checked her email notifications on a regular basis and responded to administration, parents, her colleagues and her students in a timely manner. She even text messaged her teammates to remind them to check.

After one year, Brenda developed a bad habit of skimming her emails and was selective even when she sat down to read them. She was no longer thorough or consistent and didn't follow the socially acceptable, "respond within 24 hours rule." It seemed she was sucked into the "I'm not a freshman anymore" mentality and this unprofessional mindset altered her professional habits. It just so happened that she missed an important email two days prior from her administrators about a change in a safety procedure that was due to the rising number of school shootings. As a result, that morning, her students were not properly prepared for the safety drill and the confusion quickly led to tears. The embarrassment and apologies that followed were enough to reboot her email reading habits. Reading emails in a timely manner is an expectation for adults in a school. This bad habit that Brenda slipped into of ignoring professional duties and deadlines had negative consequences on her career.

Lesson Plans

"If you fail to plan, you plan to fail," rings in my ears as I write this chapter. Once again, ignoring our professional responsibilities is not what is best for students even though the responsibilities sometimes seem so far away from helping students.

Consider Dante, a sixth-year teacher in Dover, Delaware. His students loved his math class for five years running. He even had a waiting list of parents who wanted their children to join his class for the past four years. Dante had five years in a row of engaging lessons under his belt and he was always invested in his students' growth and well-being.

Year six seemed very different for Dante, unfortunately. His lessons were hit or miss and he often appeared unprepared during walkthroughs, even to his students. It appeared that Dante got sucked into the "I've got tenure now" mindset and it significantly changed his habits–something that Tracey writes about in her previous chapter.

No matter how many years you have under your belt, planning effective, engaging, relevant and differentiated lessons is an expectation for teachers at any school. As Dante relied on his past years experiences and neglected to plan for his lessons, his efficacy did not carry over. His learning targets were not succinct or communicated. His exemplars were no longer present, and he was not connecting the content to current events or interests of his students. This bad habit occurred one week too many and his students' learning and perception of him sunk that very same year. He did not realize that his choice to ignore professional deadlines had negative consequences that could have easily been avoided.

It is easy to go from hero to zero when teachers ignore their professional responsibilities. A mediocre mindset is a synergy killer for sure.

Ann Hlabangana-Clay is a presenter, consultant and a grades 1-7 instructional coach in Delaware. She is the host of "Coaching You through All Things Education" podcast and is passionate about providing equitable opportunities for every learner by building relationships, capacity and resilience, one educator at a time.

Stop Being Unwilling to Carry Out a Reasonable Request
ROBERT F. BREYER

In every school there are teachers who are willing to do anything and everything that is asked of them. They are not afraid to go above and beyond for their students, or school. In their minds, every request made is doable and they will move forward and never look back. They are part of a community and willing to serve. Conversely, you have those teachers in your building who feel like every request made is absolutely ridiculous, a waste of time, or it is simply just not important enough to worry about. We all know socially toxic teachers like this. We have overheard them in the hallways or in the teacher's lounge, talking about how they are not going to do something so pointless. "Don't they know I have more important things to do, such as teach my students?" We all know this person, or group of people, in our schools that not only dig in their heels to reasonable things, but sometimes become downright passive aggressive about what they don't want to do and this must stop.

Whining Won't Fix the Problem

Every school leader wants to make changes that positively impact the students in their building. Yet, I can admit that I am completely removed from the front line, or "trenches" as it is often referred to, and I may not always know what will work best. As a principal, I prefer to spend time with the teachers to ask questions and gain more insight on what they believe is going to be successful or what they feel needs to be done immediately in order to positively impact the school or the students. I understand that this may not be the case in every school. If you believe that you have a valid concern about a

159

request that you feel is unreasonable, then go through the proper channels (or chain of command that Matt writes about in his previous chapter) with your concern. One thing that we know for sure is that whining and complaining won't fix the problem. For better results, be proactive and bring a solution to the table, not just a gripe. There are times when the request may seem impossible. This deserves a conversation and addressing the situation, professionally.

Discuss it, Argue it, then Embrace it

Many times, colleagues are a great support of the bigger picture and you may be able to work out a solution by working as a team. Once a decision is made, it is time for you to roll up your sleeves and just get it done. No one comes to school thinking that they do not want to do what is best for children. Decisions are often made to enhance the learning environment or, better yet, the student experiences at the school. Keep that in mind when you are asked to do something. It is time to stop complaining about the request and just move forward.

I have worked with principals who established a norm around decision making by saying "discuss it, argue about it and when the final decision is made, it is time to embrace it." We are in a profession in which there is never enough time. So, what are some examples of reasonable requests within a school setting?

- Stay off your cell phone when you are with students.
- Keep a close eye on your students while they play on the playground.
- Eat lunch with your students to build connections and relationships.
- Stand at your door to greet students.
- Don't allow young students to travel the building alone.

One cannot possibly argue that these are unreasonable requests. If you think so, then you may want to fast forward to Chapter 100.

Embrace the Rule Don't Modify it

My friend's kindergarten daughter had an executive functioning disorder and was considered to be developmentally delayed by two years. She was not a runner, but she was a curious young lady who was easily distracted and would wander off to explore. She was pulled daily for specialized services and the principal had set the expectation that the classroom teacher would walk her down to her special education teacher each day. Due to a tight schedule, the classroom teacher self-modified this rule and walked the student only halfway. The child would get distracted and wander around outside until someone found her. This resulted in a daily hunt for a missing child. Sadly, this was not a one-time occurrence. When you receive a very reasonable request, such as walking your students back to class each day, short cuts are not appropriate.

It's Just Part of Your Job

Most reasonable requests are just common-sense directives and are just a part of your job. Unfortunately, schedules, time restraints and other responsibilities and expectations laid upon teachers make it enticing for them to skip doing the right thing. Sometimes, teachers dismiss doing the right thing because they put their own needs first.

What can you do today to start embracing reasonable requests?

- Be a team player who is willing to work with everyone in your school to ensure that you are setting the stage for excellence in your school. Be mindful that what is best for you may not be best for the school overall.
- Be more respectful of others in your school! You will find that over time, your school will be more productive, have an increased morale and your students will flourish in a more positive environment.
- Remember "if everyone in your school had your attitude, what kind of place would it be?" Adjust your attitude and remember that you are an integral part of the success at your school.

In the immortal words of Maya Angelou,

"If you do not like something, change it. If you cannot change it, change your attitude."

Keep pushing forward by getting better every day because your students deserve nothing less than your best and, yes, that does mean complying with reasonable requests.

Robert F. Breyer is an elementary school principal, author, leadership coach and the host of "The Guiding Principals" Podcast. He is passionate about helping others overcome barriers in order to maximize their impact.

Stop Using Sick Days as Punishment to the School or District

ANDREW BROERE

So, you're going to stick it to them by staying home, right? I get it: you are feeling under the weather. Everyone experiences this from time to time. You were not feeling 100%, so you took a day off. Another time, you weren't feeling as bad, but you put in for time off anyway. Then, one day, you decided that you had a rough stretch and put in another request for time off. Then, you didn't like something that your principal said to you, so you took another day off. If the cycle unfolded that way for everyone, there would be no one left teaching our students.

Is it Really That Big of a Deal?

Sick day accumulation is really meant for you to be protected against long illnesses without pay. Those days were not meant to give you an entitlement to use them whenever you want.

At some point, something inside you may have changed. Somewhere along the way, you were passed over, short changed, or disenfranchised. What drew you to the classroom is now no longer enough to combat the distinct forces that drive you out of the building when you decide to call in sick.

Perhaps you look across the landscape of national, state, district and local achievement testing and you find yourself sick. You are tired of entitled students, helicopter parents and absent administrators and quite frankly, you have had it! What led you into the profession isn't enough to keep you in it today.

But, the pension is decent and you've only got a few years left, you tell yourself. So, you continue to use an eight-hour sick day for a one hour doctor visit and you add in a mental health holiday here and there and you've convinced yourself that it's not that big of a deal, that your students will be fine and you're not hurting anyone. This kind of cycle of no return does not contribute to the synergistic school system. It weakens it.

Tired of Caring

Let's deal with things one at a time. First, there's nothing wrong with going to the doctor, getting a physical, or taking a day off to spend with your aging parents. You need to take care of your physical, mental, emotional and spiritual well-being. Balance is essential. There's no prize for burning out!

Second, teaching is tough and politicians, media, society and other factors do not help you to feel better about much of anything. Much of what a teacher does daily is often periphery to actually teaching the content. You are busy with documentation, conflict mediation, district mandates and more. You are tired of the professional responsibilities that Anna writes about in her chapter and you just don't have any more energy.

Third, I understand that some illnesses require the need for extended time off requests in those special cases and circumstances. I have personally seen the effects of cancer, dementia, major surgeries and other medical issues in the lives of my colleagues and staff. However, even though teaching is laborious, you must be honest with yourself and make sure that you are not sticking it to the wrong person as a passive aggressive means to an end. If something angers you or is upsetting at your job, you are only sticking it to the students. You are fooling yourself if you think otherwise.

Attempt #343

Maybe you approached your district with your thoughts and concerns about a specific topic or idea. Perhaps, you had informed a colleague who might be sympathetic to your alarms. You presented to the board, shared stories with the central office and you continue to be turned down. No one bent a sympathetic ear to you. The program you want to build just won't happen. The resources your school desperately needs will not materialize. You feel scorned.

In your mind, no one cared, and you are done trying. You are done caring. You are done hoping. You are done teaching.

Your Wrongheaded Solution

You decide not to show up to work. At first, not showing up took the form of pulling away from groups and committees you would normally take part in. But, after a while, you begin to pull away from your students. You no longer fielded questions or held after school help sessions. You reduced the amount of time lesson planning. "I am a veteran teacher," you told yourself, and you sold yourself on your ability to teach without planning.

Your Options

If you have made it this far, it's possible you see some mistakes made in your recent past. Allow me to suggest two logical choices as you go forward. Both are honorable, equally right and gracious to your students and yourself.

The first option is to wrap things up at the end of this year. It is okay to be finished fighting. This option is not akin to quitting; rather, you are allowing someone else to pick up the mantle you have left. This fight you have been waging, this back and forth with the district, is no longer worth it. But, punishing the district by taking excessive time off only hurts the students in your class. At the end of the day, a good district must consider the impact of your excessive absenteeism on the student population, and at some point, may make the decision to let you go. This option gives you the opportunity, the power, to walk away on your own terms.

The second option is just as difficult a choice to make. It is demanding and costly. Stay. Do not just finish up your years until retirement. Rededicate yourself to the mission of serving your students and community. Get involved in extracurricular activities. Volunteer for another committee. Consider becoming a mentor teacher.

Do not simply count the years until retirement; instead, make your years count! Do not punish the district by taking excessive time off. I am the inner voice inside you making you feel guilty.

Andrew Broere serves as the Assistant School Administrator at Fourth Baptist Christian School in Minneapolis, Minnesota. He is passionate about making a difference in the lives of students, parents and staff every day.

Stop Coming to Work Tired or Sick

CHRISTOPHER DODGE

The work of educators is a calling and work of the heart; we give and give until there is nothing left, often sacrificing our own well-being. We are internally driven and motivated, never asking for more than the respect and value that we deserve. As Andrew wrote in his previous chapter, there are times when you cannot come to work so long as you are not using your absences as punishment towards administration. Here, I need to discuss the importance of taking care of yourself at all times, pandemic, post pandemic, no pandemic.

The Perception Ping Pong

The same public that was once honoring us for what we did during the pandemic is now telling us we are selfish and that if we really cared for our students and families, we would "get back to work." It feels like a ping pong game where one moment society believes teachers should be honored and the next they are filled with shaming criticisms. It is hard to keep score. I am not foolish enough to think that we will ever gain the appreciation and the respect we deserve, but I am saying that the same thing that brings us to the work and drives us could also be the thing that allows such poor treatment. We take it and take it and it may be time to start standing up and taking care of ourselves so we do not truly burn out.

I am fully aware that this chapter also comes with some slight hypocrisy as I was the teacher that had to be pushed out the door at night and who tried to stay in my classroom when I was sick so the nurse wouldn't find out and send me home. Even as a principal, I am the first to preach self-care and wellness, but I do not do a good job of practicing what I preach. So, I am going to spare you (and me) the "you can't pour from an empty cup" jargon and give some straight talk to both you and me in hopes that together we can do a better job of taking care of ourselves and draw some boundaries between ourselves and the work that is all-consuming. In this way, I am going to identify the messages that I tell myself about why I can't take a day off and attempt to counter it with some hard truth. I assume that you tell yourself similar things and my hope is that you can relate.

When You are Out, Stay Out

If you are reading this book, my guess is that you are a high performer in your school. You are the one who leaves detailed sub plans with every minute laid out and options so there is no down time for students to take advantage of the new person in your classroom. You know every student so intimately that you leave a list of strategies that work for each student and possible things for the substitute to look out for. You've even contacted your grade level colleagues to let them know you are out and to check in with your substitute throughout the day. Even while you are out, you aren't really out. You are checking your email and texting your colleagues, asking them how the day is going. I am telling you to stop. In every other profession, when you are sick and need a day off, you take an actual day off. Leave the best plans for the day that you can, leave your computer at school and stay off it. The school will not burn down.

When You Return, Move On

Here's the other thing you need to stop doing: spending a day after a sick day "fixing" all the things that went wrong while you were out. Give yourself permission to move on like the day never happened. You and your students know that things are different when you are out and the expectation to mirror a typical day is foolish. Adults behave differently when their boss isn't around so why do we expect kids to act differently? Last thing: take everything your students did while you were out and toss it in the trash. The work is not going to give you any reliable data that will inform your practice and, again, you were out and shouldn't be making up work from your day off.

Here's a hard truth: you aren't as important as you think you are. If you disappeared today, your school would find a new teacher and life would go on. I am going to assume that if you are reading this, you are a high performer in your school. You are on every committee that the district offers, you mentor new teachers and your classroom is the one that every parent wants their child to be in. The mere thought of taking a day off gives you anxiety. You get involved in trying to manage every minute you are out and you also don't want to cancel on the other commitments you have that day.

You may also notice that the overachiever in you is starting to grow bitter towards your colleagues, as you have taken on many roles while others do not take on any. You watch others take more than their share of days off while you are busting your butt day in and day out. As a principal, I can tell you this with quite certainty: you are a high performer and everyone knows it. I can also tell you this: your colleagues do not work like you do. You are the one on staff who barely ever takes a day off, but then worries when you take more than one day because you wonder if your principal is getting concerned. I will tell you now that your principal is concerned about your well-being and wishes you would take more time for yourself, but knows that sometimes you won't help yourself. Relax, stop blaming yourself and don't look back.

I have been in the profession long enough and been in enough roles to know that high performing educators everywhere at their core are caretakers and do-gooders with the ultimate goal of being a role model for students and preparing the next generation of humans to take care of our planet. Be careful: your all out commitment could be leading you to being taken advantage of, both in your local workplace and in our profession as a whole. You are also not being the role model that you want to be. You preach to your students about self-care, social-emotional health and physical health while you run yourself ragged. How can your students take advice from someone like that? And if you don't think your students notice, guess again. So, let this be a call to action for all of us. Let's stop being hypocrites and playing the victim. Later, Evan will talk about martyrdom. Read his chapter carefully. Let's be strong enough to stand up for ourselves and each other by drawing healthy boundaries and being the role model that we always wanted to be and claim to be.

Christopher Dodge is the Pre-K-6 principal of the Orange Elementary Schools in central Massachusetts. He is a heart-centered leader who seeks to strengthen school cultures, both for adults and students and has a passion for bringing equity to underserved populations. He is also a consultant for Seaside Educational Consultants.

Stop Showing Up Late to Work
ALLISON KLEIN

You don't value your students or their education.

You don't respect your coworkers' time.

You're seemingly careless about the burdens you impose upon others.

You get away with it and no one stops you.

You get special treatment; you are the principal's pet.

This is how you are perceived. These are the messages that you are sending when you show up late to work, regularly. Perceptions and integrity matter. Perceptions are the building blocks of your reputation.

Perceptions are the Building Blocks for a Reputation

Things happen, I get it. Your son doesn't wake up for school, your dog crapped in the house, or you slept through your alarm going off. But when your life becomes a runaway train of so-called emergencies, you become less and less credible to others and others grow to resent you. You unwittingly stigmatize anyone else who has a legitimate emergency; subjecting them to added scrutiny and fear of backlash, causing them to make great sacrifices all because you hit the snooze button one too many times. Students can't rely on you and they feel disrespected. They start disrespecting you by acting out in your class, shutting down and disengaging. Their perception of you as a synergistic and dependable teacher dissolves. When you send the message that punctuality no longer matters, students may stop showing up altogether and view you as a hypocrite when you try to address tardiness or absenteeism. You groan when they are late to your class, but you just got there, yourself. People are running around to cover your class while you waltz in. You've made your fellow teachers' jobs ten times more difficult because they now must sacrifice their prep period to cover for your classes and address your students' concerns without throwing you under the bus. You have become a liability to your employer because you're not reliable enough to be where you're expected to be each morning: supervising students and ensuring their safety. This impacts your reputation and all credibility as a teacher.

I don't know anyone who has a perfect track record of timely attendance, including myself. This isn't about a rare or atypical occasion. This is about a habitual unprofessional trend that you are getting into. The good news is, there's a fix for tardiness. When you build time into your schedule for all those things that could go wrong, you are prepared for the inevitable.

Waking Up in a Flash

I was a first-year teacher in 2004 in the Midwest. I slept later than usual, so I rushed to get ready for work. I took a lightning-fast shower, got dressed, brushed my teeth, grabbed a few packaged snack items and sped off to work. I pulled up to the school just as my cell phone rang–awakening me from my dream. I was still in bed, daylight blocked out by my blinds and the clock read 8:15am as I reached to answer my phone. It was the school secretary "Are you okay? Are you coming in today?" I was mortified and assured her I'd be right in. "Take your time and don't rush, Principal Davidson is covering your class. Be safe." This time I actually DID rush to get ready and did all those things that seemed so real the first time around, only this time in hyper speed. I showed up to work . . . late and I felt guilty. I apologized to my principal, to my students and to the secretary; I felt indebted to them for the worry and inconvenience I caused them and for the missed instructional time. That was the one and only time I ever showed up late to work. I was mortified and made a concerted effort to ensure that it would never happen again.

Fast forward to 2016 in a mid-sized school district on the West Coast. As any new site leader, I was thrilled to lead and support teachers in the best way I could. I looked forward to applying everything I'd read from so many great books written for educators that are out there. Those courageous conversations didn't seem so far out of reach for someone like me who leads with empathy and kindness. I quickly started getting complaints from veteran teachers about the new teacher on the block who was routinely showing up late. I investigated their concerns and confirmed this teacher's pattern of tardiness. Even students complained as I unlocked the classroom each morning and covered for the class until the teacher's arrival. If you think it's heart breaking to hear students lament that their teacher must not value their education, their time, or them as a whole, it's possibly more heart breaking to hear students express genuine concern, worry and empathy for their teacher (all the while knowing this is another case of an alarm clock that was slept through). I was guilt laden that I hadn't caught on to this pattern before it was brought to my attention by his peers; but his peers initially voluntarily covered his classes until he arrived in an effort to handle the situation at the lowest level possible.

Teachers and students tragically grew to resent this new teacher before the first semester concluded; he didn't stand a chance of being welcomed back by the staff. Despite my courageous conversations and the teacher's remorse, the pattern continued as he showed up later and later to work and often not at all. Eventually, this led to a conversation about his job and the teacher left the field of education.

In other career fields or businesses, there is a time clock. But when we sign up to be educators, we're inherently held to a higher standard. As a teacher, your work is your students. You're their role model. You might very well be the one person they look forward to seeing each day–the one person they can count on to be there, to take an interest in them and to serve as their springboard to a better life. You may represent their one shot at improving their life and achieving success. This may sound dramatic, yet it's all true. As a teacher, you carry a great burden. Your students need you there consistently and on time.

Just as you plan for instruction, plan for "life." Set multiple alarms. Prep your meals. Fill your gas tank in the evenings. Build in time for those things that happen to all of us, sometimes, but don't be that person that those things happen to all the time or your reputation and even your career will suffer in the end.

Allison Klein currently serves as the Director of Human Resources at a local technical college in Georgia. Prior to that, she served as a high school administrator in California and a middle school teacher in Kentucky.

Stop Playing the Role of Martyr
EVAN WHITEHEAD

Have you ever felt the need to do everything for everyone, consistently putting the needs of others before your own? Have you ever felt like you are physically, mentally and/or emotionally drained as an educator, but you push through anyway even though you are putting yourself at risk physically and mentally? What is the reason or excuse you use for just pushing through? "My students need me. If I don't do it, who else will? If I can just save one student or help one family, I feel I have done my job then I can take care of myself? As a leader I have to set an example: if I call in sick to work, how will that appear? I have to make a good impression as a first-year teacher." The list of self-critiques can go on and on and on . . .

If you have asked yourself any of these questions, you are not alone. I too, made these statements both publicly and privately. My own mind provided an excuse to not take care of myself and helped me rationalize what I was doing because it was always for others. It was like a free pass, to not prioritize my own health and well-being.

One of the fastest ways to cripple and disable the highest achieving teachers is playing the role of a martyr. What is even more dangerous than that is a teacher playing the martyr with imposter syndrome. These complexes destabilize and wear out even the best teachers.

Professional Martyrdom

Educators with a martyr complex often blame other people or situations for the challenges in their personal or professional lives. Traditionally, a martyr is someone willing to die for something they believe in. Within the context of this book and the educational profession, a martyr refers to someone who constantly puts the needs of others before themselves even to the detriment of their physical, mental and emotional well-being.

Martyrdom is extremely complex to self-regulate within education because educators are often fixers, givers and helpers by nature. Teachers typically have the personality type that places the needs of others before their own. What adds to this intensity is the increased environmental stressors such as poverty, crime, understaffed schools and districts, underfunding and the pressures placed on us when working with high needs students. When martyrs are working in this kind of high-stress educational environment, teachers are at an increased risk to burn out fairly quickly.

Imposter Syndrome

Martyrs often suffer from the imposter syndrome. Dr. Valerie Young categorizes imposter syndrome into four subgroups through the use of the competence types that actually create the imposter within us. Take a look at the profiles below:

1. The Perfectionist

Perfectionists set excessively high goals for themselves and when they fail to reach a goal, they experience major self-doubt and worry about measuring up. Whether they realize it or not, this group can consist of control freaks who feel that if they want something done right, they have to do it themselves. Dr. Young provides the following questions to determine if the "Perfectionist" applies to you:

- Have you ever been accused of being a micromanager?
- Do you have great difficulty delegating? Even when you are able to do so, do you feel frustrated and disappointed in the results?
- When you miss the mark on something, do you accuse yourself of "not being cut out" for your job and ruminate on it for days?
- Do you feel like you work must be 100% perfect, 100% of the time?

Young states that success for this type of person is rarely satisfying because they believe they could have done better. However, this way of thinking is neither productive nor healthy. Young further says,

"Owning and celebrating achievements is essential if you want to avoid burnout, find contentment and cultivate self-confidence." The reality is that there is never a perfect time, perfect place, or one that is 100% without flaw. We are human beings and there is a difference between striving for 100% success and viewing failure as anything less than 100% all the time.

2. The Superhero

The superhero often pushes themselves to work harder and harder in order to measure up. This cover-up can cause harm to your mental health and potential relationships with others. Superheroes take on the world and carry everyone's burdens on their shoulders. Dr. Young provides the following points to determine if the superhero applies to you:

- Staying later at the office than the rest of your team, even past the point that you've completed that day's necessary work.
- Getting stressed when you are not working and finding downtime completely wasteful.
- Letting your hobbies and passions fall by the wayside or they have been sacrificed because of work.
- Feeling like you have not truly earned your title (despite your numerous degrees and achievements), so you feel pressed to work harder and longer than those around you to prove your worth.

The superhero is actually addicted to the validation that comes from work, not actually the work itself. So they are actually seeking validation and self-worth within a maddening cycle. This feeling can be dangerous because no matter the source of the validation, they are constantly looking to fulfill the need.

3. The Natural Genius or Expert

The Natural Genius judges their competence based on how easy something is or how quickly they can accomplish a task. This is challenging because the measure of success or accomplishment is only based upon if it comes easy or "natural" to them. On the other hand, anything that is difficult or takes work, they view as a failure. With this in mind, a "growth mindset" is almost an impossible concept for the natural genius to comprehend or rationalize.

- Excelling without much effort.

172

- Has a track record of getting straight "A's."
- Referred to as the "smart one" in their family or peer group.
- Dislikes the idea of having or needing a mentor because they can handle things on their own.
- When setback occurs, confidence tumbles and shame is felt.
- Avoids challenges because it's uncomfortable to try something that is new or challenging.

The natural genius may be naturally intelligent but lacking emotional intelligence can sometimes exacerbate the problems of martyrdom.

4. The Soloist

The soloist views asking for help as a sign of weakness and embraces the idea of "I can do it all by myself." The soloist displays the following characteristics:

- Firmly feels they need to accomplish things on their own.
- Help from others is not desirable.
- Frames a request in terms of the requirement for the task or project, instead of their needs as a person.

Consider an airplane with one pilot and no co-pilot. Who is going to fly the plane if the pilot becomes ill? For me, I happened to fall in each one of the subgroups of imposter syndrome at one particular time or another and suffered from a martyr complex at the same time.

You may look at my professional work history and my climb to the role of an assistant superintendent at age thirty-four and believe that I have had a successful career. In some aspects I have blessings, but not without consequences and sacrifices. Educator burnout, compassion fatigue, and secondary traumatic stress are all very real.

I was no different because I often didn't have a balance in my life between work and family. I thought I had to do everything to get it done correctly. I even went as far as coaching the youth sports teams that my children were on. Even though I knew I always didn't have the time or energy to do so, I was the martyr.

I was also very bad at setting personal boundaries. I had a very difficult time saying "no" to starting clubs, groups and programs, which include the gospel choir and the college and career readiness/mentor program. I had to learn the hard way that it's OK to say no and you don't have to agree to everything for anyone and everyone.

My biggest professional and personal challenge I had was not taking a break and not setting aside time for myself or my family. There was a time that my family and I would go on vacation every year, but that stopped. I rarely took sick days or vacation days.

We must change the narrative of martyrdom within our profession. As educators, we are compassionate, empathetic givers and fixers by nature. We sometimes care more about those we serve than we care about ourselves. We often lose balance, seldom adhere to our personal boundaries and feel guilty about taking a break. We need to allow ourselves permission to prioritize ourselves and stop feeling like we have to take on the world.

Evan Whitehead is a district leader in Illinois and a national consultant. He is also the creator of #BalanceBoundariesandBreaks.

Stop Buying Stuff for Your Classroom

JEFF KUBIAK

Close your eyes. Imagine walking into the classroom of your dreams. What do you see? Look at the floors, desks and seating arrangements. What is on the walls? How do you see it decorated, designed and styled?

Now, think about how a student would view it? What would they like to have in their dream classroom? Do they have any input on the design?

Every Square Inch Was Covered

I have been in hundreds of classrooms throughout my career. While they all may vary somewhat in content or theme, one trend that really stood out to me was the sheer volume of wall-to-wall coverings. I remember leaving one classroom shaking my head wondering how the classroom even passed a fire inspection. In my discovery of classrooms that were gaudy, I noticed that most classrooms had some similarities, such as:

- Predesigned math times tables
- The "writing process" posters
- Yards of "colored borders"
- Prepackaged posters with motivational sayings
- Parts of speech and grammar rule posters
- Packets, worksheets and workbooks from the "Teacher Store"
- Cubbies, plastic shelving and desk organizers

A classroom with pre-made, inorganic, unoriginal "space fillers" is not conducive to child-focused, "kid-centric" classrooms. Where is the ownership? Why don't students get the opportunity to co-design the very space that they spend the most time in each day? Teaching has become so commercialized that students do not even have a say in what things should look like. Stop buying any more "stuff" for your classroom.

Co-Create & Ideate

What do students want in their learning environment? Did you ask them? Do they have any say? Is this their workspace too? You have amazing artists, mathematicians, designers, writers, coders, builders, scientists and much more in your class. Let them help you to create their learning and work space to model *what* they are learning. You will be blown away by the ideas they come up with as they put their creative innovations to work.

Imagine the power in gaining real world, hands on experience if, at the beginning of the year, they co-designed the learning space for efficiency. Let them pitch their ideas and then investigate those DIY Pinterest organizers and space savers. When students invest in the construction of their space, (or at least vote on it), they have skin in the game and ownership over their domain and become more invested in their own learning. Companies that profit from you buying into their own commercialized "stuff" places students at the back of the line. Save YOUR money for YOUR life outside of school.

How can you let your students help design your shared space? Think of the things that are motivating, inspiring, valid, useful and essential for teaching. Do not clutter the room with things YOU may think are cool, handy or "in" at the time. It is their space too, shouldn't they get a say in the walls they must stare at eight hours per day?

Instead of spending your personal income, consider partnering with parents, community members, alumni and local businesses or utilizing Donors Choose or other grants. Classroom design is an actual major in many high schools and colleges across the world. Use what you have and be resourceful for the rest of your classroom design needs. Remember, it's the relationships you have with your students that is most important. Ask the students for their vision. Share your mission and passion. Figure it out together, save your time and, instead, invest in co-creation and co-investment. Keep your money. Enjoy your classroom knowing that students are happy and learning in an environment they have always dreamed of.

Jeff Kubiak is an anti-racist educator, award winning children's book author and motivational speaker. He is committed to equity, inclusion and compassion in education and aspires to make the world a better place for all.

Stop Staying Late at School
SUSAN MELBYE

It has taken me years to learn the importance of not staying late at school. It has taken me missed time with my family and friends to finally understand the importance of leaving school at a reasonable time. In my early years of being a young educator, I almost felt that I had to stay late. I am here today as a more seasoned veteran educator to tell you that "No, you do not have to do this." What possibly could be so important that it must get done at that exact moment and can't wait? Often when I stayed late, I was simply more anxious and even more stressed out about the tasks that I had to work on.

It's Not a Badge of Honor

Being the last one to leave the school building is not a badge of honor. That badge comes with tired eyes, a lack of focus and the occasional mismatched shoes or earrings. What did we really accomplish for ourselves when we routinely stayed late? What did we really learn or earn? All that time spent at school was just more time away from loved ones and enjoyment, relaxation and time with friends and neighbors. There are no trophies for "last" place–last in this case, being the last one in the building.

Paperwork can wait and if you have that much paperwork to grade, then you may want to rethink how you teach. The paperwork will be there tomorrow. I have never seen a news story where someone broke into a school and stole all the teachers' papers that needed to be graded. Your loved ones (kids, families, friends, or significant others) are missing valuable time with you.

Ways to Stop Staying Late

If you are like me, sometimes you lose track of time. So, sometimes you stay late not even meaning to, but you just get so wrapped up and enthused about a project that you forget what hour it is. The good news is that time efficiency has the power to transform.

Give Yourself a Time Deadline

An easy remedy for breaking this cycle of time distraction is to simply set an alarm on your phone. Set it for every single weekday and put a message saying, "It is time to leave." If you are really stubborn about leaving, then set a second alarm. This one needs to say, "No, now it is really time to leave." It may be beneficial to put the loved one's name in the time stamped message. I have often put, "Your girls need you." That gets to me every time; it makes me realize that whatever is in front of me is not as important as my three daughters.

Find an Accountability Partner

Make it a priority to have an accountability partner in your school. Choose someone in the building that swings by your room and tells you to go ahead and pack up your bags. Make a pact with each other that you need to walk out the door together. This will help to hold you accountable each day.

Create a Tomorrow List

Make a list of everything that you need to accomplish for the *next* day. You get to start fresh every morning and you can see real accomplishment in being able to mark off completed tasks. It does so much more for you to get a good night's sleep than to constantly push yourself by burning the candle at both ends. When you have your tomorrow list, you can relax your mind and get ready for a new day.

Find Your Freedom

We know that being an educator is who we are at the core, but you cannot lose yourself to your profession. You are someone's loved one and you're their reason for coming home every day, on time. Your time, your health and your life are too precious to spend solely in the school building until late at night. Give yourself the freedom to walk outside with joy about what is on the horizon. Focus on the time you get to spend filling your cup with the freedom of family, friends or children and reflect on just how much more you could get out of life by leaving earlier. Give yourself permission to not be the last one in the building. Give yourself permission to wake up refreshed and recharged the next day. Give yourself permission to be YOU outside of your school building.

Susan Melbye has taught, coached and led in all grade levels, preK-12 throughout her career across various states. She is also a national consultant for a multitude of training topics in education and leadership.

Stop Working Long Hours on Schoolwork after You Arrive Home
JEFF W. EVENER

Now, let's take what Susan writes about and go one step further. Do not pack up your bags with all sorts of take-home work, either!

Consider this story about Jon who is a seven-year veteran teacher in a rural school district. He is the father of three children. Jon teaches 7th and 8th grade American history, and he leaves for work one hour early each day and arrives home two hours after the school day has ended. Once he arrives home, he often checks his cell phone for emails while playing with his children. Once his children are in bed, he logs into his Google Classroom and begins grading essays and providing feedback for his students. Each evening, Jon is not completely present for his family and part of his mind is always thinking about the work that still needs to be done. This is honorable in that he cares deeply about his students and is invested in their individualized success, but working late into the night is completely unnecessary and will creep up on Jon in the end.

Set Clear Boundaries

Jon is not alone with a constant focus on his work while at home. Like many teachers, he has a need for boundaries. There are many reasons teachers overwork themselves once they get home. First, in America, we have glorified being busy. Everyone is busy and must tell others how busy they are. I see people throughout education telling each other how busy they are, how many essays they need to grade or how many emails they get and need to respond to. Second, working 10-15 hours a day is not healthy. Taking care of students for seven hours each day is exhausting, in itself, and then working more hours at home can take a toll on anyone. Third, working long hours at home takes time away from family and/or personal growth.

So, what can be done about this? Why should teachers stop working long hours after they get home? When we are on our deathbed, no one will remember all the long hours we worked or our perfect attendance. On the other hand, people will remember what kind of person we were and how we made them feel. This is an important point to remember. Teaching is what we do; it is not who we are.

The Benefits of Kicking this Bad Habit

There are many benefits to knocking off the bad habit of working long hours at home. Leaving work at work allows teachers to re-energize. In our profession, we know that each day may bring trials and tribulations that come with teaching and having plenty of energy and a calm mind is an asset. The daily life of a teacher is sophisticated and intense. Teachers take on a constant barrage of decisions, questions and conversations. This pace can take its toll on anyone. Time is needed to recharge our batteries on a daily basis. We cannot leave it to the weekends to recharge. Our bodies need to be recharged, daily.

Another benefit of free time at home is that we see things differently, we access different parts of our brain and we release happy chemicals that infuse joy and excitement. It is healthy to invest in time away from the intensity of work. Teachers spend lots of time solving other peoples' problems. Sometimes, decisions can be made about problems in real time during the school day, but others take time, energy and attention to solve. The time away from our work provides perspective on problems and creative inspiration to arrive at school with a renewed mindset.

In today's information and technology driven society, teachers are bombarded with emails, texts, phone calls, and "adminis-trivia." Communication comes fast and furious during a typical school day.

Many teachers feel that they need to respond to every communication before they leave work otherwise, they will have to continue to whittle down the emails at home. As a teacher, you have the right to respond when time allows. A good rule of thumb is to respond to emails within 24-48 hours. This is a respectable amount of time. Teachers should not spend exorbitant amounts of time at home answering emails even though it is a responsibility that Ann wrote about in her previous chapter.

The workday must end at some point. The job requires a complete focus on children for seven to eight hours per day. Teachers deserve to turn work off once they go home. Constant mental exhaustion and physical fatigue can have grave consequences for a teacher's overall health.

The best reason for teachers to stop working long hours on schoolwork when they get home is to set a good example for their students. Mental health for students is just as paramount as the content they need to learn. If the adults are constantly working and the students are constantly working, it takes its toll on the entire school culture. Teachers and students need to be their best selves every day.

The poem, "The Dash," by Linda Ellis appropriately explains why teachers should stop working long hours when they get home. The poem talks about the importance of the dash on our headstones. The dash represents the life we lived. She writes,

For it matters not, how much we own, the cars… the house… the cash. What matters is how we live and love and how we spend our dash.

We do not remember the best teachers because all the long hours they worked. We remember the best teachers because of the relationships they created with us. You are a teacher, but you deserve to live your "dash" without it defining your entire life.

Jeff Evener has served as a teacher, director of curriculum, athletic director, principal, and most recently, assistant superintendent for a small city school district in Central New York. Jeff's expertise includes servant leadership, climate and culture building and equity for all students. He prides himself on taking care of the people who take care of the students

Stop Confusing Your Family with a School Family

GREG MOFFITT

When my daughter was in the 4th grade, her teacher wanted to see what the class knew about digital presentations and assigned them a project to create an electronic presentation about their families. My daughter's slides about herself and the family dog were pretty awesome (I'm her dad so I'm a little biased). She changed the background. She added images and animation. The slides looked great. Most importantly, they captured her love of soccer, competitive swimming, reading and helping others. Not to mention, she accurately depicted how our dog is an absolute terror.

Her Words Hit Me Hard

My daughter's slide about her mom was just as accurate. It read: "Things I love about my Mommy... 1.) She snuggles with me; 2.) She helps me all the time; 3.) She cares about and loves me a lot. Then my daughter added a slide about me: "Things I love about my Daddy... 1.) He works hard; 2.) He helps a lot of people at his school; 3.) He's kinda funny." Her words hit me hard. It was clear to me in reading my daughter's presentation that I was confusing my school family with my very own family. I was spending too much time taking care of other people's children and not nearly enough time taking care of my own daughter.

Being an educator is who I am, but it isn't my entire life, as Jeffrey wrote in the chapter above. It's an important part of how I identify, yes, but so is being a caring father and a loving husband. Yet, those weren't the words my daughter used to describe me. In her eyes, I was someone who worked hard and helped others, but she didn't view me as someone who was on the forefront helping her. Something needed to change. I was spending so much time at school with my school family while my actual family suffered.

Tax Season

For sure, there are moments in all our lives when work will be a priority: the first days of school, the last few weeks, or report card time. These are the days that we feel like it is our "tax season." But every minute that we are at school (or focused on school) is a minute that we aren't focused on something else. And, if we're OK with that, great. If the people in our lives are OK with that, great. If not, it is time to do something about it.

Your Co-Workers are Not Your Family

Your co-workers and your colleagues are just that: your co-workers and your colleagues. They should absolutely support you and encourage you, but there are boundaries and limits that should be set. You may feel close to your school faculty and they may even feel like a family, and if that's the case, I'm thankful that you've found such an incredible group of fellow educators. But, you still have people in your life outside of work. When you get home to them, be sure that you have something left to give. Be sure that you make them a priority.

For those of you that are reading these words and don't have supportive families at home, or that don't recognize or value who you are, I'm so sorry. If you've found a work family that honors and accepts you, I'm truly happy for you. If your school family allows you to be your true self, great! But, sometimes your colleagues might not have much to go home to. They may see your faculty as a family, but that doesn't mean that you have to, as well.

Our identities are complex and personal and I don't pretend to know what will work best for anyone else. We are comprised of hobbies and talents, neighbors and communities. Life is complex and we are much more than our jobs. When we lose sight of that, we lose sight of who we are.

An Ongoing Effort

I wish I could say that I've figured out how to make work and home fit together perfectly. I haven't. Some days, I still confuse my school family with my real family. But each day, I strive to be a better dad and a better husband. It is a process and an ongoing effort. Some things have helped, however. Some things have made a huge difference in my life. Here's just a few of the suggestions I've worked on, myself:

- Stop looking at work emails in the evening. First, we're not getting paid. Second, it can wait. Third, there's rarely a good email sent after 9:00 pm, anyway.

- Stop and pause before walking through the door of your house. Take a deep breath (or a few) and let whatever happened at work stay outside.
- Stop being distracted. Place your phone in a drawer. Be present with the folks in your life. If your kid wants to play Uno for the 1,000th time, play Uno. If your partner or spouse wants to go for a walk, go for a walk. If the dog wants to play catch, play catch.

Will these things dramatically change our lives? Probably not. Will they help us stop confusing our school family with our family? Maybe. It's been a few years since my daughter created her Google Slides about our family for her 4th grade teacher. I'm not sure what she'd put on them today or how she would characterize me. The dog is still a terror. Her mom is still one of the most caring and compassionate people I know. My daughter is still passionate about helping others and changing the world. Hopefully, in her eyes, I've changed my priorities and I've stopped confusing my school family with my own real family. Hopefully she still thinks I'm kinda funny.

Greg Moffitt is an elementary school principal in Northern California. He believes students and educators can make the world a better place with their beliefs, ideas and action.

Stop Dressing Unprofessionally or Distastefully

TERENCE TONG

At school, stop dressing like it is Saturday morning and you are off to Home Depot to pick up a few things before settling in to do some work around the house. You may be within the official rules and guidelines of your district policy handbook, technically, with your worn-out shirt and partly torn pants. No, you cannot rock the same stretched out, faded t-shirt you wore two nights ago while walking the dog. Say no to those tattered, "but they are comfy!" sweats you lounged in binging Netflix last week.

The way you dress reflects your values and self-perception, so why wouldn't you want to showcase your best self? Why wouldn't you want to dress so that others view you as confident and inspirational, like you have it together? The way you dress sends visual communication about your professionalism, competence and attention to detail.

Dress Professionally and Tastefully

Don't go to school dressed like someone in need of a fashion intervention. "Woe is me; I need a wardrobe makeover!" No, the Fab Five is not going to drop in for a surprise visit. Not one person will feel sorry for you and your sad disgrace of a wardrobe. Your colleagues will just gossip behind your back and make you the butt of water cooler jokes.

Teachers cry out at the disrespect afforded to the profession–but, we have no one to blame but ourselves if we dress like garbage. We bring it on ourselves. Take a good look in the mirror Monday morning when you go to work. Who is going to respect teachers when you show up to school dressed like you are off on a late-night jaunt to the convenience store? Do you need to dress like you are going to dinner at a five-star restaurant? No. But for crying out loud, dress professionally and tastefully. Use whatever metric you need to set the bar for yourself. Dress like you are going for a job interview, dress like you are going on a first date, or dress like you are going to meet your potential in-laws for the first time. Anything less than that and you're just doing the profession (and yourself) a disservice.

Legitimately Dressing Down

Yes, there will be occasions when there is a legitimate, warranted need to dress down. As a middle school educator, I get that. I live and breathe it with "life in the middle." Does this make me a hypocrite? Nope, not at all. There is always the occasional spirit or theme day sprinkled in here and there throughout the school year. Sure, I rock a tacky elf sweater for winter holidays and, please, do get in the Halloween spirit by dressing up as your favorite superhero. Support your favorite team by wearing their garb during the playoffs. Yes, some teachers, based on what they teach, have to dress for their position (you know I'm talking about the physical education teachers or the makerspace and visual Arts folks), but that doesn't mean you should rock a dingy 25-year-old Def Leppard hoodie or tattered basketball shorts to school.

The Professional Cross-Fit Classroom

One might argue that teachers need to be comfortable. Teaching is akin to CrossFit at times, I know, and teachers need to be able to move around their classrooms and move freely in order to engage with their learners. Yes, teachers want to be comfortable, absolutely. There is no denying that. However, why is professionalism and good taste sacrificed in the name of comfort? Why must comfort and professionalism be exclusive of each other? Comfort, professionalism and good taste can be synergetic. Modern designs and wrinkle free "stretchy" textiles allow you to move around and engage with your students without having to worry about a tale-for-all-ages "wardrobe malfunction."

A General Rule of Thumb

Any item of clothing that is more than five years old should be taken out of the work rotation. You should not be wearing that item to work (unless it still looks new). It does not mean you have to trash it; it just means you should not wear it to work. You do not need to spend a small fortune to be professionally and tastefully dressed for work. You just have to be purposeful in the pieces that you purchase. Go with items that will not only age well, but also items that are age appropriate. Yes, teachers have to be young at heart, but you don't need to dress like you are still in high school. Stop shopping for your work clothes at the same fast fashion stores that your students shop at. If you are pushing it up or letting it hang out, you will not receive much respect.

What can you wear? Here is a simple guideline to follow: your day-to-day work outfits should be contemporary, clean, appropriately fitted and free of large logos. Your wardrobe communicates your values. By dressing professionally and tastefully, you signal the value of the workplace and our profession. Just like "dressing up" for interviews; you want (and need) to make a good first impression.

> "Almost everyone will make a good first impression,
> but only a few will make a good lasting impression."
> –Sonya Parker

Every Single Day, Impressions Matter

I would encourage you to treat each school day as an interview, another opportunity for you to make a positive, lasting impression on the learning community you serve. How you dress (and, thus, how you present yourself) determines the type of interactions you will have and how you will be judged by students, colleagues and parents. Whether you like it or not, impressions do matter, whether it is the first, the twelfth or the 847th impression, impressions matter, period.

Envision going to a rehearsal of a drama production and then envision going to the same production on opening night. The wardrobe of a production has a tremendous impact and influence on the audience experience. Characters' wardrobe not only needs to convey a reflective authenticity, it also affects the audience's ability to connect with them. This holds true for educators, as well. The way you dress has the power to influence your audience whether your audience is students, colleagues, parents or community stakeholders. Ill fitted, distasteful and unprofessional clothing will only serve to distract your audience and undermine your credibility. No matter how imminently qualified you are, no matter how earth-shattering, paradigm shifting your message is, your audience will not care about what you have to say unless you dress the part.

> *"Clothes make the (person). Naked people have little or no influence on society."*
> –Mark Twain

The clothes you wear to school must represent and bring out the best in you. Your outfit should make you feel confident and inspire confidence from others. The visual image you present needs to exude professionalism, competence and attention to detail. Ultimately, respect the community you serve, respect the professional you represent, but most importantly, respect yourself!

Terence Tong is an aspiring administrator with extensive teacher leadership experience in Canada, Kuwait and South Korea. As an ardent believer and advocate of "Life in the Middle," Terence is constantly on the lookout for unique and diverse opportunities for middle school learners.

Stop Writing with Fear and without Boldness
BRITTANY SCHMIDT

> *"Don't forget: no one else sees the world the way you do,*
> *so no one else can tell the stories that you have to tell."*
> –Charles de Lint

I remember when I was in 6th grade, we had to write a story. There weren't really any guidelines; we just had to write a fictional story. It was around Halloween, so naturally I wrote a horror story with a killer clown since Stephen King's movie, *It,* was extremely popular at the time. This was not my best story and I made up the names of the setting locations after boys I liked and took elements from scary movies I'd seen. One day, I walked into class and made my way to my desk, organized my books and stole a glance at the chalkboard. To my absolute horror, the first two paragraphs of my story were written on the board just waiting to be discussed and critiqued in front of the entire class. I was mortified! Who did this teacher think she was to display my story so publicly without my permission? I felt the heat rush to my cheeks, the sweat began to form at my hairline and tears began to well up in my eyes. As I looked down in my lap, anywhere but at the board or at my classmates, I tried thinking of absolutely anything else in the world.

Write from the Heart

Why is the thought of sharing our writing with others scary? Writing is thinking. It is your own thoughts, feelings, experiences, ideas and hopes on full display. Once made public, it is open to hate, critique, unwanted feedback, opposing opinions and straight-out meanness from others. On the other hand, it is also open to love, support, a listening ear, well-meant advice and lifelong connections. Those first thoughts that come to mind when thinking of making our writing public or being bold in our writing and writing from the heart, is what keeps many of us from sharing what we genuinely want to share. It's what stops us from saying what's on our minds and, instead, forces us to put up that protective shell and play it safe. What have you ever gotten out of playing it safe?

There are two ways in which educators need to stop writing in fear and start writing from the heart. The first of the two is on social media and public platforms. The second is in front of our students.

On Public Platforms

Stop writing in fear of what other teachers may think. If you are on social media, such as Twitter, you know what I'm talking about. We're all guilty of it; typing out a tweet that shares a frustration about education and then not submitting it or deleting it after more consideration of possible responses or reactions. Stop second guessing yourself. What you have to say matters. There will always be trolls or people who are just looking for ways to bring others down, but more often than not, there will be people who relate to you and who feel a sense of relief when they see and read what you have to say. Writing takes a lot of courage especially when making your writing public. Sharing your thoughts, ideas, fears, accomplishments and doubts requires you to be vulnerable. It may not feel natural sharing your private thoughts with others. However, when you do, something happens. When you see those first positive reactions from complete strangers who tell you they support you, they share your thoughts, or they want to hear more of what you have to say, you become empowered. You become heard. Your words begin to impact others in a way that you never thought was possible. Never, ever let your doubts or fears lead you through life. The more you share, the more opportunities you will encounter.

Apart from social media, start being bold about how you self-reflect, publicly. When I began blogging, I looked at it as a way to share what I am doing in the classroom–with a sort of digital portfolio mindset. The more I get into it, though, the more it is becoming a means of getting everything off my chest and I am left feeling relieved and heard. Start small by writing about something you have tried in the classroom that went well or maybe something you were excited about that didn't go so well. Writing about your daily teaching life will make you become a better teacher and by sharing your writing on a public platform, you will grow your professional network and credibility as an educator.

In Front of Students

Stop writing in fear of what your students may think. Teaching middle schoolers how to write has proven to be as difficult as it sounds year after year. What I have learned is that if I want my students to be vulnerable in their writing, I have to model that vulnerability and be bold in my own writing. For example, we write personal essays at the start of 7th grade–which is a very new form of writing for many students. I want them to have the courage to share some anecdotes from their lives that may not be the easiest topics to discuss. If we want students to share life lessons they have learned that go deeper than "What I have learned by playing volleyball" or "My vacation to Florida" then we need to model what deeper writing looks like. The beginning of the year is the time to start this courageous journey with students because it sets the tone for the rest of the year. It tells students that their teacher is going to be straight with them and tell it like it is.

My first writing that I share with students is my personal essay on the topic of suicide with anecdotes about my cousin who took his life when I was in 8th grade. That was a long time ago, but I choose to share that topic because I was their age when this life changing event took place. My students display empathy and emotion while I read my work. Every time I read my essay to students I get the same reaction: absolute silence, glassy eyes, engagement and interest. By being vulnerable, I hook my students into wanting to share their stories and be brave with me. If I shared about what I learned from a vacation I've been on, the boldness of writing would fall by the wayside. By sharing this extremely personal experience, I have learned so much more about my students than I ever would have if I chose to not show vulnerability in my own writing.

By being bold in your writing when you choose to share something publicly with other professionals or with your students, you will begin to grow more confident in your own practices. If you choose to write with fear and just play it safe, you are choosing to be OK with being OK. And nobody wants to just be OK.

Brittany Schmidt is a grade 7 ELA teacher from Greenville, Wisconsin, an aspiring administrator and writes on her blog, "Oscar Worthy Teaching."

67

Stop Making Promises that You Can't Keep
AMY MACCRINDLE, Ed.D.

We've all been there. You're in a meeting talking to a colleague or on the phone with a parent and your stomach drops. You feel a heavy heartbeat and queasy stomach as you realize that a ball was dropped and that you were the quarterback or receiver of an empty commitment or false promise. The problem is generally related to a commitment we did not uphold, a deadline we didn't meet or an expectation we didn't fulfill. Accountability and commitment are core to professional success and a synergistic school community.

When this kind of misstep happens, our response is either being paralyzed with fear, speechless and unable to respond, or quickly making excuses by covering up the error and by placing blame elsewhere. While people who break promises don't normally do so intentionally or maliciously, the result disappoints other people. This has direct and collateral effects because this can damage your integrity, trust and relationships in every nook and cranny within your school organization and community. Let's take a closer look at five "breaking promises" scenarios and possible solutions.

Scenario 1: Vague Communication

Three weeks into a new school year, a parent in your class is concerned that their 4th grade child is reading two levels below the norm. The parent believes that the student's 2nd and 3rd grade teachers failed to support the child's reading growth. You quickly respond, guaranteeing that you will work with supportive services and making it your personal goal to help the child catch up with their grade level. Fast forward to the parent/teacher conference later that year and the parent is angry because while progress has been made, their child has not yet caught up to their level. You believe that you delivered on your promise: you engaged extensive reading intervention from a highly trained reading specialist and independently coached the student with additional weekly reading practice. The parent, however, believes that you didn't keep your promise of their child being caught up with their grade level peers.

> **Solution:** Make certain your communication sets clear expectations, goals, objectives and standards. Validate understanding by asking the other person what they heard and their interpretation. Make sure that both parties agree to the promise and commitments being made before jumping in to the problem solving process.

Scenario 2: The People Pleaser–The Fear of Saying "No"

You are meeting with your fellow math department teachers, department chair and Principal. The tone is tense as you review newly released SAT scores and there was a decline in the student percent meeting or exceeding expectations. As a cooperative PLC, you are asked to create a SMART goal and action steps to close this gap. The team creates plans that you know will not work in your classroom due to the characteristics of your students, but you do not speak up. You want to be perceived as a team player, to please others and avoid conflict at all costs. You commit to the recommended plan–almost certain you won't deliver. While your intentions were positive, you made a promise you couldn't keep and feeling pressured to say yes, you compromised your professional judgment.

> **Solution:** Learn how to set boundaries. If you cannot master this skill, you might end up taking responsibility for something that you know you can't do. It is always better to say "no" early, than to be resentful later. Why is it hard to say no? Saying no can feel like a huge risk. You might worry that your decline could elicit rejection. Remind yourself that saying "no" when warranted is respected and honored by those who are thoughtful. Own that integrity then there is no pressure to explain. You do not have to go along with something just because you do not want to create ripples in the water.

Scenario 3: Over-Romanticizing/Underestimating

You are about halfway through completing a Master's degree and the Principal talked about building a team to plan a school walk-a-thon in order to raise funds for the local food bank. Knowing that this is a highly visible and meaningful project for students and the school community, you get overly excited about the walk-a-thon. You have passionate ideas about ways to engage students and parents. You can visualize walk-a-thon t-shirts, food booths, and even how to obtain a deejay. By the end of the meeting, you have volunteered to serve as the project co-chair. While you were caught up in the excitement of the project, you failed to rationally recognize the project requirements, timelines and the amount of work, not allowing you to give it your full focus. With good intentions, you made a promise you couldn't keep.

> **Solution:** Remind yourself that we often get overly excited about a new project, but forget that we have prior commitments to balance in our lives, as well. This can result in last minute urgency and a poor job done. Pause before you make the promise. Before you commit, take some time to visualize the many steps and deadlines between start and finish. After this pause, if you find even the most tedious details exciting among your already full calendar, the project just might be right for you.

Scenario 4: The Need to be in the Game

You were recently hired as the new head coach at a high school in your small town. You bring a lot of experience to the table with your background in working in a larger district. The superintendent and principal charge you to turn their program into a state winning program in the next three years. You say "yes" and provide specific examples of what worked for you in your prior roles: working with youth feeder programs, building a program that students want to be a part of and connecting with the larger community so they see the importance of your program. Fast forward four years and while you are making progress towards this goal, you are nowhere near meeting the goal. While you believed, at the time, that you could make that happen, realistically, it could not be accomplished in the short time period, thus resulting in you making a promise you couldn't keep.

> **Solution:** We live in a competitive world and it is easy to promise anything just to get a chance at the game. However, if we don't deliver on our promise it can be devastating to our reputation and cause great losses over the long haul. When committing to specific aggressive deadlines,

add some margin-of-time to your plan. Successful people allow for this and then come to the finish line looking like it was easy. It wasn't easy, but they allowed extra time to cover their setbacks.

Scenario 5: You Simply Forgot

You committed to representing your teaching team at the fall festival on Saturday. Not having your cell phone or laptop handy, you wrote the date on a Post-it Note to update your calendar when available. The note dropped off your bag, was eaten by your dog and the date was never added to your calendar. You spent the day enjoying time at the apple orchard and pumpkin patch. On Monday, your team asks you how the fall festival was and if the kids who attended enjoyed the game the team created. You look at them with a blank stare because you made a promise you couldn't keep.

> **Solution:** There will be times when we do not honor our promises because we are stuck in traffic, have a family priority, or simply forget. In these cases, be honest. Immediately admit to the dropping the ball, apologize and commit to do better. Honesty and an apology go a long way in supporting integrity.

In each of these examples, the intention was 100% altruistic, yet actions and results did not honor the promise. The pitfalls: we did not realize that we'd made a promise, we didn't have the time to make it happen, we didn't remember the commitment, we didn't realize that following through would be so difficult or we didn't have the authority to make it happen. Broken promises and commitments impact you as much as those you disappointed and you have the power to stop these things from happening.

It is okay to be selective about the promises you make. We often end up spending more time putting out fires than we would have if we would just learn how not to over-promise and under-deliver. Trust your instinct and don't give in to self-doubt. The challenge is just creating the motivation to start and continue to the finish line. When we make this a habit, then you will truly find your own balance while using your integrity to generate trust in yourself and others.

Dr. Amy MacCrindle is a proud mother of four, the wife of a high school math teacher and coach, a Director of Curriculum and an Adjunct Professor in Crystal Lake, Illinois. Her expertise is in change management, curriculum and instruction, literacy, innovation and school culture.

Stop Mocking Parents

AMIE LAWLESS, Ed.D.

Stop mocking parents. Stop making fun of parents. Stop making assumptions about parents. Parents are your biggest partners in education and when you mock them, you are responsible for inhibiting the potential for a flourishing partnership. This is a top synergy zapper within an organization for sure!

Early in my career, one of my principals would remind us that parents are sending us the best children they have. They are not keeping the perfect, high achieving children at home and sending us the more difficult, struggling ones. They are sending their greatest treasures each and every day. Parents want their children to be successful and to learn as much as they can. You, as their teacher, want children to be successful and to learn as much as they can. You both want the same thing for their children. The parent is the expert on their children at home and you are the expert on their children at school. In Chapter 6, Rebecca writes about the importance of not blaming families. Mocking them is even worse. Synergy will only create five-star schools when teachers and families work together as respected experts. This combination produces unbeatable student success!

Mockery Reflects Inner Character

When you mock a parent, your professionalism decreases each time. When you mock a parent, you are showing others that you do not put children first, even if you claim otherwise. When you mock a parent, you are revealing your true character. When you mock a parent, your colleagues do not think you are funny.

My first job as a head principal was a challenge for many reasons. I began in January 2014 as an elementary principal in a very affluent suburban school. While on the outside it looked like the dream school (high achievement scores, pretty building, etc.), there were some areas needing immediate attention. One of those areas was a trio of teacher bullies and Jane was the ringleader.

I had been on the job for approximately six weeks when we attended parent teacher conferences. Our parent/teacher organization was so good to us that they provided dinner for the staff during one of those long nights. While the entire staff met in the cafeteria for a quick bite to eat and break, I was unable to join the group in the cafeteria because I was handling an issue. After the dinner ended, a teacher named Ann showed up in my office looking horrified. She wanted to know if she could share something that was bothering her with me in private. I assured her that whatever she told me, I would be keep private.

Ann went on to share with me that Jane (who was a close friend of hers outside of school) had been sharing a story about one particular parent teacher conference to a group of colleagues who were sitting next to her at the dinner break and the parents were within earshot of a terrible story. Jane was describing how a parent was asking for advice on how to get his child off of an IEP. Jane said, "What I really wanted to tell him was that your child is so stupid, she'll never be getting off her IEP." While she was relaying this story about the parent, Jane laughed and mocked the parent. To this day, I am still horrified at the thought of a teacher talking like that about a child and parent.

By the end of the evening, three of Jane's colleagues had sought me out to share their discomfort with how she was mocking this same parent and making fun of the child. Since Jane was known as the leader of the teacher bully group, no one felt comfortable addressing her actions in the moment without becoming her next target.

Address it or You are Condoning it

In all my years of education, this example of a teacher openly mocking a parent is at the top of my list of terrible incidents. It still horrifies me and makes me wish I could hug that parent and tell her that her child is amazing and precious. I am proud of those teachers that had the moral compass and ethics to stand up when their colleague compromised the established school values and core beliefs. Had these teachers not come forward, or had I not addressed it at all, we would all have been just as guilty as Jane. Our students deserve us to be brave and do what's right, especially when it comes to mockery.

Mocking parents happens across all settings; no school, no demographic, no socio-economic area is immune. I have come across colleagues who mock parents in every setting I have ever worked. Mocking parents does not show your intelligence or your knowledge. It shows your true character. It undermines your relationships and partnerships with parents. It undermines your relationships with your colleagues. Mocking parents and making them the butt of your jokes does not raise your value in the eyes of your colleagues. Mocking a parent does not make you funny. It only makes you the bully. Stop condoning any type of poor behavior–whether you are the one spreading garbage or are just settling on not picking up the garbage and ignoring it.

Dr. Amie Lawless has served in education for almost 30 years as a classroom teacher and administrator in Kansas. She has a passion for equity, relationships and innovative learning.

Stop Thinking that You are a Rock Star

TODD BROWN, Ed.D.

Teachers, regardless of if you want to admit it or not, love to hear that they are a student's favorite teacher! Who wouldn't? After all, it is human nature to feel approval and praise. It is also understandable that being "Teacher of the Year" is an honor and a duly noted recognition for all of one's hard work. There is absolutely nothing wrong with recognition. Celebrations of milestones and accomplishments, along with recognizing strengths and notable awards, is a cornerstone of synergistic five-star schools.

When Awards Incite Division

Celebrations, recognition and awards are the heart of motivation and synergy until they become an underpinning for division between the "haves awards" and the "have nots awards." Until the compliments or the wooden plaque is on the wall, the golden spoon or the traveling trophy begins to inflate a teacher's ego from a band-member to a self-declared rock star, you are not one.

We all are continually bombarded by a society that focuses on rewards and extrinsic values. These include wealth ("Hey, great job, you are highly effective, so here is a financial reward."), competition for more ("Here's another trophy or certificate because you're a real rock star.") and consumption ("My time and my class are more important than yours."). This competition is a byproduct of social pressures and an indirect result of state-driven testing. The combination can pit schools, departments and even teachers within the same department against one another. This is the fuel that ignites egos and creates derision and divisiveness amongst colleagues.

Teachers are Part of a Band; They are Not Solo Artists

A competition mindset is also the opposite of education, much like being in a band. Being a great guitarist, drummer, or lead singer is fantastic, but without the accompanying members, or the support system like songwriters, stage managers and promoters, the band suffers and will never reach its full potential. Schools of synergy embrace this band mindset to help foster intrinsic values such as competency, being authentic and human connection encompassing common goals for our students. The minute one individual is placed above the group, synergy wanes, negative perceptions creep in and teachers begin to feel like they are better than anyone else. When you allow yourself to become a rock star, you lose sight of your bandmates, the stage manager and others that helped to support you.

Pink Floyd

Awards are outstanding, but now listen to Pink Floyd's song, "The Wall." Take Jennifer as an example. No complaints ever. Not a peep. She worked her butt off every single day and always threw caution to the wind, jumping into cross-curricular lessons and collaboration on a whim. Students loved her, her class, and believe it or not, even loved math (can you imagine?). Suddenly, Jennifer became the teacher of the year and also went on to become the national teacher of the year at the middle school level. By the end of the year, she became more reclusive and did not want to share what she had created with others in her department or school. She withdrew into her own awesome classroom engaging in very little collaboration or working with others. By the following school year, she stopped collaborating with everyone because they didn't know how to teach. She eventually left the school because she did not receive a large enough raise considering the awards she had won during the previous year. She had suddenly gone from a collaborative team-centric five-star teacher to that of a stuck up rock star teacher who had a superiority complex. Jennifer lost sight of why she was there and what education was about. She went from someone that students loved, and teachers worked with, hand in hand, to becoming just "another brick in the wall," according to Pink Floyd.

Do Not Screw Up the Pronoun

I love me some Queen, but make sure you don't screw up the pronoun. Mike was a quiet teacher who did very well with his students in his own unique way. He was not super creative or flamboyant in his teachings, but the students enjoyed his class and achieved at high standards. At some point, Mike became sick of his classes because his students weren't scoring as high as the students in the other classes of the same subject area in the same department. He had enough. In his mind, this became a competition and not a team effort that should focus on student learning instead of test score results. He proceeded to not work with the other teachers in the department and even went so far as to promise his students a reward if they scored high enough to beat the other teachers. Eventually, Mike's competitive nature escalated. His attitude seeped into his students' mindset and they began refusing to study with other students from different classes and even resorted to talking crap about their "enemy classmates" and how terrible the other teachers were. Ultimately, the scores came out and Mike's class outscored the other teachers' classes on the test by 1.5%, overall. Mike quickly emailed the other teachers to let them know how he indeed "won" and how much better off the students would be in his class than in theirs.

Ultimately, Mike screwed up the Queen lyrics and declared that "HE is the champion," instead of "WE are the champions."

We all know there are more stories like this and we can all relate in some fashion, but we should stop with the competitions, egos and rock star mentalities if we are to embrace award winning synergy. Teaching and education are not about YOU. Education takes a tremendous amount of teamwork, support and focus on someone other than yourself. Education is a band, not a solo act.

Dr. Todd Brown is the founder of The Inspire Project and the co-creator of Operation Outbreak. His primary work and goal is to connect and immerse students of all ages in real world applications.

Stop Using Social Media to Look and Feel Good about Yourself
ALLISON SLADE, Ed.D.

The boom in social media has provided an outlet for the creation of alternative realities in our personal and professional lives. Consider what you see when you scroll through any social media outlet: smiles, beautiful scenery, family harmony, funny or perfect quotes and the marketing of ideas to promote oneself. How does the person posting decide what is "post-worthy"? Why is there such an imbalance in what we witness online versus what is actually occurring in our real lives?

Responses and Likes Make Me Feel Good

While I, myself, admit to using various types of social media to document life events and promulgate that which I believe to be true and important in the field of education or politics, or even to seem "smart" to others by following or re-tweeting high profile posters, I have learned to stop, breathe and consider these questions: "Am I using this post to receive admiration from others? Do I NEED strangers and friends to respond to me? Do I still feel a sense of self-worth and meaning in this event without a post? Is my self-worth tied to the response of others in this post?" If I'm honest with you and myself, sometimes it is. Sometimes, I want to feel connected to others when things happen–good or bad. Sometimes, I want to share experiences with others and, yes, their responses make me feel good about myself.

Self-Perceived Success Is Disingenuous

The internet and various forms of social media, however, have provided an outlet for educators to use social media to look and feel good about themselves, without actual accountability for making a difference in the lives of students, families and communities. In the most extreme cases, it has even taken away our need to tell the truth. This leads to the removal of the experimentation nature of teaching and learning because we only post those the five star topics or victories. In order to alter the perception of our profession, we must stop using social media as an avenue to receive constant praise.

Does this mean we need to delete our social media accounts? Of course not. But, it does mean that we, as educators, have a responsibility to think more critically about the image that we create and continually reinforce online and how this connects to our general feeling of self-worth when we are not on the web. When social media highlights the mere illusion of successes, then the authenticity and genuineness of our profession is compromised.

Here are two "real-life" examples of individuals who use social media to look and feel good about themselves, and how they need to stop and reframe their social media persona.

Meet the Narcissist

Reyna is a dual language teacher of Hispanic descent, who posts regularly on Twitter. Everything she posts has an origin in the ambitious teaching and learning she supports; however, every single post has a picture of herself, close-up and with perfectly placed hair and make-up.

On the first day of Hispanic Heritage month, Reyna tweeted a picture of herself with the words, "I'm celebrating Hispanic Heritage month with my Mexican-made sandals and top." Every single reply made a reference to how beautiful Reyna was. No one asked a question about Hispanic Heritage month. No one replied to celebrate or uplift other countries, beyond Mexico, that share in this celebration. She continued to engage with those who replied by replying with "Thank you!" rather than focusing on the symbolism that she was purporting to "celebrate" in her post.

Researchers have demonstrated that social media can increase self-esteem, but also damage it at the same time. The more replies and responses that posts get, the more the post feeds into replying and increasing this type of crowd approving behavior.

The FOMO (Fear of Missing Out) Teacher

Amy is a teacher in her late twenties who spends a significant amount of time on social media, although she doesn't post too often. She trolls social media looking for the "perfect" classroom. Since these avenues of social media often enable people to only show their "best selves," "best work," and "cleanest part of the classroom," the comparisons Amy makes between what she sees on social media and her own classroom is only stress provoking for her.

Amy feels the need to "keep up" and spends significant amounts of time trying to perfect what she's going to post. In an effort to show others how good she looks and feels, Amy is actually becoming a more anxious person–concerned about whether people like her or think that she is a good teacher. This inhibits her ability to grow and develop as a new teacher. Amy has a FOMO.

Both the "Narcissist" & the "FOMO Teacher" may need outside help to process their personal need for admiration or acceptance. Or, maybe, they just need regular social interaction which often decreases when the use of social media increases. Either way, using social media to look and feel good about yourself, specifically as a teacher, destroys the vulnerability and courage it takes to be an educator in the first place and can have negative impacts on creating trust and collective efficacy among staff. It deteriorates the professional environment and impacts student well-being and achievement.

Dr. Allison Slade is an educational innovator whose disruption of the educational status quo is exemplified in her founding of Namaste Charter School in 2004 in Chicago, IL. After 14 years as a school leader in the city and suburbs, she has moved to impact future leaders as the Director of Instructional Leadership at Roosevelt University where she is redesigning the program to create a new view of the principalship in PK-12 education.

Stop Chasing the Latest Buzz Words, Fads & Trends

LISA PAGANO

Fads and trends exist in all aspects of life–from fashion to music to toys. Fads and trends are often a lot of fun. As a child of the 80's, I fondly remember my Cabbage Patch Kids and Care Bears. I also remember the Beanie Babies craze in the 90's and the Macarena dance that took the country by storm. Now, we see short lived fads go viral on Tik-Tok and other social media platforms. These fads lose their luster and novelty while their popularity is brief. Fads come in fast and furious; they are hot and here today, then quickly turn cold and disappear. Unlike fads, trends tend to have just a bit more staying power. Sometimes they fade into obscurity and we never hear about them again and sometimes they resurface after a long period of time or relapse. Hello to high-waisted jeans and scrunchies and goodbye to them until they resurface in another era. What was once considered old becomes new again.

Effective Instruction Is Not a Buzz Word

The field of education is no stranger to fads and trends. Along with these fads and trends come "buzz words." Education is known as a field that is peppered with buzz words along with a large dose of acronyms, jargon and "Edu-speak." In fact, new buzz words and acronyms seem to crop up on a daily basis, making it difficult to keep track of exactly what it is we are focusing on at any given point in time. It also makes it close to impossible for a non-educator to follow. Personalized learning. Whole language. Balanced literacy. The science of reading. Differentiation. Growth mindset. STEM. STEAM. IEP. FRA. LRE. Synchronous and asynchronous. How can anyone keep track and keep up?

We must move beyond the buzz words. Many teachers talk the talk utilizing the latest acronyms and trending topics, but then fail to execute and deliver effective instruction. Many of us are incredible during job interviews because we know our jargon, but it is one thing to say it and another to do it and do it well. Teachers may say they are differentiating, but then there is no evidence in the classroom of effectively meeting the needs of all learners all of the time. You can't preach about the importance of having a growth mindset to your students, but then come into a professional development session displaying resistant and combative behaviors that contradict the growth mindset you try to instill in your students. Stop linking articles and blog posts about innovation and collaboration in education on your Facebook wall when you have your students sit in rows while you stand and deliver your lesson, followed by doling out worksheet after worksheet.

Effective Instruction Produces Results

The same applies for educational leaders. What you say doesn't matter nearly as much as what you do. Talking and doing are two vastly different things. Educational leaders tend to preach and tell us about the "what" but rarely show the "how." The "what" is easy; the "how" is not. Where is the action? Where are the practical applications, solutions and strategies? Stop dropping buzz words in conversations and start doing the work.

I am not saying we need to close ourselves off from what is happening in the world. It is certainly important to remain current on best practices and new educational research; however, I believe there are certain tenets in education that will be timeless. We will tire ourselves out and spin in circles if we constantly chase after the new buzz words, fads and trends. After all, they will eventually go away. They do not have staying power and what is trendy, cute and fun won't move the dial for student learning or create the lasting impact we desire.

There is no "magic bullet" in education. If there was, someone would be getting very rich, graduation rates would soar and we would continually churn out future ready students. We have to stop running after the next new, shiny tool or curriculum that makes lofty promises but ultimately fails to deliver, like so many before. You see, what goes into great teaching is more than just a "thing" and it certainly is not just a curriculum or tech tool. What really matters most are teachers and what they *do* with their students.

Effective Instruction Cultivates Positive Relationships

Relationships are at the heart of everything we do in education. Trust and safety must be established with our students. Knowing them beyond their data points is critical. Sure, we need to know where they are and how to be responsive to data, but we must also connect with them socially and emotionally. Students are, obviously, more than what their assessment results indicate. What are their interests, skills and talents? What is their story? What is their family life like? Building strong connections with every student is critical. Your students will remember you long after they move to the next grade level or building but they will not remember your jargon.

201

Teaching thinking skills will never go out of style and serve students well across all content areas and disciplines. Developing strong relationships and layering in opportunities for critical and creative thinking can lead to high student engagement.

Relationships and critical thinking have lasting power and last within in-person, remote and hybrid teaching models. They are the essential elements of educational style and should be part of every teacher's practical go-to wardrobe–like the staple black dress or blue pinstripe suit that you might find in your classic closet. So, let's stop chasing the new buzz words, fads and trends and start sticking with the tried & true classics, while adding some fun embellishments along the way.

Lisa Pagano currently serves as the AIG & Talent Development District Lead Teacher for Charlotte-Mecklenburg Schools in Charlotte, North Carolina. She is a National Board Certified Teacher and is passionate about growing both teachers and students to positively impact learning and teaching.

Stop Talking Crap about the Profession
MICHELE RISPO HILL

Did you know that the brain is wired to see negativity as a defense mechanism in order to keep people away from danger? It makes sense, right? But, if we are wired to see the negative, what exactly do we do with that information? Well, for many people it results in people, "talking crap" about the very profession that they work in each day. What is designed to be a safety feature in our frontal cortex to warn us of danger, makes its way into our mouths and we spit it out as negative communication. We talk about politics, religion, other people and even our jobs. While I'd like to believe that the intention of the "crap talker" is not to spread negativity, it happens just the same and to be clear, it happens in every profession.

Every job has its ups and downs, but not all are as emotionally charged as being an educator, possibly because those outside the profession of teaching are not working with children all day long. You would think that because teaching is a vocation that people are called to, they would shine a bright light on the profession and elevate it with warmth. You are more than likely to see colleagues trashing our profession, even on social media.

202

Crap Talking Types

Over the years, I've witnessed different types of crap talking done by educators. It always amazes me because I'm a positive person. I wouldn't say that I live in a fantasy world with rose-colored glasses, but I actively choose to be positive in spite of the challenges that I encounter each day and education sure has its challenges! You could classify "the crap" being dished out into three categories: talking about other teachers, talking about the school, and talking about the students.

Teachers Talking Crap about Other Teachers

Rick is especially devoted to this same exact topic and goes into even more detail in a later chapter. Allow me to take a moment to give you a slice of my thoughts on this topic since it fits into my chapter. Talking crap about other teachers is one of the three categories that feed into bashing the profession, at large. Everyone likes to let off some steam at times and that most certainly includes educators. Recently, I was at an event with a friend of mine. After pleasantries, people started to talk about their profession. One of the guests revealed that she was a teacher, and without much prompting, she unabashedly unleashed stories and information about her colleagues describing them in the most unflattering way. She talked about the physical education teachers who really doesn't teach all that much, the lazy ones who have the same lesson plans and resources for the past twenty years and the new teachers who aren't committed and don't want to do anything extra. I stood there with my mouth agape not believing what I was hearing. After declaring that I was also a teacher who was fortunate to work with some incredible educators and was sure that the ones that she spoke of were the minority, I politely excused myself and thought, "I wonder why the public perception of educators is what it is. Now I know!"

We owe it to our profession to elevate the reputation of our colleagues. Let us commit to being part of the solution with our colleagues by mentoring, assisting or giving grace during difficult times. Through support and encouragement, you and members of your staff can turn around a struggling teacher. When someone improves their pedagogy, we all rise as a profession and for goodness sake, we all have opinions, but it is not necessary to share those opinions about your colleagues with others. They do not have the backstory or details to make an objective assessment of whether or not the information you spout is valid.

Teachers Talking Crap about Students

Jim Smith, a middle school math teacher, started every day off with complaining about his students while doing hall duty. A typical positive "good morning" from Mr. Smith consisted of any of the following crappy statements about students on any given day:

- "These kids can't even get to homeroom on time, so how are they going to make it in the real world?"
- "I gave a quiz today and none of these kids studied; they are so lazy!"
- "Kids today are different; they just don't care."

Mr. Smith's colleagues weren't the only ones impacted by him; often, the students overhead him and were devastated. What a terrible impression from a teacher. When teachers or administrators engage in conversations that include negative speech about students, they are giving educators and the whole profession a bad rap.

Teachers Talking Crap about the School

For some people, complaining is just part of their character. They will find fault with everyone or everything. Sometimes, there is more than just one or two of them, there is a group of them, so watch out! Teachers within the history department of an inner-city high school that I know of seem to thrive on complaining. The weekly department meetings turned into futile venting sessions that bashed everything from the lack of support from their administrator(s), to the lack of resources available to them, to class sizes being too large, to not enough time to go to the bathroom in between classes, to boring faculty meetings and so much more! These complaints only create a picture of a dysfunctional system to those who are hearing about it. When you openly talk negatively about your school, you invite others to pass judgement and make assumptions that may not even be true. Who knows who is watching and listening to you?

Make no mistake about it, each one of these types of verbal condemnations are detrimental to the profession, thus impacting the overall culture and reputation of the school and the profession in a negative way. They are synergy stealers. If we genuinely want to improve education, let's start by working together to identify the issues facing education and come up with solutions.

Please stop "talking crap" about your own profession. We need to protect the profession by engaging in positive speech and probable solutions. People are looking to the experts in the field and that is you!

Michele Rispo Hill is a speaker, trainer, blogger and passionate educator who is currently serving as the Coordinator of Admissions and Strategic Marketing for Burlington County Institute of Technology. Michele is on a mission to support educators in their professional journeys.

Stop Debating about Public, Charter, Private & Home Schooling
DAVID FRANKLIN, Ed.D.

I spent five years as a principal of a traditional public middle school in California. After accepting the position, I walked my campus and discovered something unexpected. Right in the center of the campus was a small school of choice. We will call it "The Academy" in this chapter. It was considered one of the seven middle schools in our district, but it was able to operate a little differently. Much like a charter school, attendance boundary guidelines did not apply to this school. Students from anywhere in the district could apply for admittance into this school regardless of their address or traditional school boundary if they lived within the wider- margined district boundaries. They were able to offer interesting elective classes that we could not create due to fiscal constraints.

The Academy

I quickly discovered that my staff members were not happy about "The Academy" being on our campus. The common complaint was that they siphoned off all the best students from our school and other schools within the district in order to increase their own test scores, parent involvement and status within the community. Students did leave our school throughout the year as spots opened at "The Academy." In truth, many of them were students who performed well on standardized tests, had little to no disciplinary issues and had involved parents. Each time a student transferred out of our school, my teachers made another comment about losing another good student and caring family to "The Academy."

To be fair, my school did not have the best reputation. Our test scores were low. Our suspension rates were high. Our teachers did not have high expectations of our students. That all needed to change.

I also did not like the fact that "The Academy" was on my campus either. They were outshining us in every way. I needed to change the narrative, however. Instead of complaining about them, we needed to offer a stronger academic program, more varied elective classes and have high expectations for all students. So, that is exactly what we did.

We spent two years revitalizing our school. We lobbied our board of trustees to allow us to create a more robust catalog of course offerings. We worked with local agencies to reach out to our families, increasing communication and support structures. As an administration team, we instilled a belief as part of our core values that everyone on campus embrace high expectations of both our students and we as educators. We pledged to hold each other accountable to our new vision of excellence.

Two Years of Hard Work

It took two years. Two years of hard work. There was plenty of blood and sweat plus a whole lot of tears. The start of my third year as a principal also marked first year that "The Academy" was not on our campus. While turning around our school, we made the small school of choice obsolete. Students from my site were no longer being added to "The Academy's" wait list. Parents were happy with our program. They did not feel the need to move to a small school of choice or a charter school.

At the end of the day, parents just want the best educational and social experience for their children. They do care about the school's label or if it is public or charter. Yet, the bottom line is all about results. Sadly, the conversation about public vs. charter schools is not about results. This debated conflict is about politics. As educators, we must recognize that if a process, program, or organizational structure is working and beneficial to children, then we shouldn't automatically dismiss it just because it is uncomfortable or in opposition of your preferred political platform.

The charter school movement began for an important reason. Traditional public schools were not working for some students. Parents wanted more flexibility in courses and scheduling. Educators wanted more control over funding. While the media is quick to point out when charter schools fail, we must also recognize that most of them are well run and are supporting students who are traditionally underserved by public institutions. Many charters are considered public schools, as well.

I do not believe that there is anything wrong with some healthy competition in education. Without it, we become complacent. School systems must continue to grow and adapt to the changing world around them. Charter schools started out in areas where the public-school systems were failing students. If a different organizational structure can support students who were unsuccessful in a traditional school system, then why should we try to shut them down? For private school students or schools where religion is stressed, how could we take those experiences away from children, likewise? How could we discount home-schooled students? Education has all sorts of forums.

The debate should be about how we can all work together to support all students, no matter the type of school, so please stop amplifying the debate and focus on where you are or where you want to be as an educator. Focus on the students, not the politics.

Dr. David Franklin is an award winning school administrator, education professor at Colorado State University, curriculum designer and presenter. He is also a Marzano Research fellow trained in high-reliability schools, instructional rounds and building effective collaborative teams.

Stop "One-Upping" Others or Trying to Be the Principal's Pet
HOLLY MARCOLINA

Your school existed long before you came on board. Realize that history did not begin when you signed your contract. Please do not act dismissively toward your senior colleagues; they have spent decades doing things you know nothing about. I recall a younger teacher once condemning an older teacher about not attending union meetings during a contract negotiation year. What that younger teacher did not know is that the veteran had run the entire union's scholarship program for decades even before the new teacher was born. She had been there and done that. There is no need to "one up" anyone. We are better than that.

Be Quiet and Observe

Looking back on starting our teaching careers together, my colleagues and I reflected on the unwritten rule that we were to not speak up in meetings until we were employed by the district for ten years! There is some wisdom to that. Any comment made to flatter oneself or promote oneself will come off exactly that way. Nobody will be impressed with you, including your students. Do your job and love your students without broadcasting it. Make your own professional goals and demolish them privately. Let your life and your teaching speak for itself; you don't have to.

You Need Your Colleagues

You really do need your colleagues--not just in the collaborative sense, but you may need your co-workers for the simplest things, such as getting something from your classroom for you when you are sick. Teachers are social humans and as a school with high synergy, you laugh together at the end of the day as you blow off steam, you provide a stash of candy for each other throughout the day and, yes, you bounce curriculum ideas off one another. You spend a lot of time at work and very often these co-workers become part of your life. We are all in this together. Stop looking down on your co-workers who are not tech savvy or the one who leaves immediately after work. Most likely you don't know their personal circumstances as well as you think you might. Be gracious, humble and loving with your co-workers. Love them as the amazing people they are, not as potential competitors.

Everyone has a Story

Each person at your school was hired for a specific purpose, including you. When you interviewed, the district saw something that they wanted in you. They also saw something in your colleagues. Five-star schools, fueled by synergy, take the time to get to know one another's stories. Once you understand the perspective, history and strengths of your colleagues, a foundation of culture and success is established. There is no need or benefit to your students to prove anything to your co-workers.

Everyone has an Identity

At the core of "one-upping" is your identity. Who are you without the accolades, without the groups of admiring students, or the likes on social media? "Busy-ness" can drown out your own internal compass. Confidence cannot come from your job, position, or your own performance without putting your full self, your full identity into what you do. A career is temporary and, yes, as educators, we have a sacred trust. Perform your duties with excellence and take pride in your job. Keep your own intellectual fires burning and love the students in front of you. It really is about them and not you.

The Principal's P.E.T. (Power - Espionage - Truth)

Power

Principals are middle management leaders. They don't have as much power as you might think because the buck does not stop with them. They work for a superintendent who works for multiple supervisors--their board of education members. During the summer of 2020, I was flooded with requests to bring students back to the school building in the fall after conducting school remotely. That decision had nothing to do with me. The requests for certain courses, supplies, a new classroom, or whatever it may be was something I could look at, but not always approve. Often, things are completely out of our hands. When you go into the office, you have no idea that your principal may have just been in a meeting with law enforcement about a child abuse case. A principal might not recall something that is urgently on your mind or might not have seen the email you sent two minutes prior to coming to his office because he just returned from accompanying a suicidal student to the hospital. You are probably unaware of the sheer volume of phone calls your principal has received and taken the blame and been screamed at in an attempt to deflect some of a parents' wrath from you. Surprisingly, principals do not hold the keys to the kingdom; we just try to keep the peace in our schools. Power does not ultimately lie with us; it lies with your ability to be the best that you can be without one upping or becoming the principal's pet.

Espionage

You might be a mole and not realize it. Some principals spend years trying to figure out the social circles in their buildings and strategize whom to make alliances with as they struggle to survive each day. This sounds like it is straight from a blockbuster movie and in some cases, navigating a school is truly political "survivor." Some teachers feel like they are part of an inner circle when they find themselves friends with members of the administrative team. Sometimes, these friendships are genuine and sometimes they are not. In your attempts to cozy up to your principal, you might be being played, yourself. Be mindful of the information you share and the questions you are being asked. This may sound cynical, but be cognizant that this dynamic can exist as a two-way street and playing field where capitalizing on one person's information or status can go both ways, sad to say.

Truth

The truth is that your principal is human. Be genuine and human with your principal. Create a space for her to be the same with you. Ask about your principal's weekend plans, wish him a happy holiday, invite her into your classroom parties or save him a piece of cake. These simple gestures recognizing humanity are important. Before they were principals, they were teachers like you. Principals have a whole history and network you are unaware of. Administrators tend to not stay in one school for an exceptionally long time. Working together, you have an opportunity for a friendship that will last long after tenure at your school, it does not have to be an artificial attempt in becoming the principal's pet.

One upping your colleagues to get ahead and move closer to the office of your principal or other supervisor is a narrow-minded chess move. Look more closely at your real intentions that do not need artificial support.

Holly Marcolina has served in public high schools throughout New York State for nearly twenty years as a social studies teacher, Dean of Students, and currently a secondary school principal. She is pursuing a Ph.D. in Curriculum, Instruction and the Science of Learning at the State University of New York at Buffalo.

Stop Gossiping and Violating Confidentiality
JENNIFER BUTTERFOSS

Perhaps the title of this chapter should just read, "Stop Gossiping, in General." It is a bad habit. Gossiping might help you form a quick, instant bond with another colleague in the staff lounge or over drinks, but that one quick little laugh comes at the expense of your long-term credibility and trustworthiness. Do you want to know what most people are thinking when you start to share the tiniest bit of gossip with them? In the back of their minds, they are making the connections that if you are willing to talk about a student or colleague behind their back and reveal personal information, you might one day gossip about them, as well.

I have found there are three main types of gossip that run rampant in schools across the nation. There is gossip about administrators, colleagues and students and their families. Each of these have their own intended and unintended outcomes. Some are even against the law, according to the Family Educational Rights and Privacy Act (FERPA). If we are to produce synergy in five-star schools, then we must deconstruct this bad practice and figure out how to stop it, altogether.

210

Gossip about Administrators

One of the most pervasive types of gossip, even in my own career as a teacher was about our principal. I must confess: I took part in gossiping about her too. We were so frustrated with some of her decisions and being overworked, underpaid and completely overwhelmed first-year teachers, that we delighted in the tiniest bit of news about her personal life and struggles over happy hour each Friday.

What purpose did this gossip about our boss serve? Perhaps it bonded us closer to one another and helped us justify our own feelings of insecurity and inadequacy in the classroom. Maybe it helped convince us that we did not need to work as hard to meet the needs of our students because our school leadership was "so terrible." Maybe it provided a bit of drama and entertainment for the evening.

Then I became an administrator and suddenly, the rumor mill started swirling about me. A few teachers would occasionally stop by my office and attempt to "fill me in" on what was being said. I heard everything from my lack of experience in the classroom to my prior reputation at other sites as a "hatchet lady" and a few far-fetched tales that were completely untrue.

I remain grateful to those teachers who clued me in to the gossip about my family and me. It gave me the chance to model truthfulness and transparency with my staff. These small gestures of outreach allowed me the opportunity to address some elephants in the room. It was through this kind of openness and communication that I could move forward with my staff and ensure we stayed focused on serving students.

Gossip about Colleagues

We have all had colleagues and fellow teachers in our buildings that may have given us some concern. Whenever a teacher is going through turmoil or hardship in his or her personal life, it can often spill into and affect the classroom environment. So, what do we do? We whisper, we shrug, we shake our heads, we find a few coworkers to share concerns with and often it ends there.

But, do we ever get brave enough to speak directly to our colleagues about the rumors and gossip about them? No. Who does that end up hurting the most? Students. Year after year, students bear the brunt of adult challenges and hardships and none of us were brave enough to do the very thing that might have helped intervene most effectively: having an honest and open conversation directly with the person we are quick to gossip about.

211

Gossiping about Students and Families

Earlier, Amie wrote about mocking parents. Her chapter really raised my own eyebrows. As a teacher and school administrator, I dealt with my fair share of student bullying, fights and incidents of violence. The parents of the alleged victims would inevitably ask about the other student or students involved. They wanted to know names, background and consequences received. In their eyes, it only seemed fair and appropriate that they get a small window into the other children causing their own child pain, perhaps as a means for understanding the cause, but also for a sense of justice being served.

When I became a parent and received that dreaded phone call after my daughter's first day of preschool that another child had bitten her, I was curious how the school would respond. To my utter shock, the director called the child who did the biting over to my daughter and me during parent pick-up that afternoon. She wanted the four of us to engage in a restorative conversation. His mother was not present, nor did I see any attempt to gain consent. Not only did I learn the name of this young boy, but once he left, the teacher took it upon herself to inform me that he was adopted and that this was not his first incident of aggression. I could tell she wanted me to have a deeper empathy and understanding for this child and maybe be more forgiving of the school for allowing this incident to occur, but instead I left with a heavy heart, knowing that this family's basic right to privacy and confidentiality was violated by an adult they trusted.

Let us all agree to stop disclosing confidential information about students and families to other students and families, no matter how eager desperate or justified a family feels about knowing these details. We are bound by law to comply with confidentiality standards. If a family asks about another child or wants to know about a consequence for an alleged incident, the following should hold true:

1. I'm sorry, but that information is confidential and I cannot disclose that.
2. We are handling this incident to the fullest extent possible.
3. We are in close touch with the other family and will work with them directly on this matter.

These kinds of standard protocols should exist to ensure the information being disclosed is out of educational necessity and not simply "water cooler talk."

Before disclosing information about a student or family to another colleague, ask yourself the following questions: Does this staff member need this information to best serve the particular student and family? Does this staff member currently have direct contact with this child and family? If I refrain from sharing this information, could there be possible negative consequences in the future as a result of this staff member not knowing this information?

If you can answer "yes" to all three of the above questions, then yes, you should feel confident about disclosing the information you hold to the other professionals at your school that may need to know the specifics to do their job well. Otherwise, please keep it to yourself.

By being a bit more discerning in what personal information you choose to pass on and to whom, you can build up your credibility and trustworthiness at your school. If you still find yourself desperate to learn some juicy gossip about someone else, I suggest you go purchase a subscription to *People* magazine or check out the latest episode of *TMZ*.

Jennifer Butterfoss is a leadership coach for school administrators and a writer for Golden Gate Mothers Group Magazine. Prior to this, she served as a school principal, assistant principal and a teacher for 18 years in the California Bay Area.

Stop Talking Crap about Your Colleagues
RICK JETTER, Ph.D.

Not a single person in ANY school can convince me that crap-talking does not exist in EVERY school and district, *everywhere*. Crap-talking is toxic. That is why we had a few authors attack this important STOP element in a few of our chapters, already. Remember Michele's chapter a little further back when crap-talking schools were addressed? Jennifer just introduced a great chapter on gossip, as well. If educators are willing to talk crap about their school, then most likely they are also willing to talk crap about YOU (like Jennifer stated) and I have a bit more to say about the crap that others will shovel on you without hesitation.

Adversity Will Rear Its Ugly Head

If crap does not appear at your doorstep or involve you in any way, that's GREAT (for now), but who knows if adversity will rear its ugly head in the next hour, week, one year from now OR creep up on you when you least expect it. So, if you are not involved in crap (which is usually drama-injected), it is still probably happening within your school right now and involving others–where you may or may not even be privy to the details of such wild adversity campaigns, anyway.

I do not accept the idea that "people will be people" and that education is such an intensely emotional profession that teachers will, inevitably, get out of hand, from time to time just like anyone else. *Do not believe this nonsense for one second.* The in-your-face reality is that people bring about adversity inside and outside the workplace because they have issues of their own and are not willing to look in the mirror to reflect on becoming a better person.

Talking crap about another teacher involves a certain amount of inadequacy, a bit of jealousy, or the exact opposite: feeling that some sort of injustice is taking place within the system and the poorly skilled teacher is still, unfortunately, allowed to be around children while a failed administration will not address the problems of the alleged "problem teacher." Therefore, talking crap takes place across a full spectrum of teacher competencies: the teachers who receive crap are either too competent and will make other teachers look bad because they are so good at what they do OR the teacher is so terrible that something must be done to get rid of that teacher. Forced removal might take place when the system finally does something about a terrible teacher or removal by choice might take place when a teacher cannot take any more of the crap, so they just end up quitting and going somewhere else on their own.

Two Categories of Crap

I've seen two major kinds of crap being dished out to other teachers (even though there's more, I'm sure): one that takes place *in front of kids* and one that is more *subtle*. In the end, however, both types of crap take a toll on teachers and the system in which they work together.

Crap-Talking Type 1: In Front of Kids

Jennifer, a seventh-grade math teacher in Springfield, Illinois, is a terrific teacher. She goes out of her way to help kids, establishes incredible relationships with them and will go through the fire to protect them all. She knows her math well and is brilliantly tactical when it comes to her instructional practices. Jennifer's so-called friend and colleague, Amanda is an average special education teacher who pushes in to Jennifer's class each day. She is there as a consultant teacher in order to help support some students who are mainstreamed in Jennifer's class. Amanda knows that Jennifer is a brilliant teacher, but Amanda has a fragile perception of herself and has not received great evaluations each year, so her insecurity is even more heightened. She is simply jealous of Jennifer's skill-set, but this should not matter since they are both there to help their students, after all. This is certainly an "Amanda problem" when you read more below.

One day, Jennifer needed to take a personal day in order to drive her mother to the hospital for her cancer treatment. While she was absent from the classroom, Amanda took over and ran Jennifer's math class for the day. While some students were struggling to grasp the review concept of the Pythagorean Theorem, Amanda uttered to the class, "Well, you didn't do it the right way because Ms. Galant moved too quickly and never showed you how to break things down. I will show you the *right way* to look at this problem." Students may perceive Ms. Galant to be less than expert in what she does. It has the potential to turn off the students to math and not provide them with as much faith in the skills of their teacher as before. This kind of crap needs to stop and, yet, it happens often.

Crap-Talking Type 2: Behind their Backs

Randy, a technology teacher in Bronx, New York, is fed up with Jim, a new technology teacher who works in the same school where the students absolutely love him. Randy has been assigned to mentor Jim and has been very frustrated with Jim's lack of lesson planning and preparation of materials and resources. Randy often says nasty things to other teachers about Jim behind his back because he wants him gone. Behind-the-back tactics often make it to the forefront when the subject finally finds out about it, anyway. Randy doesn't want to deal with Jim any longer, so instead of trying to mentor him a bit longer or getting additional support, he just badmouths him time and time again. Jim transferred to a new school once he learned about the crap campaign against him, so Randy got what he wanted. But now students are left with a substitute teacher until the school can find another replacement in an already bleak pool of candidates.

Both types of crap are toxic to the professional environment and can have devastating impacts on student well-being and achievement. Even an innocent comment thrusted upon your students telling them that "they should have learned this from last year's teacher" can do damage to the culture.

According to a brief survey that I ran last year about crap-talking, 846 teachers out of 1,110 responded that "speaking negatively about colleagues in the workplace" (a.k.a. talking "crap") is a problem, so stop talking "crap" about other teachers. If you are one of the good ones who does not engage in this type of terrible behavior have courageous conversations and be a voice of integrity. Even though it may feel awkward, in the long run, halting toxic conversations for that of student focused success will always net respect. At a minimum you may generate discussion and personal reflection that shifts the energy from toxic to dynamic off-the-charts achievement.

Now, go ahead and photocopy this chapter and place it in the mailbox of a teacher you know who talks crap about others. Now THAT is a real behind-the-back tactic that might generate some discussion or even some personal reflection.

Dr. Rick Jetter is a co-founder of Pushing Boundaries Consulting, LLC; author of 9 books for educators, speaker, trainer and Asst. Head of Schools at Western NY Maritime Charter School in Buffalo, NY. Rick is also ranked #17 in the World's Top 30 Global Gurus in Education for 2021.

Stop Backstabbing Colleagues
MENA HILL

Rick presented a realistic and boundary-pushing chapter about crap-talking. Sometimes a courageous conversation nets positive change, while other times it ramps up passive aggressiveness in some colleagues. Sometimes, deescalating a situation just isn't in the cards and your colleague will skip passive aggressiveness altogether and move straight for a metaphorical jab in the back!

Working with others is challenging. Individuals in any work environment show up with a variety of experiences, values and identities. Not only are we expected to get to know our students and their families, but we are also tasked with getting to know our colleagues. Sometimes getting to know and relating to your colleagues can be a challenging job because of time limitations or immediate differences. In order to become five-star synergistic schools that impact students, teachers must learn how to best work together to effectively meet organizational goals and support the development and growth of students.

Blindsided by a Backstabber

With so many different personalities, I am sure you have seen both functional and dysfunctional teams within your own experience. Backstabbing within relationships is, unfortunately, something that many of us have dealt with in our careers. Consider the following story:

Jan, an elementary school teacher, just got promoted to a new grade level. She was identified as a teacher leader and was training to take on some leadership responsibilities for the following school year. Jan worked closely with the grade level team leader, Sara, to understand the ins and outs of leadership and the expectations of that grade level role within her school. They developed a positive working relationship where Jan felt like she had someone in her corner she could trust and depend on.

At one point in the school year, Sara invited Jan to have lunch. Within twenty minutes of dining, the casual chatting took a strange turn. Sara announced, "Okay, now we are going to do some professional development." Sara began to list all of the things Jan needed to improve on to become a better leader. Under the impression that they were both just having a casual lunch, Jan was completely caught off guard. Trying to maintain professionalism and not wanting to compromise her potential leadership opportunity, Jan lowered her eyes, took notes and kept quiet. Jan felt embarrassed, exposed and violated by the intensity of what Sara was telling her. Jan left that lunch feeling as though her relationship was now different with Sara and that future conversations may have some sort of strings attached. Jan did not say anything and continued to partner with Sara. Throughout the year, little moments like that continued to happen between Jan and Sara, but Jan was still slated to become the grade level team leader the following school year.

Later that year, there was a team meeting with administration. The meeting began with a haughty speech from Sara talking about the importance of professionalism, leadership and poise. The principal then chimed in, "With that said, we have decided that Jan will NOT be our team leader for the following school year." The words burned into Jan's ears. "WHAT? Where did this come from?" Out of nowhere, without any indication that she was performing poorly, other than that odd lunch date and brief offhand remarks, Jan was blindsided. Stunned, Jan attempted to save face and hide her hurt and shock with a fake smile on her face. That was that. The meeting was over and Jan was broken. She had no idea as to why that decision was made or what she could have done differently. Little did she know that Sara was running a backstabbing brigade behind her back the entire time.

217

A Violation of Trust

This story illustrates multiple layers of backstabbing. There was a violation of trust and a faulty sense of self that was set up by Sara so she could promote herself and keep someone down. Actions and words that result in backstabbing your friend or colleague ruin relationships, forever. It causes a ripple within the working relationship that cannot be repaired and it permeates throughout the school, simultaneously. It is imperative that we do not allow ourselves to stoop to the self-promoting, power hungry levels of backstabbers like Sara. Backstabbing only promotes dysfunction for teams and produces dreadful outcomes. There is no place for backstabbing within five-star synergistic schools.

Backstabbing Can Happen Anytime, Anywhere

Reflect on this situation and ask yourself, "Am I a Jan or a Sara?" Recognize who is in your corner. Learn how to identify the self-serving, self-promoting, ladder climbing and power-hungry people within your organization. Have a game plan to extend professionalism with boundaries. Advocate for yourself. Identify your intentions, goals and the things you need to be successful. Establish professional boundaries. Develop awareness to consider how your actions and words impact others. Align your thoughts, beliefs and feelings with your actions. Be open to growth, but ALWAYS be true to yourself.

Jan left that school at the end of the year feeling that she was not supported or cared for as a person or professional. Backstabbing can happen at any moment and at any level. Be aware that backstabbing exists and one of the best ways to curb backstabbing is to have open conversations about it as a staff. Backstabbing has consequences and students suffer, sometimes directly or indirectly even while careers suffer for the adults involved. Backstabbing needs to stop and you can be part of the plan to eradicate backstabbing at your five-star school.

Mena Hill serves as a Curriculum and Instruction Coach for Lawrence Public Schools in Lawrence, Kansas. She is also a doctoral candidate at the University of North Dakota. Her main professional goal is to partner with educators to support personal growth and transformation of their practice.

Stop Comparing Yourself to Other Teachers

JAMES WHITFIELD, Ed.D.

Teaching is an extremely complex and multifaceted profession. While there may be some very solid educator preparation programs out there, there is nothing quite like stepping into your own classroom for the first time. All the emails, lesson plans and scenarios that played out so well during your coursework might not pan out the same way once you're in the thick of it.

When you are handed a set of keys to your own classroom and it becomes real, you feel a rush of responsibilities, such as:

Real students.

Real families.

Real colleagues.

Real supervisors.

Real lesson plans.

Real IEPs.

Real responsibilities.

I have such deep and profound respect for the work educators do each day. Over the course of my career as a teacher, administrator and educational consultant, I have been in hundreds of classrooms. Each with its own unique vibe and character. It is quite fascinating to experience.

Comparisons Sow Seeds of Envy

Day-in and day-out, teachers straight up perform magic in their classrooms. Yet, so often those magicians don't seem to quite understand just how amazing they are or how much of a difference they make each day. I could share so many examples of how this is represented in our schools. Teachers, who do so much to go above and beyond for their students, get caught up in the comparison game, diminishing the work they do in relation to someone else, which is a dangerous way to live.

I was visiting a school I had been coaching in south Texas. This school was all too familiar to me, almost an identical school to the one where I was a principal. The school had landed itself on one of those statewide lists of schools that "needed improvement." Any time I went on a coaching visit there, I would sit in my car in front of the school for a few minutes and observe the start of the day. While it doesn't necessarily paint the entire story, you can tell a lot about what is going on inside the school by watching students enter the school building in the morning. Inside, I found Mrs. King.

Everyone Knows Mrs. King in Room 310

Mrs. King knew everyone. The music in her classroom was pumpin'. She engaged students with hugs, high-fives and special handshakes. I watched students flow into the building and there wasn't a second that this teacher wasn't smiling, grooving and engaged with, not only students, but adults who entered the building too. I had to meet this person.

The school bell rang and that was my cue to enter the building, where I was to meet briefly with the campus principal before starting my day observing classrooms. After discussing the goals for the day and areas administration wanted me to observe, I asked "Who was the teacher greeting all those folks this morning and busting out the music?"

The principal smiled. "Oh, she's been here a while. That's Mrs. King. EVERYONE knows Mrs. King!"

"What does Mrs. King teach?" I asked.

"8th grade science" the principal said.

"Does she have a class right now?"

"Yes sir! She's in room 310."

I made my way up the 3 flights of stairs, caught my breath and headed to room 310 frantically.

When I arrived, I witnessed poetry in motion. The flow, the energy, the authenticity, the rigor, the relationships, the joy, you name it, this class had it. There were moments of redirection, moments where things didn't go as planned and Mrs. King had to rewind and run it back, but as the bell rang I looked at my watch and couldn't believe I had spent the entire class period in this classroom. She was amazing. Absolutely amazing!

The other classrooms were not as dynamic as Mrs. King's classroom. She had a special sauce–a talent that I've never seen before. Yet, comparing each of the other teachers to Mrs. King would be unfair. So many talented teachers who were doing great things had their own styles. Yes, Mrs. King was one of a kind, but that is OK. No one can truly be someone else.

Own It

While I was meeting with a different teacher at that school, she went to great lengths to pick herself apart and compare herself to whom she was not: Mrs. King.

I finally had to tell her "Young lady, you've got to stop! You know that person you have in your life that, no matter what you say or do, they have something better to say, you know, that one-upper friend?" A huge smile graced her face and she chuckled "Yes, I've got a few of those kind of friends!"

"You are being that person right now–to yourself." I gently said. "No matter what shine you have going on, you are constantly devaluing that because of what someone down the hall does. What does that have to do with you? You are a phenomenal teacher, staff member and community member, so just own it!" She perked up a bit and we continued our discussion before I had to visit with another teacher.

You Are Uniquely You

We have met people just like Mrs. King who, while they are exceptional teachers, might make us feel that we are inferior because we beat ourselves up over what we think we should be like. You are uniquely you. One of my mentors once told me "James, don't get caught up trying to be someone you're not or you'll be chasing something that is unattainable."

Comparison is the thief of joy. The more you try to measure up to others, the more you will miss what is right in front of you: your own greatness.

Dr. James Whitfield is an educator and national speaker based in Hurst, Texas.

Stop Ignoring Your Own Biases

DONNA SMILEY

Differences in ideologies often impact how teachers interact with students, colleagues and families. On any given day, situations arise in our schools and in haste we make decisions favoring one thing over something else. Unknowingly, these quick decisions can lead to making great errors. Without realizing it, educators may even display varying forms of bias when engaging in conversations with others. To quickly solve a problem and move on, we let our personal biases influence quick decisions that later could be considered unfair or inequitable. To ensure that we do not fall into the bias trap, we must stop ignoring our own biases and figure out the root cause of our beliefs. Our individual ideologies are formed and developed over time based on life experiences and backgrounds; yet, we must be willing to consider other's perspectives in order to grow impartial and deliver equality in what we do.

Bias Ownership

There can be no true self-discovery if there is a failure to acknowledge and understand how being biased affects our thoughts and actions. Each day provides us with an opportunity to take ownership over our own self-reflection and mirror into ourselves. Nothing constrains the ability of a teacher to reach the highest heights of fulfillment quite like a heaping dose of denial. When teachers pretend that there is no such thing as bias, they restrict the flow of personal and professional development. It is important to discuss the word "bias," especially if you are determined to prevent your own bias from seeping into your own decision-making or how you treat your students.

No matter how covert you are, your body language reveals a lot about your beliefs. If you have researched your own mental concepts and embraced why there are differences, you are one step closer to connecting with the fact that owning your bias does not make you a bad teacher. Teachers must use their position to model how we can all embrace the topic of bias but renounce the negative energy which flows with its presence.

Possessing the willingness to take ownership of personal bias is a great display of power, not weakness.

Teachers cannot avoid engaging in difficult conversations just because they breed discomfort. Teaching should provide opportunities for authentic communication governed by an understanding of self-motivation. It is an adequate understanding of your belief system and a willingness to place bias in its proper perspective that can push individuals into better places. A teacher can never say that their decisions are not made with some level of bias. Once those biases are pulled out into the open, a greater level of scrutiny can take place. Great levels of truth are enjoyed when specific patterns that evoke bias are stripped of their power.

Biases can range from gender and racial biases to size and weight biases to cognitive biases. The list of biases run deep and wide. What is most important to understand is that if we make decisions and consider people using such labels, then our own biases drive our perceptions rather than possess a limitless unbiased view of what each person can ultimately become. If an obese person is dismissed by us as someone who just simply overeats, then we are missing the mark about that person's possible reality of having health conditions, such as diabetes. If a student who was suspended from school is labeled as "bad," then our bias over the incident that led to the suspension does not afford that student a chance to be restored with any kind of future hope.

Confronting my own biases allowed me to ask, "What are my students capable of when I intentionally remove my own bias out of the situation and view them through the lens of possibility?" Those who dare to plunge into this type of internal scrutiny are destined to thrive. Owning your own biases creates opportunities and leads to solutions, resolutions and dynamic off-the-charts achievement despite the size of the problem.

Donna Smiley is a 20 year veteran in the field of education. She currently serves as a high school administrator in Hoover, Alabama. Donna is also the mother of two awesome children and a strong advocate for supporting cultural competency in all areas of education.

Stop Responding Emotionally to Complex Problems

KAREN CASWELL

"When you react, you are giving away your power. When you respond, you are staying in control of yourself."
–Bob Proctor

I regretted the sarcastic tone the instant the words came out of my mouth. The accompanying sigh, eye roll, turning on my heels and walking away in anger sealed my fate too. What I am thinking or feeling tends to be written all over my face. I am sure my exasperated expression was the icing on the cake for the person who was abruptly left with a view of my retreating back. Deep inside, I knew I was reacting emotionally to the situation that I found myself in; yet, I felt unable to control my behavior. I was enslaved by my emotions.

As educators, our core business involves interacting with others daily. Inevitably, within the myriad of situations we face, issues will arise. Some are quite simple to resolve, but the issues we encounter in education are becoming increasingly complex and are influenced by a wide range of factors. It is easy to become overwhelmed and there are many people, words, opinions, or situations that may provoke an intense and excessive emotional reaction within us. It is always a choice how respond to these scenarios or whether we emotionally react to them.

Emotional Triggers Enslave Us

Everyone, to some extent, is a slave to their emotional reactions. For the past few years, I have struggled with becoming aware of my emotional triggers and it has been a long journey to divert such reactions. With a learning curve also comes failings along the way. I tend to react with less grace than I would like. I am driven by emotions which can overwhelm me and make it difficult for me to express myself articulately. Often, the size of my reaction does not match the size of the problem or I react to one aspect of a complex issue without being able to see the big picture. Over time, the realization dawned on me that I needed to put in the effort in exploring my emotional triggers. The more aware I am of my emotional triggers, the less likely I will be ruled or enslaved by these stormy forces within me.

Emotional triggers can include people, words, opinions, or situations that provoke an intense and excessive emotional reaction within us. Common emotions that we experience while being triggered include anger, rage, sadness and fear. Depending on our beliefs, values and earlier life experiences, virtually anything can trigger us, such as the tone of voice, a type of person, a particular viewpoint, or even a single word that we loathe. Psychologists say we suffer from emotional triggers for three main reasons: opposing beliefs and values, trauma and ego preservation.

The Ego of Our Self

When our egos are challenged or hurt by others, we are prone to becoming immediately triggered. Personally, I have identified that I am triggered by ego preservation. The ego is the sense of self we carry around, composed of thoughts, memories, cultural values, assumptions and belief structures that we have developed in order to fit into society.

We all possess ego, and its primary purpose is to protect us by developing elaborate "self-protection" systems in the form of beliefs, ideals, desires, habits and addictions. As a people pleaser whose greatest armor is perfectionism, I am often triggered when my sense of self is damaged. I vividly recall the feeling of shame that washes over me when I believe I have disappointed others. A tingling sensation surges throughout my body as a result of a spike in cortisol and adrenaline. My heart races and I become short of breath. My stomach clenches and I feel physically ill. My face becomes flushed and I hang my head, hunch my shoulders and I shrink in order to take up less space. On the flip-side, this is also a desperate feeling of defensiveness that hijacks my rationality when I feel I have been rejected, unfairly treated or judged as unworthy. The moments when I am at my most vulnerable and exposed are those when my need for fairness, acceptance and being valued are not met—and this is when I am most likely to react *emotionally*. If I were to catalog all the occasions when I wish I had responded intentionally instead of reacting, the list would be incredibly lengthy.

When Our Needs are Not Met

Perhaps being emotionally triggered always goes back to not having one or more of our deepest needs or desires met. It is vital to take time to think about which needs or desires are being threatened: acceptance, autonomy, attention, love, safety, fun, consistency, respect, peacefulness, and predictability. We want to be liked, feel needed, be right, feel valued, be treated fairly and have some sort of control over our situations. When we reflect on the resurfacing of our unmet needs or desires that are constantly reappearing, we can be more in touch with how we respond versus how we react to something. Unfortunately, what makes it hard to refrain from responding emotionally is that our brains have evolved to react (not respond) to stressful interactions in ways that are unproductive.

Regulating Hijacked Emotions

When we are hijacked by our emotions, we tend to personalize things, make the other person's behavior about us (when in all likelihood it might have nothing to do with us) and focus on the problem. Becoming aware of our body, thoughts, unmet needs and desires and certain people or situations that set us off will help to prevent us from acting out the next time we are in a fiery situation.

When we are not aware of our emotional triggers, let alone how to handle them, our lives follow damaging paths. Identifying our emotional triggers is vital because without bringing to consciousness what provokes extreme responses, we will be a puppet where our emotions constantly control the strings. Relationships with colleagues and supervisors will be turbulent or sabotaged, relationships with students and families could be strained or ruined and our days at school will be a never-ending rollercoaster of discomfort, suffering and pain.

But what happens once we have already responded with a knee-jerk response because we were emotionally hijacked by someone or something? There are plenty self-regulating strategies we can implement when hijacked in mid-flight with no parachute in hand. Even in this extreme emotional situation, you have the power to think on your feet and take charge of your emotions. You may want to consider these self-regulating tips.

Breathe

Remove your attention from the person or situation and focus on your breath. Focusing on breathing in and out for a few minutes can make a world of difference. If your attention goes back to the triggering person or situation, pull your attention back to your breathing since it is always there. Such focus is a common form of mindfulness.

Go to a Different Space

Take a break. Remove yourself from the situation. Walk away for five minutes and cool down. If you are speaking with someone, excuse yourself temporarily and say that you need to go to the bathroom or someplace else. Return when you are feeling more centered and calmer. If possible, delay a reply, especially to emails. Take time to compose yourself and your response.

Talk to Yourself

Ask yourself why you are being triggered. Our emotional triggers have a way of blinding us, so to counteract that, be curious. Ask yourself, "Why am I feeling so sad/angry/anxious?" Understanding why you are being triggered will help you to regain a sense of calmness, self-awareness and control.

Focus on What You Can Control

Think of at least one thing that you can do on your own (either in the moment or at a later time) in order to have control over preventing your worst-case scenario. Try to see the other person's behavior as originating from their own limitations or from a "benefit of the doubt" explanation of their motivations.

Delay Your Emotions

Do not bypass your feelings, but delay acting on them, either. Repressing or trying to "control" your feelings is not the answer; however, you can delay your emotions. For instance, if you are feeling enraged by someone, instead of exploding at them, consciously set those feelings aside to experience and unleash later in a healthy way, such as heading out for an intense emotion fueled workout. Whatever the case, be incredibly careful of repressing your emotions. There is a fine line between consciously delaying your emotions and unconsciously suppressing them. This is why it's so important to practice self-awareness.

Education is already an incredibly emotionally challenging and complex landscape to navigate without also reacting out of anger, jealousy, embarrassment and other emotions that can control our lives if we permit them to. Knowing your emotional triggers can help you avoid the problems in the first place. Responding intentionally will enable us to turn negatives into positives, communicate and connect with others positively and effectively and experience emotional fulfilment. So, stop responding to everything emotionally. We are higher level beings with the intelligence to self-regulate.

Karen Caswell is a grade 4 teacher and Collegial Coach and Beginning Teacher Mentor at a primary school on the Gold Coast, in Queensland, Australia. She has also worked as a Learning Support Teacher, Special Education Teacher-In-Charge, Instructional Coach and Head of Curriculum.

Stop Apologizing for Being a Teacher

LEE ARAOZ

Teaching is not just a job; it is a calling, a purpose, a career some have dreamed of since they were young and, in some cases, a serendipitous moment that chose us. So, why do many teachers find themselves apologizing for who they are and the noble profession that they have chosen?

Many educators are made to feel guilty about having summers off. Friends and neighbors say things like, "You're a teacher? Having all that time off must be amazing. There are only 184 teaching days! You only have to work half the year!" These critics do not realize nor value the time and dedication teachers put into their jobs. The amount of paperwork can be daunting. Other jobs end when the clock strikes 5:00, but teachers' jobs just get started after hours. Teachers take the demands of their job in stride because we realize exactly how important what we do is. So why do some apologize or respond to others that they are *just* a teacher? The word "just" deprofessionalizes any profession. I am *just* a teacher. I am *just* a Supreme Court judge.

Teachers Seek the Best Possible Outcomes

A dynamic and effective teacher modifies and personalizes instruction for each student and works to uncover what motivates and engages every student. Teachers are chameleon-like in their educational approaches as they adapt to every situation to ensure the best possible outcome. During any typical day, a teacher may morph into a cheerleader, taskmaster, negotiator, mediator, detective, parent, or even a stand-up comedian. With artistry and precision, teachers raise the level of concern in their classrooms and motivate students to demonstrate deep and rigorous thinking; yet, we distill our importance by telling others that we are *just* teachers.

Teachers Never Stop Learning

Teachers are passionate about their profession and most intentionally seek to improve upon and add to their pedagogical repertoire on a daily basis. The best teachers are also the best learners and they strive to learn as much as they can about education in the 21st century. So, the next time that someone tries to make you feel bad for having more time off than the average worker, take a deep breath and remind yourself that you gave each student your "all" last year.

Out of every profession in the world, teaching is the one profession that creates all other professions. What happens or does not happen in the classroom can affect students in the short and long term, both inside and outside of your classroom. Teachers are one of the very few professionals who must be able to triage the needs of each student, monitor and adjust their instruction in real-time, all while promoting a safe learning environment. We are responsible for not only highly effective academic instruction but also the social-emotional well-being and interpersonal relationships of those we work hard to mold and influence for life after graduation. Teachers are people strengtheners and there is no other profession on the planet like teaching. We are not *just* teachers. Perhaps, everyone else *just* has a different career and are not fortunate enough to be one of us?

Lee Araoz is the Director of Technology and Learning Analytics at East Rockaway Schools, in Nassau County, New York. He has over 30 years of experience working with elementary, middle and high school students, teachers and administrators. As a national speaker, director, coordinator and classroom teacher, Lee infuses cutting-edge educational technology into the already rigorous curriculum to amplify and enhance learning.

STOP Making Everything About You

This Nonsense Prevents Dynamic Off-the-Charts Achievement

Stop Thinking on a Small, Local Scale

ELISSA GOOD SMITH, Ph.D.

We love thinking that we are special, that our school is unique and that our students are one in a million. However, viewing education through this lens is limiting our ability to create dynamic, off-the-chart thriving communities. We are not able to fully support our colleagues, our students and their families when we remain in the four walls of our own classrooms. Five-star classrooms and schools think big, dream big and partner strategically to elevate their success on a bigger networking and impact scale.

Cultivating Quality Relationships

Professional learning networks and professional learning communities (PLNs and PLCs) have continued to gain value over the past decade in education, especially with an increased use of technology as a connective tool. They exist in a spectrum and regardless of where you are located, there is room to improve or increase how you work with others. In *Phi Delta Kappan* (2018), Andy Hargreaves and Michael O'Connor explain that the most successful and sustainable efforts draw on both expert knowledge and strong collegial relationships, creating what the authors call collaborative professionalism. Michael Siciliano (2016) notes in *AERA* that simply collecting social connections will not yield much improvement, though; a focus must be on cultivating quality relationships.

Expand Your Sphere of Influence

Big-minded educators are the ones that set out and plan for far-reaching audacious goals. I am not suggesting that synergy is produced merely by having big audacious goals but rather, the bigger you plan, the bigger you impact. Consider expanding your sphere of connection through networking both inside and outside of education, inside and outside of your district and state. Seeking out professionals who have expertise to offer or another point of view aimed at success is high added value. When you connect and collaborate for the purpose of dynamic achievement scope of efficacy broadens and synergy takes root. Seek out educators and professionals with exceptional drive and success in their respective fields that will influence the improvement of community impact. Consider STEM professionals, local businesses, authors, or classrooms across the globe that can provide ideas and feedback to current challenges. Magnetic and synergistic educators possess the ability to take a step back and absorb the big picture (instead of thinking on a small, local scale). Innovators and influencers shed their narrowed minded view of proximity and expand their impact to their entire district, region, state, country or global landscape.

The Benefit of Working in Industry before Teaching

Jesse, a teacher in Virginia, transitioned from being an occupational therapist in a hospital setting to early intervention OT while moving across the state. She initially felt that her professional connections were focused on rehabilitation and eldercare and could not help with lesson planning and IEP goal support. While her former colleagues may not have specialized in three-year-old pre-K pedagogy, they were able to build connections through empathy and compassion with a strength-based approach. Jesse easily picked up on lesson planning with support from her new colleagues while at the same time was able to share customer service and strategies that built on dignity and strength. Industry practices are high added value to new solutions to our classrooms. Jesse is now active in multiple online groups, a subscriber to an online forum and collaborates with her new hire group regularly. A victory took place.

Content Singletons Seek Out Support

Kelly from Iowa is a singleton teacher in a rural school, where she is the only person teaching business: "When you're in a community that does not have access to many local businesses and you're the only business teacher, it's certainly not easy," she shared. If you sit around and only teach what is on the syllabus that you inherited from your predecessor and you're not open to new ideas and updates, your students aren't getting what they deserve. It is on us, as educators, to build professional relationships to strengthen our students' learning." Danette Parsley (2018) shared additional tips for building a successful rural network, written about in *American Educator*, including investing time in planning your group, recruiting with care and considering ways to manage growth. Kelly's extension of her career and craft created a wider audience for support and assistance when local interests were not there for her. Another victory took place.

Leadership Roles can Extend Far beyond the Walls of their School

Teri, from New York, is a literacy specialist who has embraced the science of reading and recently shifted into a leadership role as an instructional coach. She was surrounded by colleagues who were not trained and experienced in academic research focused on high impact instructional best practices. She was not as confident in coaching and supporting teachers as she would like to be and was invested in learning and growing. Teri attended an national conference and was surrounded by professionals who were eager to share evidence based best practices that were a hit within their own grade level, buildings and districts. That very same national convention brought in thousands of colleagues from all over the world that were invested in effective instruction. They too were seeking connections to both learn and share dynamic achievements happening around the globe. The conference led to creating an online community of like-minded professionals whose mission was to support educators with the science of reading instruction through brain-based research. Another victory took place.

Advocating and Persevering as a Superintendent

Ron, a superintendent of a school district outside Chicago and spanning a large geographic area, struggled with ensuring students had access to internet during a recent closure. Broadband and Wi-Fi were not available in multiple areas within the district. He attempted to call digital Wi-Fi companies to seek out a solution to the deficiencies in broadband access among his students. After sharing frustrations with neighboring districts, the superintendents collaborated to write a letter to the editor of a local newspaper and began using their connections to reach out to politicians and state level and national advocacy groups to leverage their voices as a cohesive group. Another victory took place.

Climbing to a 40,000-foot aerial view of your current situation is not always easy. It is not practical to think you can immediately or drastically impact a challenge without support. Stepping back or climbing higher offers another vantage point and perspective to your current situation. If you are focused on your personal classroom, look at your grade level team. If you are focused on your building, what is happening in your neighboring school districts? If you already work with a local consortium of schools, is there a state or regional team you could reach out to for more collaboration?

You are not limited by your demographic. Connect with other schools in the same demographic, a different demographic, with similar values or issues. Sometimes the same demographic is facing the same challenge and stuck in a rut too and the collaboration may net a new solution. Or a connection with a school completely different from you may have protocols, strategies, and community solutions that you might not have otherwise considered. Network and connections both inside and outside education are ahigh added value. Start by making a list of what you care about within your own classroom or building. What are the things that make you passionate about where you teach? What are the specific improvement opportunities that your classroom or school should focus on?

Once you have your list of values and issues, set out to find your team! The easiest way to do this is to start with social media platforms. Search social media groups based on your keyword list. Keep a list of hashtags that align with what you care about and follow them like breadcrumbs to lead you to others searching for and sharing information. You can also reach out to your regional and national professional associations and ask for support to build collegial connections.

There is more to connecting than getting what you need. Collaboration is a two-way street. When you join an online community, be sure to reply to help others, not just ask a question and demand others do the heavy lifting for solving a problem for you. Give and take and then give some more wisdom. Offer to mentor a new teacher within your school or through a professional organization. Consider reaching out to your alma mater to see if you can support their network of professionals.

Finally, if you cannot find what you're looking for, then be brave and start your own group! Others will thank you for filling the gap. Remember, the only boundaries that prevent you from moving forward are the ones that you set up, yourself. Stop looking through a microscope and start looking through a telescope if you are in pursuit of dynamic off-the-charts achievement.

Dr. Elissa Good Smith is a Pre-K-6 Principal at Lyndonville Central School and served as an Educator Voice Policy Fellow. She currently sits on the Board of Directors for the Rural Schools Association and NYS Pre-K-3rd grade Administrators Association. She is an avid grant writer with nearly 20 years of experience teaching primary through college level students.

Stop Planning PD that Isn't about Teaching & Learning

SHERRY ST. CLAIR

Several years ago, Mrs. Moffit reached out to me as a seasoned school administrator seeking specific leadership feedback on her efficacy as a principal. Mrs. Moffit was a highly reflective leader with high student achievement at the forefront of her personal goals. She had reached a point of frustration because her school was not showing the academic growth that she had hoped for. When she called me, she shared that she was seeking specific feedback on the effectiveness of her school's professional learning and development plan as well as their instructional coaching implementation. I was up to the challenge and excited to work with a principal who was so open and willing to take risks and make changes.

I remember the first day that I met Mrs. Moffit. She had a soothing and comforting demeanor and you could tell she was loved by her students and staff. She discussed all the goals she set for her teachers and students, the dozens of strategies she taught them in professional learning sessions and all the ideas she had ready to share with them. Despite all her support, she said, "The teachers are just not making the academic gains with their students."

Classroom Walkthrough Feedback

Through our hearty conversations I could tell that Mrs. Moffit was instructionally strong. She knew her stuff. She was passionate and caring and had an arsenal of high-quality ideas and strategies in her instructional learning and development tool belt. She shared with me a list of the classrooms and grade levels that we would be observing and provided a rundown of many of their strengths. The second list she shared with me was a list of trainings the teachers had received in the past two years: Kagan cooperative learning, depth of knowledge and questioning, the trauma informed classroom, writing impactful objectives, essential questions, brain breaks, STEM in literacy, second language learner strategies, partnering on IEPs, PLC cycles, school safety, Google classroom and so much more. The list was extensive and robust, and the expectations set forth by Mrs. Moffit were high.

With clipboards and forms in hand, we set out to visit classrooms in the K-5 elementary school. During our walkthroughs, I mentioned the sheer volume of strategies and expectations that had been placed on teachers. It was hard to know what to look for trending from one classroom to the next because the menu of expectations was so varied. Even though all the above topics were important to the art and science of teaching and relevant to this school staff, it was a lot to keep track of and implement effectively.

The Debrief

As we were walking back to her office, I turned toward Mrs. Moffit and said, "I noticed that your teachers are overwhelmed. With so many goals and ideas for them to embrace, are they able to effectively prioritize? Do you think this may be a reason that you aren't seeing the academic growth you had expected?" She paused for a moment and I could tell that she was really processing the classroom observations and replied, "I've always lived by high expectations and offered professional development and training support for teachers, but now that you say it, I can see how that might be overwhelming to them." We continued talking about the value of focusing deeply on one overarching goal at a time and connecting classroom strategies and expectations to their school's core beliefs. What was happening was that the teachers were attempting to please their boss but were losing sight on why they were implementing so many strategies in the first place.

For professional learning and development to be effective, it must not only be intentional, but also aligned with the school's core beliefs or overall vision which should be highly focused on teaching and learning. When professional learning and development is not attached to a core belief or overall goal, then it may just become a checklist of things to do. When professional learning and development is intentional, focused and rolled out in a methodical pace, it provides time for teachers to practice, grapple and achieve dynamic synergistic five-star success focused on the art and science of teaching.

Evidence Based Professional Learning and Development

Merely throwing a new strategy or tool at a teacher is not necessarily always focused on teaching and learning. Giving teachers only one week to practice a new strategy, without also checking in with them to hear how they have progressed and providing coaching support and feedback, the professional learning will not become sustainable nor automatic.

One of the primary goals of professional learning is to unlock collective teacher efficacy (CTE). Studying the effect sizes of programming or instructional topics that either support or prohibit powerful learning, John Hattie defines CTE as, "The collective belief of teachers in their ability to positively affect students' [learning and achievement]." But, most importantly, he adds that it must also include "the evidence of impact."

Four Practices to Optimize Professional Learning and Development

When learning organizations intentionally infuse the following best practices, they establish professional learning that optimizes teaching, learning and development through collective teacher efficacy.

1. Establish a Growth Mindset Culture

Part of a growth mindset—and a true learning organization—is a culture that welcomes and encourages taking risks in the name of growth. Educators must feel safe making mistakes and supported in learning from them. Fear is antithetical to both a learning organization and growth.

2. Create a Shared Vision and Goals

In order to achieve this, a school first needs a vision. A true learning organization will have an identified vision that explicitly pertains to student learning and success.

3. Establish Strategic Intentional Systems

Team learning draws its strength from the trusting relationships and sense of accountability among team members. It is optimized when teachers observe each other, exchange respectful feedback and share resources. In addition to focusing only on high effect size strategies (aim for .4 or higher), all professional learning that takes place in the school should be strategic and related to targeted evidence-based instructional strategies.

4. Embrace Teacher Voice and Choice

Safeguarding intrinsic motivation demands that instructional leaders do not require teachers to focus on a new strategy or goal each week. Instead, it asks that instructional leaders create a safe space for teachers to struggle productively, make mistakes, fail, learn from their team members and ask for and receive help. A true learning organization acknowledges that teachers are learners, too, who also need time to process new information and access scaffolded support when needed.

Stop losing sight of what matters most: teaching, learning and dynamic off-the-charts student achievement. The days of hiring motivational speakers who will put on a show and make you feel good will simply lose their luster when they exit the stage and when there is nothing to implement in the classroom to raise student achievement. All students deserve a classroom of targeted growth.

Sherry St. Clair is president of Reflective Learning LLC and the author of: Coaching Redefined: A Guide to Leading Meaningful Instructional Growth. She coaches instructional leaders, globally, with the aim of helping administrators, coaches and teachers create the optimal learning environment for students.

Stop Teaching without Robust Lesson Plans
RAE HUGHART & BRYAN ZWEMKE, Ed.D.

Teaching is Like Running a Full Marathon

Ugh, do you hear that? It's 3:30 a.m. and your alarm woke you up in a tizzy. You've been preparing for this for eighteen long weeks. Bag packed, you drive into the city. You did not even need coffee this morning because the excitement for the day already has you energized enough. *This is the day of your first marathon.*

BRYAN

In 2014, I ran the Chicago marathon for the first time. I had set the goal for myself about a year prior to this date and had spent every moment of the week leading up trying to back out of what I had committed to: 26.2 miles around the city--was I crazy?

Just a few years earlier, I was proud of myself for carrying one of my children upstairs, after falling asleep on the couch, without disturbing them. I was a novice weekend warrior at best running some smaller events, but never a marathon. This race was going to be a bit more challenging.

The night before, I packed my bag.

Shoes . . . check.

Socks, you know the really good ones . . . check.

Hydration . . . check.

Shoes, socks, hydration . . . recheck!

I tend to recheck repeatedly, even though it sounds crazy. It is a habit similar to my ritualistic recheck of keys, wallet and cell phone before walking out of the door. I simply cannot run without those items. To be honest, it is the peace of mind that I require to set myself up for success.

239

Backward Design

I had been a novice runner for the past few years before that big day. But, I learned early on in my running career that I wouldn't have been able to reach this point without preparation. I used a training plan, relied on the experts and built a network of supporters to help me accomplish my goals in running.

While some of us may choose to label ourselves as runners and others may be comfortable with our coffee drinking connoisseur titles, many moments in life are crafted from planning and seeking a goal well before executing what we need to do in order to fulfill that goal. At the time, my marathon goal seemed so far out of reach, until I used backwards design in my running, just like I would in my classroom.

The backwards design, introduced by Grant Wiggins, is a simple but brilliant concept. You begin with a goal–or for many it's a class standard or target–and you work your way backwards. What small steps are needed to achieve the goal? For example, if you want students to understand how to add multi-digit integers, they must first understand the foundational components of number sense and addition. Every standard at every grade level has scaffolding requirements and those elements should then bleed into an educator's daily lesson plans.

But what would happen if we ignored the scaffolding needed and what if we didn't consider the end goal of our instruction and, instead, taught without a lesson plan or a unit? Well, wouldn't that be the same as the marathon early morning riser waking up the day of the race without having prepared for the big day? No lesson plans in teaching is equal to no training in running.

RAE

The Chicago marathon had its own segment on my favorite radio show. I listened to it on my way to school each morning. Every year, the radio hosts would call out to their network to find someone planning to run THE biggest race of the year, but had not prepared at all. Each year, the stories would get more and more ridiculous! I remember my jaw hitting the floor when they found someone who had not even bought their shoes yet for the race which was a mere two weeks away.

It is what it is?

"Are you worried about your lack of preparation at all?" the radio host asked.

"Eh," the contestant seemed to shrug, "It is what it is."

It is what it is? Really? You are going to attempt running 26.2 miles around the city of Chicago with an "It is what it is" attitude? Good luck buddy!

An attitude rooted in an "It is what it is" mindset may be fine when the repercussions of your actions do not affect others. For example, you missed your turn on the way to work, but you are already 10 minutes ahead of schedule. Eh, "It is what it is . . ." and I'll take the next turn and it will all work out. But what about when there are other components on the line or others' lives being affected?

Consider how an 11-year-old student will be influenced by their teachers. If that same student graduates high school and pursues a four year degree, they will enter the workforce about 11 years after their middle school class concludes. The world can shift in a blink of an eye and, yet, educators choose to take on the impossible task of preparing students for a world they cannot even dream of because teachers understand the power behind providing every student the foundation of a strong education that can make a difference in our world. Therefore, we must choose to prepare our students with both content skills and adaptive skills.

In many cases, teachers are severely overlooked, mistreated and misunderstood. Teachers are important. Teachers deserve to be respected. Teachers have powerful jobs to shape the minds of future generations. So, how can teachers move throughout this enormous responsibility with an "It is what it is" approach?

Your students need you to think ahead. Make a plan, set your alarm and pack a bag just as marathon runners do, because for teachers, every day is race day. Every moment of instruction matters. Every finish line is another student's future success being celebrated by roaring crowds. This work matters. Stop teaching without planning.

Creating lesson plans for your class does not mean you are formally typing up the well-documented template you were handed in college. Rather, you simply need to have a method to understand where you want your students to be headed and the type of information you need to plan to get there.

Five Questions to Eliminate an "It is what it is" Attitude

Consider these 5 questions when crafting your next lesson plan to stop teaching with an "it is what it is" attitude:

What is Your End Goal?

Every moment of planning must begin by knowing where you want to end. Therefore, consider your standard, target, or final assessment to determine what your finish line looks like. Then, build your steps backward. In utilizing this practice, you can have the confidence that your daily instruction is setting up your students for a successful end point, either by meeting a grade level state standard and/or mastering an essential skill.

Who Is Your Audience?

Knowing your audience is an essential element to your lesson plan puzzle. Building relationships with your students to best understand their needs and background information is essential for daily instruction. The background of your students who enter your classroom will act as the foundational pillars of your future instruction. Therefore, get to know your audience and use that information to craft not only the way you design a lesson but also what elements you utilize to engage your learners. Surveys, pre-tests and interest inventories are key elements in knowing your audience. Review both the qualitative data you have learned about your students and the quantitative data you have access to. Both are loaded with information about your students and should be used in designing instruction. You cannot teach those you do not truly know just as you cannot run in a race that you have no clue about the terrain that will be beneath your feet.

Where Can You Differentiate?

Consider the areas that you can add dimension and differentiation for your students. While you cannot differentiate for students until you know what students truly know and what skills they already have, do not assume what you think your students know or can do. This may be as simple as providing different modalities of instruction to adopting a fully mastery driven approach with The Grid Method. Either way, get thinking about how you can differentiate for each individual learner.

How Can You Gather Feedback?

Without intentional feedback, your lesson plan will always be a flop. So, craft intentional moments in your lesson plan to not only provide students feedback on their understanding, but also allow for students to share feedback with you. Why? Because learning is fluid and conversational.

Feedback can be gathered from multiple methods, but should not be limited to formative assessments, performance assessments and summative assessments. Open-ended questions beyond recall can be given to small groups of students can garner an understanding of a student's skillset. Consider scaffolding questions using Webb's DOK and then allow for the conversation to evolve. No one said providing and gathering feedback would be easy, but it will level up any lesson plan.

Where is the Equity of Voice?

The teacher and students must share the space in the room to allow for equity of voice. Teachers deserve to not be the only voice in the learning space and they also deserve to not be the only leader in the room. Allow your students to take hold of their environment and possess ownership in the success of your classroom. Equity of voice goes beyond how much time a teacher or student is speaking.

Students should model being leaders for one another as well as advocating for needs daily. Building a classroom community is part of a larger comprehensive plan that puts the student at the center of the room. A student should be able to explain why they are learning the skill and what the implications are to future learning.

Learning is a two-way street, and you should not be the only driver on the road. Whether you are a runner or a professional couch potato, parallels can be drawn to teaching as every person sets the sights on something bigger for themselves. The preparation for the large event is the culmination of a series of smaller events. Great pain would come to the untrained marathon runner with lasting injuries. Stop teaching without plans because you and your students deserve better. The network that you plan with, the plan you follow and the ability to adjust the plan along the way ultimately determines the outcome.

Rae Hughart is a middle level math educator in Illinois, the Chief Marketing Officer for the Teach Better Team, Vice President of the Association of Illinois Middle Grade Schools, host of "Teach Better Talk" Podcast and author of Teachers Deserve It and Teach Better. After being inducted into The Illinois State University Hall of Fame in 2017, Rae was awarded the 2018 First Place Henry Ford Teacher Innovator Award for her innovative educational impact through mastery learning and community engagement strategies.

Dr. Bryan Zwemke is an instructional leader serving as a high school principal focusing on student voice and agency. Bryan earned his doctoral degree at Aurora University and is dedicated to supporting school-wide social media communication campaigns.

Stop Treating Art, Music & Physical Education as Inferior Subjects
SYNDEE MALEK

So, I get it. I really do. As a former elementary teacher, I looked forward to my 40 minute "prep" period (code in my head for a "break") everyday! I mean, some days I lived for them just to make it through.

I planned my minutes at the copy machine, minutes to grab coffee, minutes to stop in the office to pick up my mail and those treasured minutes in the restroom. These were just a few of the things I did while my students were in art, music, physical education or other "special area" or "activity" classes. Back in the day when we filled out our lesson planning books each week, the first thing I did was mark my prep time. Sometimes, I even used a different color to highlight this major event.

They are Highly Skilled Humanities Teachers

I would drop off my students to their special area class a few minutes early or pick them up a couple of minutes late, secretly, so I could preserve as much of my own time as possible. Looking back as I type this, my arrogance makes me cringe. See, here's the deal, all of the art, music, or physical education teachers have specialized degrees, and they possess a unique influence in their own right. They deserve respect and dignity because, as specialized experts, they add value to any school's program and enrich the lives of their students. Even the label of "special area" or "activity" devalues the teachers' expertise while disrespecting the students that they serve. They are humanities teachers, life skills teachers and essential to the growth of our children.

They Tirelessly Serve All

Collaborating with these talented expert humanities teachers will enhance any reading, math, science or social studies lessons you can come up with as a classroom teacher. Cross content connections and applying technique or learning from one class to another only creates more connections. Most humanities teachers serve every student in the school, yet are singletons when it comes to culture building events. Extend a personal invitation into your classroom and make them feel included in your classroom community.

The sad reality is that when budget times get tough, special areas are the first on the chopping block. The concerts, field days, fine arts festivals and fundraising serve the school and community. Honor your colleagues by being on time at the beginning and the end of class. Support the teachers by sharing concert or field day information in your weekly newsletter. Buy a candy bar and know that you have contributed to the magic that happens in each of their classrooms. Engage in the fun and be an active learner with your students.

Please do not punish special area teachers by keeping students from attending these specialized classes. They have worked hard on their lessons without transition times and have set lofty goals and expectations with minimal time to do much. For the student who loves painting, dancing, singing, building or running, missing special area classes hurts them more deeply than we can possibly imagine.

Art, music, physical education and so many other special area classes are not inferior to anyone else's classes. To the contrary, they are the perfect partnership for applying reading and mathematical concept learnings in these cross-content areas. These exceptional environments should be valued as incredible opportunities for students to learn. These courses are high value, high interest and oftentimes the one space that students feel successful. Stop mistreating the learning outlets that often act as the main reason why children want to come to school in the first place.

Syndee Malek currently serves as an Associate Executive Director for the Michigan Elementary and Middle School Principals Association. Prior to her current position, Syndee has served over 30 years as a teacher, principal, central office administrator and leadership development consultant for one of the Michigan RESAs.

Stop Letting Words Misrepresent You
SUE LITMAN-HALL

"Who are you talking to?"

"What are you trying to say?"

"Who hears what you are saying?"

"Did you hear what you just said?"

"Your words are like daggers."

The Words You Use Represent Who You Are

As a teacher, there is so much on your plate that you may not think that the word choice and the way you use language is important. I am not talking about language that is used during instruction, but I am referring to the language that is used both formally and informally that ultimately represents you as a teacher. We can all get caught up in a conversation, but are you really listening to what you are saying and the words that you utter that you are responsible for?

Being a teacher and being at the top of your game each day can certainly be tiring. When teachers are tired or under the gun, stress, frustrations, judgment it is so easy to let your guard down and that is when misconceptions come out. We have all been in a situation where we responded in a way that didn't bring out the best in us. Words whether written or conversational have the power to inflame, motivate or deescalate.

Words Publicize

Think about the quality of words and how they make one feel valued or heard. When you respond verbally or in written form, you are telling a story–not someone else's, but yours. Words matter and are a significant part of what an individual represents.

Your manner in delivering a message and the words you choose publicize your reaction, beliefs or presence. One may think "I have a right to say what I want." Yes, that is true in most cases, but as a teacher, we are public servants and held to a higher moral and ethical standard by sheer societal perception. Our words become a public transcript that make impressions on our communities and profession. Teachers must professionally adjust to their audience and be meticulously mindful of the tone and words conveyed through email, conversation, or phone call. Our words have the power to illuminate the magnificence of our profession and the impact that we make on future generations, but they also hold the power to tear down and destroy. Talk can be cheap, and that cheapness manifests the power to ruin us.

How many times have you heard a colleague say, "I responded to an email and then read what I wrote and deleted it?" Luckily, we are born with an inner consciousness that alerts us, "This venting email approach is not appropriate use of language and any audience deserves a professional and mindful response, a better narrative." Karen's earlier chapter about responding to situations emotionally provides a framework for why and how humans react and respond to the tone and words we choose. If for some reason you jumped ahead to my chapter, you won't want to miss reading about the in's and out's of emotionally complex problems.

Guiding Questions to Help Filter

The next time you find yourself in a conversation or responding to an email, consider how your words or response will impact that person or community. Have you considered their point of view and feelings? Are you focused on the result being the dynamic achievement and happiness of the student? Is there a way you can convey your messaging in a manner that is responsive and professional? How is your expressive language, tone or word choice representing you?

Another Set of Eyes

It is an essential practice to always have someone you trust review the written work if you anticipate the situation to be emotionally charged or just a sticky situation. This is an effective practice in any profession (or situation really) to maintain a respectful and intentional perception of your language versus letting language control you. When you are consciously concerned about the tone or impression by seeking help from a friend or peer, you are leveling up in professionalism, partnership and purpose.

Eliciting another set of eyes or ears provides a clearer picture and objectivity for both the writer and the audience. Accept the feedback and remove your embedded feelings and redirect the tone of your language and reword it in such a way that it is helpful to your audience and career.

Identify Key Points First

A technique that has saved me many times over is identifying key points. Before responding (especially when emotions are high) write down 3-5 key points you would like to make. On those key points cross out any words of emotion (remove the emotion out). Paring down the information to what is relevant will help you review and illustrate what you want to say. This practice is particularly helpful when there is a verbal conversation happening. Even in the heat of a conversation, you can reply, "I'd like to just take a moment to get my thoughts together before I respond. Would it be ok to give me just a minute to jot my thoughts down?" This on-the-spot strategy builds partnership capacity because it offers equity of voice, it portrays a clear intentional message, and it demonstrates intentionality. Sometimes pausing and breathing is enough to alter the outcome of your language. Referencing your key points validates what the other person has said, demonstrates you heard what they said, and allows for more meaningful, active participation, instead reacting and overtaking the partnership.

Just like a crinkled piece of paper, the tone and the words you use through your language use, no matter what you say or how you say it, can never be changed back to the original condition. You cannot unwrinkle a crumpled sheet of paper. It is impossible. As a teacher, you are responsible for the words you choose because they represent you, your school and the deep emotional human factor that drives our profession. Words can either mend and bind or divide. This choice is up to you. Remember, dynamic off-the-chart achievement happens when educators pause long enough to be intentional with their language.

Sue Litman-Hall has been a proud public educator for over 23 years and currently serves as an elementary principal. She is passionate about inclusive school cultures, social emotional supports and providing space for the entire school community for all stakeholders to feel valued and empowered to do what is best for all students.

Stop Teaching Entrepreneurship Incorrectly
JEFF GARGAS

In middle school, I sold toys to fellow classmates. In high school, I sold shopping services to other students, dropping party supplies off to 3-5 houses every Friday and Saturday night, earning enough money to cover my friends' expenses for the weekend. In college, I started a concert promotions company, then a record label, then a non-profit, then a management firm and even a tavern.

At this point in my life, I had started more businesses than most people will experience in three lifetimes. I also failed at more ventures than most would in their worst nightmare. I've had companies crash and burn within months and some that never even left the ground. Others have done well for a while, just long enough to get my hopes up, before sputtering to a pitiful end.

The Reality of Pain and Struggle

Yes, I have had success as well, and that's what most people see now. But what they don't see is what's most important. What they do not see are the countless sleepless nights I've spent scrambling to find enough money to keep the lights on. What they don't see are the seemingly endless days where I clocked more than 20 hours and still couldn't sleep because I wasn't sure where my wife and I were going to get the money to buy food. What they don't see are the days where we woke up thinking a storm had knocked out the power, only to realize it was an unpaid bill instead.

What they don't see is the loneliness. The stress. The frustration. The pain.

Here is the craziest thing of all; if they DID see all of that, it would be even harder to understand true entrepreneurship. Why do it? If it causes all of that pain and struggle, if it is so hard, why continue to pursue one idea after another idea? Why keep going with so many failures?

Because I'm an entrepreneur. I don't know how to not be this.

You see, I have been this way my whole life, long before it was cool to be an entrepreneur. Long before anyone was okay with a young kid dreaming about being Mark Zuckerberg, I was determined to build my own company long before I had an Instagram bio.

And . . . I will be an entrepreneur long after it's cool.

I remember when it wasn't cool. I remember being told I was childish, or silly, or just plain stupid. Why try to build something? Go to college. Get your degree. Go get a job with a good salary and good benefits. Why risk so much? I remember all the conversations with friends and family telling me I was wasting my life trying to chase another unrealistic dream. I remember being looked down on, criticized and constantly judged by people when I had to work part time jobs while I worked to create something. I remember working at Arby's while my old high school buddies had offices and company cars.

Entrepreneurship Can't Be Taught

Here's my point with all of this: I am an entrepreneur. Always have been. Always will be. I don't know why. I do not understand why I have been able to handle everything that comes with it, but I understand that I have, I can, and I will continue to fight through all of it. I don't think I'm capable of not being this way. Not everyone is this way and more importantly, not everyone should be or told that they can be an entrepreneur very easily.

We need to stop telling kids they should be entrepreneurs, start businesses and be their own boss. Before I go any further, I am NOT saying you shouldn't teach kids to dream or create. In fact, I believe instilling the confidence in students so they can dream and dream big is one of our most important roles. But, dreaming big does not mean it has to be the same dream as everyone else. It does not mean that a dream needs to have a tycoon ending. You can dream, be creative and build amazing things without ever starting a business.

I try not to say this too often, but I'm going to say it here. True entrepreneurship can't be taught. That drive, that need to create something, is within people and it is not taught. That's okay, though, because we really shouldn't be teaching kids to be entrepreneurs; we should be teaching them entrepreneurial skills, mindsets and abilities. Yes, we need to instill the confidence and strength in them so they know they can be an entrepreneur, but the truth is, we don't want all of our students to be entrepreneurs.

The Educational Buzz Word vs Reality

I believe entrepreneurship has become such a hot topic because it has been falsely displayed as some kind of lottery ticket to freedom. Who wouldn't want to control their own schedule and be their own boss? The problem is, that's not reality. Just like Hollywood stars or professional athletes, students often equate entrepreneurship with becoming the next YouTube sensation. They perceive a one hit wonder experience that just catapults them into financial success. What we fail to teach students is that when they own their own business, everything is on them, everything is their fault, they work for everyone else and their schedule is decided by the needs of the business, not the needs of their family.

I get it, picturing our kids growing up to create the next cool tech startup that raises a hundred million dollars in capital is pretty cool. That is, until you realize that 70% of tech startups fail and shut down less than two years after raising all that money. It becomes even less cool when you realize that entrepreneurs and business owners are more likely to suffer from depression, anxiety, and other mental health issues.

Entrepreneurship Embraces More Failure than Success

A study by Dr. Michael Freeman, a clinical professor at University of California San Francisco, showed that 49% of the entrepreneurs surveyed reported having a mental-health condition. The top of that list was depression (30%), followed by ADHD (29%) and anxiety problems (27%). Compare that to the general US population, where only about 7% identify as depressed. Those numbers become alarming when we think about the effects of entrepreneurship.

Look, I am absolutely not trying to rally against entrepreneurship. Entrepreneurship is important. We need people to continue to create new businesses and new jobs and we need to believe that our students can create new things. I believe most teachers are approaching entrepreneurship in a dangerous way– a glamorous *Shark Tank* way, perhaps. The truth is, telling students that they should go start a business is not only dangerous, but also unrealistic to not share the realities of the grind with them so they know what they are getting into.

I am noticing a bad trend where we push entrepreneurship on students to a point where being an employee for someone else is no longer the cool thing to do. We are making it seem like being an accountant or a human resources representative or a mid-level manager is not good enough and that is the wrong message to send to our students.

What You Should Teach Instead

Stop teaching the glory of entrepreneurship decision making. Instead, what we should teach are entrepreneurial skills, mental abilities and business-minded tendencies that call for strength, in communication skills, creativity, collaboration, teamwork, critical thinking, problem solving and leadership skills.

Stop focusing on the potential end goal of being an entrepreneur. If you do, you will be setting your students up for failure. Instead, focus on the things that will prepare students for whatever road they choose to take. Prepare them with the skills and mental capacities that they need so they can find the path that is meant for them.

Jeff Gargas is the COO and co-founder of the Teach Better Team and co-author of the book, Teach Better. He works with educators and schools to support teachers as they strive to reach more students and improve their achievement.

Stop Allowing Technology to Drive Your Instruction

MICHAEL DREZEK

We are a society that is tethered to technology. Our students were practically born with social media accounts and embedded microchips that can track just about anything. Technology tools and devices provide instantaneous feedback responses equal to the air we breathe and the water we drink. Technology is an amazing gift and tool that can streamline our lives and, in many cases, positively impact our overall quality of life. I want to overemphasize this message: Please do not stop using technology to enhance and enrich your teaching and classroom efficacy. What I am saying is: stop allowing technology tools and apps to hijack or replace high quality classroom instruction. Some teachers are putting their efforts into simply using software programs rather than co-constructing high quality content learning through student voice with the intentional selection of tools that support the learning.

Without People, Technology is Useless

As a District Technology Integration Specialist, I have the privilege of observing the creative and innovative ways teachers embed and integrate technology in every content area. I've seen students with learning disabilities master digital accessibility tools. I have witnessed students feeling enlightened while collaborating with students in other countries. Learning with technology excites me and it can be a positive contagion for so many of the educators I support in the classroom. I love apps, websites, software, hardware and all of the technology that makes my life as an educator easier and more streamlined. Technology helps me inspire students, leverages my connection to others and motivates students to share their passions while making content connections.

Do you know what is even more amazing than technology alone? People. That's right. You. Me. All of us. Without people, technology, alone, really isn't all that special. Don't get me wrong, people can also play a part in making mistakes on their educational technology journey. There are time when technology negatively impacts students and detracts from the depth of content learning in the classroom. Dynamic off-the-chart educators ensure that they are doing all they can to be on the right side of using technology in the classroom and not let technology use them.

Pedagogy is the Driver, Technology is the Accelerator

Michael Fullan said that, "Pedagogy is the driver. Technology is the accelerator." In my district educational technology newsletter, I put this quote related in the header, front and center, for all to see. I revised the first sentence to "Teachers are the drivers." I wanted our teachers to know that they are and should be steering the car. Their ideas and their planning efforts make learning take off. Technology is there just to help. It guides. It accelerates. But, as the driver, I'm leaving teaching, learning and achievement to the professional educators who are trained in the content, art and science of teaching and know what students need. If we are not intentional in our work, technology can become the driver. When we lack intentionality, it can happen unknowingly. The excitement of the new shiny or trendy technology gives us that shot of dopamine that we enjoy, but at the same time can backfire and induce anxiety. When we are caught up in the excitement, we can lose our vision and direction and when we lose pedagogical focus, we can easily miss the destination. I am all for taking risks and trying new things in the classroom with technology. The best educators do this regularly and bounce back when things don't go as planned. Taking risks sets a powerful tone and should not be discouraged. However, we must stop letting technology drive our instruction.

When Technology Becomes a Distraction

There are many places you might learn about new technology: a colleague, a professional development workshop, a webinar, a conference, a blog, a social media chats, social media groups, a podcast and anywhere in between. In every one of these spaces, there is usually an additional buzz generated around that technology. That buzzing is often smoke and mirrors, however. It is a distraction. If you are introduced to a new technology, take a few minutes to digest what it does and how it might help you. Ask yourself if the tool offers any additional leverage than what you can already do in the classroom. You can take notes on paper or take notes on the screen, but there is no pedagogical leverage. What does the new tool offer that will increase complexity in thinking or application to the real world? After considering these things, don't do anything. Sit on it. Don't rush in. Add it to your toolbox. If the technology is that good, it will still be there ready for you when you are ready to implement it to enhance the learning of your students. If you have an instructional technology coach or specialist in your district, bring it up in conversation and see where the conversation leads you. Sometimes the latest and greatest technology trend has minuses and when we take a step back and let the smoke from the initial fireworks clear, we discover it did not help the learning at all, in fact it may have slowed it down. You may want to consider sharing a post on social media asking others: "How are you using this technology in your class?" When we use technology for the sake of using a bright new shiny technology tool merely for the novelty and not for accelerating quality learning through empowered learners, everyone loses. *We can do better.*

Sometimes the best technology for a lesson is still a pencil. Sometimes the best technology for a lesson might be an augmented or virtual reality tool. It all comes down to the learning objectives. I like to consider a few important questions: What do I need my learners to be able to know and do at the completion of this lesson? How will I help get them there? How might I hook them and spark their curiosity? How will I assess their learning? Technology may very well be the solution to some of these questions. But asking the right questions and starting with questions is key. Just like Rae and Bryan discuss in their chapter, starting with the end in mind and planning backwards is often extremely helpful.

Technology Standards is the Driving Manual

The International Society for Technology in Education (ISTE) Student Standards (https://www.iste.org/standards/for-students) is like a car manual. You need to know how all the functions work together to drive the car, and ultimately to arrive at your destination. These standards provide a context, purpose and intention for high-quality instruction. I like to start with the students and then check myself through the ISTE Educator Standard of Designer which ensures that educators: "Use technology to create, adapt and personalize learning experiences that foster independent learning and accommodate learner differences and needs."

It's not a matter of using technology or not. It's a matter of knowing when to use technology and most importantly when to not lead with it. Technology when implemented effectively turns what was previously not possible, into possible. But let's pause and make a pledge–a pledge to read the manual before opening the car door and a pledge to stop letting technology drive instruction. Leverage your standards, students and instruction by allowing them to press the accelerator so that you all will arrive with an off-the-charts dynamic win at the finish line.

Michael Drezek is the District Technology Integrator & Teacher Leader for the Lake Shore Central School District in Western New York. He is also the recipient of the 2016 NYSCATE Lee Bryant Outstanding Teacher Award and a former math teacher.

Stop Ignoring Helpful Feedback

SHAWN BERRY CLARK, Ph.D.

"Some people feel the rain. Others just get wet." –Roger Miller

On the holiday of Shemini Atzeret, Jewish people make a special blessing for rain because water is essential and beneficial to life. Feedback can be just like rain; it can come to you as a drizzle, sprinkle, drops, downpour, thunderstorm, or monsoon. Feedback can be non-existent or sparse and hit you like a drought which leads to no growth. Whichever form the rain takes, like feedback, feeling the rain is necessary for growth and productivity. Feel blessed when you are provided feedback no matter what the content or context is or from whom feedback is given. You can either dismiss the reality of that moment or you can absorb the feedback in order to thrive and grow.

You Can't Escape the Weather

Meteorologists attempt to predict rainfall and forecast weather conditions just as you can predict the type of feedback you might get following an observation, parent conference, or evaluation. The forecast shows a 70% chance of thunderstorms, so you dread putting on that raincoat and grabbing the umbrella (whose whereabouts are probably unknown) and heading to school. Or we pay entirely too much attention to the weather because it drives our choice of wardrobe or what recess may be like for the day. You can't escape the weather. You can't escape feedback. It exists as a part of the profession regardless of whether you want it or not. Feedback is different from criticism. Feedback is meant to help you become the best that you can be. If your ego gets in the way, you will not be able to recognize the areas that can make you better. And becoming a better teacher only helps your students in the end.

In the song "Ironic", Alanis Morissette sings "It's like raaaaiiiiiin...on your wedding day..." You don't want it to rain on your momentous occasion, but the rain might result in a rainbow. Generally, people may not be comfortable with getting feedback about their performance, but if you consider the potential effects that positive feedback may have so flowers can bloom, plants thrive and water is replenished to help everyone grow together. Dynamic, synergistic five-star schools thrive on giving feedback to everyone–students, teachers and school leaders.

Getting Past the Fear of Feedback

We fear feedback sometimes due to memories from the past growing up. My mother was good at throwing a backhanded compliment that criticized me, "I love how you don't care what your hair looks like." How do we get past that? Use feedback as a means of self-understanding versus categorizing yourself in a certain way. Feedback does not define you like the weather defines a geographic region. If you know it rains a lot in Seattle, then dress accordingly but don't' think twice about doing your hair. If someone gives you negative feedback, address it accordingly by listening and reflecting.

Internalize Feedback and Bloom

True growth mostly stems from conflict and taking an honest look at ourselves. You can put up an umbrella to block the rain. Filter harsh feedback with some time and space for reflecting and looking at any touches of truth that may be present. The raindrops or rain showers of feedback you may get from students, parents, peers, coaches or supervisors provide an opportunity to grow and learn.

The following scenarios regarding feedback are intended to help you accept feedback cycles.

Student Feedback

No matter what type of feedback you get from students, take a breath and absorb it because student voice matters tremendously. Students can be harsh and extremely honest because they may not have social filters or self-regulation mastered. Educators are constantly giving feedback to students, so we better be pros at receiving it too. When you criticize a student's academic work, are you trying to harm a student? Of course not.

Recently, I witnessed a student providing feedback to a teacher on a virtual platform. The student blurted out in the middle of the lesson that the teacher was looking raggedy and might want to pop on a video filter. While that could be deemed offensive and disruptive, the student was not wrong - the teacher did look pretty rough on camera that day. The teacher waited a few seconds then admitted to the student that she didn't know filters were an option on this digital video platform. She could have taken that feedback as negative and rude and gotten really upset, but what resulted from this feedback was the student showed the teacher how to use the video filter feature and the two of them had an awesome time trying on different virtual props and changing the hues of the filters.

Family Feedback

When I was teaching 5th grade math, a parent angrily asked me during a parent conference, "Why are you failing my child? He hasn't learned a thing from you!" My first instinct was to defend myself and respond, "I'm not failing your child. Your child is failing my class because he never turns in work, is absent half the time and is too busy messing around when he does come to school." What we must realize is that this mother's feedback, which was shaped in the form of an accusatory question and insult, was really a parent's only way of asking for help. My response, after I took a deep breath and paused, focused on how we could work together to ensure her child's success because we both want the student to thrive. That feedback was like a thunderstorm, complete with lightning meant to strike me down as a teacher, but it was also an opportunity to really listen and partner with that parent for her child's success.

Peer Feedback

My friend, Marie, teaches second grade and said the worst feedback from a colleague was like stepping in muddy rain puddles constantly. Marie started teaching later in life and is a mother of three. Marie was assigned to a young mentor who knew a lot about education and Marie valued her advice. Weekly mentor meetings and observations were documented, but the mentor only called out everything Marie was doing wrong, while providing little to no feedback. These constant muddy puddles of critical feedback made Marie question everything about her teaching abilities. Marie could have jumped right over the puddles and ignored the feedback from this much younger teacher, but, instead, she sidestepped most of the puddles. It took some time and space, but Marie's mentor helped her understand that although she nurtured the students as if they were her own, that she was too lenient with her behavioral expectations. Marie listened and reflected on the feedback and coupled her ability to provide a safe, loving and nurturing environment with the mentor's strategies for changing the classroom structure and boundaries. Marie discovered that it was indeed much easier to meet the needs of her students if there were consistent procedures and structures in place to manage behavior. These types of puddles strengthened Marie in the end.

Coaching Feedback

When I was a principal, one of my instructional coaches did the opposite of leaving little rain puddles of feedback. Instead, she would hit me like a monsoon and impale me with too much feedback at one time. Tons of feedback might overwhelm you. Malik was told in an observation post-conference that his classroom was disorganized and messy, that students were not engaged, that teacher talk dominated student talk and his check for understanding at the end of the lesson was not aligned to the learning target. It's impossible for a teacher to make that many changes (and do it well) at one time. So, you take that feedback, pick the one actionable item with the highest rain gauge (hurdle rate), and focus on improving that one thing, first. Instead of ignoring all of the feedback and feeling like a failure, you can gain success for you and your students by implementing one impactful change. Seek shelter from the monsoon by finding one safe place.

Supervisor Feedback

I asked a thought partner, Peyton, to recall a time when she got horrible feedback from an administrator and she immediately said, "The time my principal gave me a two out of five on the "rigor" scale when I was provided no information or professional development about rigor." Peyton was so taken back by that one piece of feedback about rigor that she completely ignored the other positive ratings. After a follow-up conversation with his administrator, Peyton used the feedback and low rating to advocate for and request professional learning related to rigor in the classroom. You, too, can push through the misty fog and find meaning in the feedback cycle even if it is uncomfortable.

Root for Feedback in All Directions

After leading a meeting in a corporate business setting, Kim Scott's former boss, Sheryl Sandberg, criticized her for saying "um" a lot during her presentation. Sheryl offered her a speaking coach to learn how not to say "um" every sentence because it made her sound stupid. Kim refused the coaching and was offended by the offer, but it turns out that this feedback was vitally important. Kim learned that Sheryl would not have told her the truth if she did not care about her and her future. Ultimately, Kim learned to provide feedback to others as she cared for her employees, as well.

Stop letting the rain do its job. Contribute to fertilizing the classrooms in your school so growth dominates our egos.

Dr. Shawn Berry Clark is a school improvement and transformation coach for the South Carolina Department of Education. She is a co-author of Using Quality Feedback to Guide Professional Learning.

Stop Acting Like a Know-it-All
KRISTEN KOPPERS

We all know them. They are your friends, your neighbors and even your family members. They are the ones who know *everything* from how dinosaurs became extinct to the mysteries of the solar system. We are talking a living, breathing human know-it-all web browser. No matter what we say, they are ALWAYS right!

Interruptions Equal Ignorance

The best part of being an educator is learning from others. With varying backgrounds and knowledge, I can learn so much from others. Learning from those around me is both overwhelming and a blessing. That is what makes learning interesting. As an English teacher, I find myself correcting others' grammar. Honestly, it comes naturally to me. I must admit that there are times that I purposely correct one's grammar based on principle, while forgetting that I may be annoying someone. *I don't purposely mean to call people out.*

What happens when someone *believes* to know it all? Understanding how to deal with a "know-it-all" really takes practice in order to not insult anyone.

A "know-it-all" does not necessarily know all the facts to something, they may know just enough to be dangerous. In fact, the worst part about a know-it-all is that they are *unwilling* to listen before spewing their own ignorance about a topic or inserting their expertise into something that no one asked them about. Sometimes, we need to gracefully hold our opinions, knowledge, or thoughts until someone *asks* for our opinions. Nobody wants interrupted unsolicited advice. Interruptions of ignorance never sit well.

Why Do They Ignore the Rain?

Take Shawn Berry's chapter and her rain metaphor and apply it to this chapter. Ultimately, the alleged "know-it-all" is the one being judged based on the super-ego that is portrayed and projected. Consider why a person would act this way: perhaps it's because of low self-esteem or the need to be the center of attention. Nevertheless, being talked down to, by anyone, does not feel good at all. We must think about the "know-it-all" raining on our parade and figure out why they interrupt only to give unsolicited advice.

Close Your Umbrella and Feel the Rain

Know-it-alls are easy to spot because they are always outfitted with umbrellas, galoshes and any weather repelling gear that they can get their hands on. Once you meet one, you can spot them a mile away in their canary yellow rain jacket and rubber boots. Below are some guiding principles and feedback that will help you take the galoshes off, take the umbrella down and feel the rain, peacefully.

1. Stop offering ways to fix everything. Being the person to solve the problem is not always the best position for you to be in. You do not know what the situation is, so do not be so quick to offer advice if it is unsolicited in the first place.

2. Stop and listen more than you talk. Instead of offering an opinion, listen to others because you might learn something new about a situation. Remember: your way of doing things may not be the same for someone else. Listening is a better attribute than always voicing an opinion and you will earn more respect along the way and be taken more seriously when you do decide to assert your opinion.

3. Stop thinking that your position is right when tackling a know-it-all. No matter what the topic is, there will always be an answer even if you are not sure it's correct. You never know who will know more than you about a given topic, so let the experts rise to the top and learn from them.

4. Stop letting your own ego takeover. The ego is one of the common problems between right and wrong. No one wants to be wrong, but an ego is a distinctive force for immediate gratification. It's okay to be wrong and not know the answer to a question. If you try to fool others with misinformation, you compromise your own reputation.

No one likes a Mr. or Ms. Know-It-All. When know-it-alls come across as the almighty knowers of everything, they ostracize their colleagues, supervisors and anyone who crosses their paths. To grow a collaborative organization of experts, we know that everyone knows *something* and when we share all of those somethings, we grow, together, instead of isolating others strictly because our egos get the best of us.

Kristen Koppers is a National Board Certified Teacher who has been teaching secondary ELA and acting as an adjunct professor for a local junior college in Illinois. Kristen focuses her teaching on differentiated learning and prides herself in her community service work.

Stop Offering Unsolicited Advice
TAIREN MCCOLLISTER

In the previous chapter, Kristen unveiled the attributes of know-it-alls and she even touched on unsolicited advice. Know-it-all's and unsolicited advice often go hand in hand. I want to spend some time on the topic of unsolicited advice. As educators, the way we give and receive feedback can make or break a dynamic off-the-charts school. No one is saying that you cannot offer advice. Problems arise and there are times when you must proceed in offering advice even when no one asked for it, expected it, or desired it. Teaching is a profession that is already filled with personal struggles of adequacy, effectiveness, and purpose in our own right. Unsolicited advice can make or break a day, a lesson, a unit, or even a simple moment.

It Feels Like They Have No Faith in You

During my student teaching, there were many veteran teachers who constantly gave me unsolicited wisdom:

"Don't smile at your students in the first marking period."

"Always ask other teachers about students when you get your class list."

"Never admit that you've made a mistake."

261

Yes, these are words that were spoken to me as I embarked on my teaching career. Offering a novice teacher this type of advice could set them up for disappointment, frustration and, ultimately, failure. How can you not smile at students? Connection is the ultimate teaching strategy. Ask other teachers about students? No thank you. Students are different with every teacher they encounter. Not admit mistakes? What are we teaching students about life when we model not admitting mistakes? Powerful teachers recognize when they are wrong and offering apologies to make it right. Apologies mend and grow relationships.

Unsolicited Advice Ruins Relationships

We can offer support to others by being understanding. Let's face it, sometimes, advice might be a form of bragging, a way to feel powerful or capable. A newbie might not be able to sift through the disguised waters of mind games. Building yourself up at the expense of others is never appreciated. Teachers need teachers; camaraderie, encouragement, understanding, humor and support can strengthen our relationships with others. Unsolicited advice can quickly ruin relationships.

In graduate school, I became friends with Troy, a second-year civics teacher in an inner city school in Philadelphia. He was creative, crazy smart and had a sense of humor too. He ended up leaving his teaching position in the final semester of our program. He was well liked by his students. He used his sense of humor to win students over and have them buy into the ideas behind powerful civics. Troy would share lesson ideas and plans with us in class and even I, the least civic-minded person you could ever meet, found myself thinking that he would be the best teacher to have if I took a course in civics. The entire time that Troy was working his magic with his students, he was constantly being advised to change his teaching style and his approach with his students. He was advised by his supervisors to reduce so much laughter because their focus should be on learning. Troy's mentor and supervisor left him feeling like he had made the ultimate life mistake in choosing to teach. Such misguided advice and wrongheaded advice ruined a blossoming career. I'll never forget Troy.

Everyone enters teaching for different reasons with different levels of comfort and confidence. Teaching students is challenging enough, but offering unsolicited advice can range from giving subtle sarcasm all the way to ruining careers. The great philosopher, Eddie Murphy, once said, "The advice I would give someone is to not take anyone's advice." Sometimes, our best asset to the profession is to simply listen, zip our mouths shut and show support. I promise you, Mr. Murphy would approve.

Tairen McCollister is currently an ELA instructor, Diversity and Equity Coordinator, adjunct professor and host of a children's story podcast entitled, The Namaste Stories™. Tairen is a trauma-informed educator and trainer with extensive knowledge of neuroscience and education, trauma and resilience and diversity and inclusion.

Stop Doing Everything on Your Own
ERIC NICHOLS

"I can do it," said the first-year teacher.

"I've got this," said the veteran reading teacher.

"Involving others just takes more time," said the social studies department chair.

"Why would I involve the new teacher down the hall in my planning? What the heck does he know?" said the elementary teacher.

Collaboration Avoidance

These comments effortlessly spill out of the mouths of education professionals for one simple reason: to avoid collaborating with other educators. Yes, involving others takes more time. Yes, you can pull yourself up by your bootstraps and do a phenomenal job on your own. Yes, there are some amazing educators who stand alone and do magical things for kids. However, there are educators who struggle inside their lonely classrooms and lonely schools.

A second-year teacher, Mary, struggled to find the answers as to why her lesson stunk. She had months of frustration with several students who were misbehaving and was ready to call it quits. Mary asked for advice, not the unsolicited advice that Tairen just wrote about in her earlier chapter, but Mary's grade level team told her that her problem was: "You are too soft. Be tougher with the kids, Mary!" Mary struggled implementing a new curriculum. She was frustrated with the new student information system and was dreading the upcoming professional learning meeting where frustrations with the principal about the training were already running wild. Mary testified: "This isn't what I thought teaching was going to be like. This sucks. Teaching sucks."

A twenty-two-year veteran teacher, Jacob, enjoyed his job for the most part. Often, he would say: "I really like teaching writing. The kids are engaged and they love to write!" As the year went on, Jacob continued letting kids write and he continued giving students feedback on their writing. For the first time in his twenty-two-year career, the students were tested on their writing. When the results came in, Jacob's students scored at the basic level. It was a gut punch for Jacob as he said, "Twenty-two years of poor writing instruction. Twenty-two years of kids not learning. Twenty-two years of no feedback for the teacher. Twenty-two years of no collaboration."

When Professional Learning is a Gripe Session

I do not accept the idea that collaborative professional learning communities are bad if the time is used properly, where educators dive into the data to create systems that positively impact teacher practice and student learning. When topics become gripe sessions, educators see collaboration as a waste of time. They run from these meetings, close and lock their doors and are never to be heard from again. Good teachers are left alone to attempt to be good teachers and ineffective educators are left alone to be ineffective educators, never shown or given the tools to get better at their craft.

Isolated Behind Closed Doors

We create this problem too. Teachers might be formally observed once or twice each year where they put on a dog and pony show for their administrators.

We hire teachers, sometimes never having seen them teach, and turn them loose into classrooms to educate our students for incredibly important future lives. Talking to many educators, it is quite common that they will have never seen another teacher teach throughout their entire teaching career. Trial and error are one way that an educator might get better at teaching. We do not control the students who come through our doors, but we sure can control what happens with education staff when they are in our schools.

Open Your Door

So, what is the solution? Open your door. Invite other educators in. Walk through another educator's door. Go see effective teaching practices. Go see why students love a particular teacher. Have another teacher watch you struggle through your tough 2nd period class where students are acting up. Talk about your struggles. Talk about how you could improve as a teacher.

Gandhi is known for this popular phrase: "You must be the change you wish to see in the world." Be the change in your world. Be the change in your classroom and school. Talk shop with others. Plan with colleagues. Talk about what is and isn't working for you and them. Videotape yourself and show it to your colleagues. Give your math test to your grade level colleague. E-mail your unit plan to your cross-state peer. What worked? What didn't? How can WE make things better? As Elissa discussed in her chapter about local, regional, national and global collective think tanks, look outside your first-order circle of friends and colleagues.

Times will get tough in your classroom. You'll have several students who don't respond to your instruction. You'll have students who don't learn even when you pull out your best tricks. Who will you turn to?

Eric Nichols serves as the Assistant Superintendent/Principal for the Silvies River/Crane Schools in east rural Oregon. Eric has been advocating for student and teacher voice while serving as a high school teacher and administrator for nearly 21 years.

Stop Studying to be an Administrator Just to Make More Money
VERNON WRIGHT

Dynamic, synergistic five-star rated schools do things for the right reasons. Although it's been years, I remember it like it was yesterday. I had been teaching for a while and had been tasked by my principal to contribute beyond the classroom in a campus leadership committee to provide feedback in creating a new school mission and vision that was focused on high student achievement. We were one of "those" schools that had failed to meet state and federal benchmarks for achievement in a perennial fashion. Needless to say, we were operating out of an adverse heightened awareness that our doors could potentially and indefinitely close. I loved the classroom and stepping up and embracing a new leadership role did not exactly excite me all that much at the time.

Potential Leadership Energy Already in Motion

The term, "teacher leader" was new to me. I was willing to help the campus beyond my teaching duties and doing so provided an opportunity for me to see more of the inner workings that make a campus function every day. However, my interest in anything "leadership related" was cursory at best.

I was approached both formally and informally about next steps in my career beyond the classroom. I appreciated the consideration, but politely declined such offers. Yet, there were some people placed in my life that were meant to be there–for a certain reason.

One of those reasons is to bring you to a higher awareness of the next level potential within you. In physics, I believe that is called potential energy and for me, maybe I was stumbling upon my own "potential leadership energy."

While in graduate school and serving as an administrative intern/aspiring leader, some of that potential energy had been converted to kinetic energy. In other words, I had been taking action and had some promising things in motion, but for the right reasons. I was not studying leadership because salaries are higher than what teachers make.

Leadership is a Noble Purpose, Not a Paycheck

I remember getting that first paycheck as an official campus administrative team member and noticing how much more it was than my checks as a teacher. Now, certainly most people are interested in money as it's the tool we use to buy goods and services, food and other things not only for ourselves but for our family. We all have bills to pay and higher salaries can often make a budget seem less oppressive. As nice as the extra pay was at the time, the motivation to do all that administrators are called to do was so much more than the increase in pay; the time spent could be figured out as an hourly wage and we would be surprised at how much we get paid if we look at things in this way and measure time and energy spent leading an organization. In some respects, leadership is a calling, a noble purpose, a cause of which a person devotes their life to–in part or in totality.

If money is your motivation for the basis of pursuing administration, then you'll quickly find out that all you are called to do and all of the hats that you will wear far outweigh the compensation that your title or position offers. In short, there has to be something else beyond the money that is your rock, your foundation, your cause and your deeper sense of self. In essence, this is your impact, your mark, your contribution or your pay it forward to make things better for your community. So, don't fumble the ball by being blindsided by dollar signs.

When Money Takes a Back Seat

I remember preparing to go to bed one evening knowing that all the duties, tasks and goals of the day were either completed or had sufficient progress made on them. I was off to a night of sound, deep sleep prepared to wake up and put on that administrative hat once again to serve the students, staff and community with very difficult issues. There's one small problem with the plan that doesn't quite deliver what we expect out of a position. Deep within my true REM sleep, my cell phone rang at 2:30 in the morning. I picked up the phone a bit irritated but found out that someone had broken into our school and had set off the building alarm.

It is in these moments that the amount of money you're being paid takes a backseat to the worries that you will have about your school, the safety of your students and staff and so much more.

There are many ways to make money. If money is your motivation, then be real with yourself and know that the job of administrator is not one driven by the money, but rather a life purpose and a calling. Be real with yourself, assess yourself and your situation and choose your career path, wisely.

Vernon Wright (@TheWrightLeader, TheWrightLeader.com, ZeroApologyZone.com) is an entrepreneur, speaker, life coach and consultant. He has over 15 years of experience in education working in large, urban school districts and has previously served in the roles of teacher, teacher leader, campus leadership team member and district-level support.

Stop Trying to Be Perfect
KYLE HAMSTRA

It had been a painstaking process, a back-and-forth, tug-of-war of pursuing perfection and letting go of trying to be perfect. Pursuing perfection comes at a cost--even to the extent to which you' are willing to let it ruin your life. Writing a chapter for a book or having a career can be an exciting, process-oriented opportunity driven by action, inspiration and ownership. With each passing day, writing this for you grew into a pressure-building, product-oriented, to-do-list task driven by reaction, shame and panic. Authoring this chapter was not easy for me.

I am proud to be a part of project this special with at least 99 other educators that I really admire. My current staff members, former students, friends, family and strangers might read this. My name is on this. It is my work, and, therefore, as a dedicated educator and lifelong learner, it requires my very *best*. Anything worth doing is worth doing well. If I'm going to do anything, it's going to be my best. If I'm not doing it, then I will ignore a high-quality product. There is no middle ground.

Then, I felt an overwhelming thunderstorm that included a mixture of relief and regret that poured down on me. This chapter is done, yes. But, it's not perfect and I must live with that. I could have done better, perhaps, so much better. What will others think of my imperfect performance? Will they be accepting? Will they still accept *me*?

Letting Go of Perfection

Have you ever stood behind the camera and taken one video after another striving for that perfect take? Who determines what perfection looks like? As educators, do we put certain criteria on ourselves that are unattainable?

With the tripod set up, the desired background in view and the script bulleted list, I convinced myself that I was ready to record the perfect example of success on a video. But here is how it *really* went:

Take 1: I forgot my lines.

Take 2: I was so excited that it sounded fake.

Take 3: A really loud vehicle drove by.

Take 4: My three-year-old was screaming.

Take 5: The neighbor ran his chainsaw.

Take 6: I forgot my lines again.

Take 7: I had to double check the learning target.

Take 8: A flock of birds flew overhead.

Take 9: There was a technology failure.

Take 10: I was interrupted by a phone call.

Take 34: It was getting dark and cold outside.

Take 52: It was almost dinnertime.

Take 77: It was not perfect, but it's done.

Once again, I just could not do it. I couldn't record the perfect video. It was so frustrating. I wanted the absolute best for our students. Video can make the lesson planning and execution much more efficient, but it will never be a perfect process. So, accept that.

Instead of getting caught up in perfection as educators, we must step back and analyze this concept of perfection for a moment:

What really mattered, here?

Was this video going to engage my students?

Did this video communicate what my students needed?

Isn't it OK for students to see us make mistakes?

Education was founded on the continuous cycle of making mistakes, we learn from past failures and build upon new learning and connections. Ultimately, learning is about persevering through imperfection while moving forward in growth. Educators are instrumental in activating and perpetuating this progress.

Empowering Through Imperfection

The number one challenge, obstacle, or barrier to letting others know that we're not perfect is ourselves. Our own fears obstruct our vulnerability and our potential shame that thwarts our progress toward empathy is real. What if we not only acknowledged our own imperfections as educators, but also celebrated imperfection and used it to empower others?

Model Imperfection

The number one reason why it is important for educators to model imperfection is because it might ultimately empower learners all around us. What could students really experience if they embraced mistakes as a pathway to success? Walk through these two classroom spaces:

Classroom A

It is picture-perfect: Student work, heavily edited with precision by the teacher, lines the walls with exact symmetry. Rows of desks could intersect each other at right angles. Craft materials are carefully stowed just out of reach. Feedback consists of yes or no, pass or fail. Upon entering the room, it's apparent who owns the space and who will eventually own the learning. Students need structure. They will rise to the level of high expectations set by the teacher. By all accounts, it all looks great on the surface or online.

Classroom B

It's well kept most of the time. Student work, heavily wrought through the writing and learning process by the students, lines the walls in all shapes and sizes. Flexible seating sprinkles the space according to individual learner needs. Feedback is frequent and ongoing. Upon entering the room, it is hard to find the teacher. Students need opportunity. They will rise to the level of authenticity in persevering through their own imperfections and the frequency of which they are allowed to make mistakes and learn from them, by all accounts, is a work in progress.

Our work and our craft is not about lowering expectations and settling for good enough. It is about establishing the culture in which others can grow and progress towards the best version of themselves. It's not about accepting mistakes and stopping there. It's about embracing mistakes as benchmarks from which to measure forward progress. It's not about commanding perfection with authority. It's about commending resilience with empathy.

Every time we expect perfection, we not only lose another opportunity for authentic learning, we create a disservice to our learners and our profession. Please, stop trying to be perfect.

Kyle Hamstra is a father, husband and 20-year educator in Cary, North Carolina. He is an ASCD Emerging Leader and former fifth grade teacher. Kyle currently serves as a STEM Specialist, After School Director, blogger and presenter.

Stop Worrying about What Others Will Think about You
DAN KREINESS, Ed.D.

Fear of Other People's Opinions

I don't know about you, but sometimes I hesitate to share ideas or resources because I am afraid of how others will perceive them. I don't' want to come across as a know-it-all like in Kristen's chapter, but then there is also its counterpart that cowers and keeps quiet too. I once heard this type of feeling described as the "Fear of Other People's Opinions" (FOPO). In my experience, the feeling has crept in as a form of what I believe to be imposter syndrome. Even though I hold advanced and even terminal degrees in education and leadership, have years of experience in the field, thousands of social media followers and a successful education podcast, I still worry about what others will think of me, my thoughts and my ideas. My goals in writing this chapter are for you to understand that having a FOPO is OK and to offer ideas to help manage and overcome these nuisance feelings. How do I combat my own FOPO?

Develop a Sharing Mentality

Many of our authors in this book discuss the importance of sharing. Before I became a full-time instructional coach, the position had never even existed before. It quickly became my mission to encourage more sharing among the staff at my school and within my district. I established a process for teachers to participate in learning walks and helped the district to rethink the way it delivered professional development by giving teachers more choice in what they learned. Celebrating the amazing talents and experiences of our internal staff can help with your own FOPO.

Platforms, such as social media and walkie-talkie apps have emerged as powerful tools for educator collaboration. Connecting with other connected educators on such platforms allows for an on demand sharing of ideas and content that is difficult to match anywhere else. Social media platforms with chat features provide the ultimate tool sharing experience. Utilizing chat features allow participants to respond to questions and engage in discussions based on other participants' responses or share content related to the chat topic. Walkie-talkie apps allow for asynchronous communication to occur among users. My journey to becoming a connected educator advanced exponentially when I connected with groups of educators using apps with this instantaneous and personalized type of tool. I have been able to virtually meet other educators whom I can reach out to any time I want with questions, answers, ideas, or just to chat.

Having a blog, podcast, or video channel can be amazingly powerful. These types of content creation tools allow the content creator to grow. Instead of using social media to grow followers or make you feel special--similar to what Allison wrote about in her earlier chapter--it is merely there to help others gain new ideas, new tools, or new perspectives about concepts of interest or support. Content creation tools when shared among educators also provides new knowledge that may occur naturally through the research, creation, editing and publishing steps in the content creation process, as well.

I believe all educators have a passion and knack for sharing information. The trick is to turn that passion into an effort to collaborate with other educators to advance the profession and defeat your own FOPO. I have wrestled with my own place in this collaborative process, often thinking that my message is the same one that other educators have heard before or that I lack original thoughts or ideas. But think of it this way: someone, somewhere is waiting for your thought, your idea, or your message. That person could be in your school district, your state, your country, or somewhere else in the world. The exciting thing is you never know who your sharing will reach or on what level it will reach them. Rest assured that it will be received and it will be appreciated, but only if you decide to open up, share your learnings and defeat your own FOPO fears.

Dr. Dan Kreiness is an instructional leader who searches for the most effective ways to advance education and produce high student achievement. Dan currently serves as an instructional coach for digital learning in Connecticut and hosts the "Leader of Learning" podcast.

Stop Worrying About Presenting in Front of Your Peers

MICHAEL LUBELFELD, Ed.D.

Just like FOPO in Dan's chapter prior, the fear of presenting in front of your peers can be real. So why do you worry about presenting in front of your peers when you do it every day with your students? Teachers acting as sages on the stage and guides on the side making magic every day for millions of school children is not any scarier than working with colleagues. From the old-school teachers to the cool hipster teachers and all the other stereotypes and archetypes in between, a teacher presenting to students has been a staple of society and culture of the school. Presenting to staff is an added bonus to the profession and it can be exciting once you get going.

A Revolution of Teacher Expertise

In general, teachers prefer to work with children, rather than adults, and they feel far more competent and comfortable presenting to hundreds of students rather than ten peers in an auditorium. Often, they freeze when contemplating curriculum night or open house with hordes of parents coming into their classrooms. It is a great time to STOP fearing this adult-to-adult presentation. It is a great time to STOP thinking that you are only effective or impactful with children! It is time to change your audience mindset and focus on the positive impact that you can have.

Don't Worry about Fear

When a teacher is asked to present at the next staff meeting, one might say: "I'm much better with my students; I don't feel comfortable presenting in front of adults." This dismal attitude and legitimate fear robs the faculty of local expertise and a culture of peer sharing that Dan just wrote about in the last chapter. The greatest talent in a school is typically staring you in the face. Too often, due to fears or apprehension about feeling like a showoff or having legitimate anxiety of sharing in front of adults or peers, prevents incredible, just in time best practices from being shared, explored and replicated in schools.

Teachers are some of the best presenters around. Teachers already have incredible confidence, and creative ways to present information and facilitate learning. My best advice on this topic is similar to Nike's slogan, "Just Do it".

Professionals seek learning and guidance from in person or virtual conferences, staff meetings, online webinars, podcasts, TED talks and so much more. You can easily shoot a video of your work and post it to social media and see how many people benefit from your expertise and you may want to simply just start there!

Your Expertise is a Gift

Stop fearing how you will be seen or how Dan defines FOPO. You will be seen by the good people as a gift! Any adults who think you are showy or who reject your ideas might have other problems that are unrelated to you and your presentation. Let's stop fearing other people's reactions and let's start a new revolution of teacher-to-teacher expertise! We are long overdue for a revolution of teacher expertise and excellence to take over. The time is now for an educator driven revolution of courageousness ready to confront "negaholics" and move them out of the way. It's time to show everyone your best. You are sitting on a goldmine of innovation. Go for it! Just do it! You CAN do it!

Dr. Michael Lubelfeld is an award winning public school superintendent, published author, national speaker and adjunct professor with a demonstrated history of working in the education industry.

97

Stop Beating Yourself Up Over Past Mistakes
JILL WORLEY

Think back to your first-year teaching. We've all been there. Each of us has made mistakes that dominate our every thought until we can determine a way to resolve them or finally figure out how to let them go. We all make *minor* and *major* mistakes.

Blitz the Blunders

Some of us have made huge blunders--, the mistakes that cause you to think, "Maybe if I change schools and possibly my name, it would be like it never happened and everyone would think that I am an amazing teacher." The perceived perfect teacher (even in your own school) has also made an exorbitant number of mistakes too, but has put forth effort to reflect, learn and grow from each one.

This is the type of educator you can be if you stop being so self-critical and let go of the cacophony of self-doubt and past mistakes echoing in your mind. Use your 40,000-foot view to swiftly erase, destroy and demolish any past mistakes or regrets. There is no need to carry this forward in your future and it does not help students if you carry this on your shoulders either.

Things Do Not Always Go as Planned

While attending an educational conference in Tampa, FL, I sparked up a conversation with a second-year elementary math teacher who looked utterly overwhelmed. During a breakout session on the best strategies of teaching measurement and data, with a sense of vulnerability, she confessed the conference was stressing her out. From her vantage point, due to her constant focus on thoroughly teaching the standards correctly and ensuring she is meeting the social, emotional, and academic needs of all her students, there remains little time to incorporate all of these phenomenal ideas and make necessary changes in her own practices. I shared what my mentor always tells me when I feel overwhelmed, "It's a marathon, not a sprint!"

We discussed the importance of attempting one new strategy or concept at a time with the understanding that regardless of the amount of planning and preparation, it has equal probability to be the quintessential idea that captivates students. But even then, things don't always go as planned and your lesson or idea might just be a flop. We have all been subjected to unseen interruptions at a time when we are supposed to shine, ranging from unplanned fire drills, a student getting sick, or a parent walking by the screen in their underwear while you are virtually working with your students.

Teaching is All about Daily Reflection

Reflection about classroom instruction is an opportunity to tweak, modify and refine yourself. Teaching is not the punishment of the past. What worked, how it could be improved, is it worth doing again, should I share the idea with my team, should I move on and pretend it never happened are all

275

common feelings and self-doubt reflections that are healthy to think about. The list goes on and on and even pushes the boundaries of unrealistic expectations. Moving forward, you will have days where you can't wait to get home and brag to your family about your unparalleled triumph. You will also have days where you drive home pondering how you possibly thought what you implemented was an exemplary idea and revolutionary in the world of pedagogy. Despite embarrassment, you have to fix the mess you created.

No one wakes up with the desire to wreck their winning streak. Each new day, we begin with the goal to present the best version of ourselves to the world. No one enters the field of education as a flawless teacher. When mistakes occur, successful educators make the choice to live and learn. The word "live" refers to moving on with the intent to make tomorrow a better day. "Learn" refers to the act of reflecting on the mistake that occurred and, when appropriate, seek out new knowledge to ensure mistakes are not repeated. So why not live and learn?

The best way to move on from the past and avoid future mistakes is to actively seek the path of a lifelong learner. A plethora of avenues exist to enhance your craft and become a stronger educator. In Dan's chapter, he explained so many great routes that you can take in your career and learning path. Continue your lifelong journey to become the best educator you can but remember that when mistakes occur, you need to stop beating yourself up about them. Your colleagues and students have bruises of their own and when you recognize that you have some too, all the pain can easily go away. Have fun, keep working hard and always celebrate yourself! You are unique and you are needed.

Jill Worley is a former elementary school administrator and math teacher. She currently serves as the Operations Manager for the International Board of Credentialing and Continuing Education Standards (IBCCES) in Jacksonville, Florida.

Stop Feeling Stupid if You Don't Know Something
JESSE LUBINSKY

The gasps were audible even all the way in the back of the auditorium. I'd been invited to a neighboring school district to hear a well-known education technology leader speak to the entire staff on a conference day. The speaker held up their phone for the crowd to see. "All of your students have these. If all you have to offer your students are facts and information that could easily be looked up on this, then you have nothing to offer your students." And while the statement was intended to get a rise out of the crowd (which it did), I definitely understood the underlying point that was being made at that moment and why it struck such a nerve with the audience.

Growing up, I remember that questioning a teacher was frowned upon and on those rare occasions where a student would correct a teacher or ask something the teacher didn't know, the vibe in the room would be one of hushed awe and disbelief. The idea of "the teacher is always right" has been ingrained in us from an incredibly young age. In many ways, it is the educational equivalent of "the customer is always right." It starts off by manifesting itself as a necessary demonstration of respect for the authority of the teacher but then transitions into an unreasonable expectation that the teacher's word is sacrosanct and beyond reproach. While this belief provides a safe haven for educators to exist in their classrooms, it flies directly in the face of everything we tell our students about learning.

The Unwarranted Fear of a Failure Mindset

In recent years, it's become popular in schools to talk about failure--not as something that students should avoid, but rather that failure is a natural part of the learning process that we should embrace. Reread what Jill just wrote in her chapter. Through failure, educators say, students gain incredible benefits such as building resilience, developing a tolerance for taking risks, learning how to be more reflective and fostering an ability to connect to others in a more open and honest manner. So, given that we all recognize the benefits of reframing failure as something that is a necessary part of the learning process which we should welcome rather than avoid, why would we, as educators, operate by the old expression "Do as I say, not as I do." rather than "What's good for the goose is good for the gander?" The answer is simple: *Fear*.

The reason that the speaker at the start of the story struck such a chord with the audience wasn't because the teachers in the crowd were in stunned in disbelief by such an offensive and absurd suggestion that they may no longer be relevant or necessary. No, they were *afraid* because it was true. The way schools have been designed, the traditional classroom positions teachers at the center of all activity as the gatekeepers of knowledge and learning. Knowledge is exactly what keeps teachers in that position. At the core of this idea, one believes that the teacher has the knowledge that the students need in order to move forward in their academic careers and that only by successfully demonstrating that they have learned all that a teacher has to offer, will they prove themselves worthy to move on in life. While that last sentence may seem ridiculous to you, if you think back on your own school experiences, chances are that you have had teachers who operated under that same belief. This fear, however, is both unwarranted and unnecessary because it will prevent you from being your best and your dynamic, synergistic school is counting on you!

The concept of the life-long learner is one that is pervasive throughout schools and education in general. One of the most common things you'll see across the mission statements of schools and districts around the world is the goal of creating life-long learners. But, if teachers and educators don't lead the way by embodying the characteristics of life-long learners, then those mission statements become nothing more than empty platitudes.

I remember being in front of my classroom and having to admit that I didn't know the answer to a question from one of my students. Did I feel vulnerable? Of course. I knew my students looked to me as the person who was there to ensure that they would learn trigonometry. But I also knew that demonstrating that vulnerability would not be interpreted as a sign of weakness, but rather as a show of mutual respect was what was going to rule my roost.

You see, admitting you don't know something only looks stupid if the only response to not knowing something is "I don't know." Not knowing something isn't a flaw if you seek a solution. If "I don't know" pivots to "I'm not sure but let's find out" or "I'll have to look that up and get back to you" then you begin to model the attributes and learning dispositions that we aspire for our students to develop on their academic journeys. We can't lose sight of the fact that imbuing students with those attributes and dispositions are the actual goal of school, rather than simply ensuring they memorize rote facts and information that they can easily acquire on any web browser.

The Fear of the Unknown

The role of the teacher continues to change and evolve. A pandemic forced teachers to rise to the occasion in ways they never could have envisioned and for which they received little to no training in order to do so. Yet, teachers everywhere persevered and did amazing things that they never could have imagined. There's always fear of the unknown. But, that's different than being afraid or simply not knowing something that you are not willing to find out. Of course, it's possible that everything I just said is incorrect and maybe I don't know what I'm talking about. If so, that's perfectly OK with me.

I'm still learning and I'm not afraid. I stopped that a long time ago. Will you join me?

A career educator for nearly two decades, Jesse Lubinsky is currently serving as the Chief Learning Officer of Ready Learner One, LLC. Jesse is co-author of Reality Bytes: Innovative Learning Using Augmented and Virtual Reality and The E-Sports Education Playbook: Empowering Every Learner through Inclusive Gaming. He is co-host of the Partial Credit Podcast and is an international keynote speaker who has presented across North America, Europe, Asia, the Middle East and Australia.

Stop Worrying About Your Formal Observations
ANDREW MAROTTA

Yes, stop. Just stop worrying about it. Sure, it sounds easy. But, what if you can't? What if you're thinking about it over and over and nervous that you're going to make a mistake or look bad during your formal observation? What if you worry that it is not good enough or your administrator will think it stinks? My hope is that I can help you with some strategies to NOT get nervous, NOT worry so much or, at least, overcome your potential nervousness and worry.

A Little Nervousness Means that You are Alive

The first thing I'd like you to understand is it is OK to get a little nervous. This means you care that your work matters. This means that you are alive. I understand. Someone is evaluating you and critiquing your work which can be a little nerve wracking. A little nervous is normal. Over the course of my lifetime, I've experienced numerous evaluations when I was extremely nervous.

When I taught middle school in Staten Island, NY in 2000 and I was getting married in 2001. I had just returned from a volunteer trip in the Tuscany region of Italy, volunteering with Augustinian volunteers and I needed a job to pay for my wedding. I was desperate. I was certified in science, but the only job they had open was teaching Italian. The principal, who was of Italian descent, asked me if I spoke Italian and I said "Sure, no problem." He hired me on the spot without doing heavy investigating on my level of Italian proficiently. What I didn't know was the grammar of the language

279

and all of the rules of the language, so I had to fake it until I made it. I was doing just fine until my observation! Oh no!

Now, I am not normally a nervous person and I've never had a panic attic, but as soon as that administrator came in with that clipboard and was staring at me, it was like a bucket of water was poured over my head. I began sweating, stuttering and rapidly calling on kids, not even knowing what I was asking them. Looking back, it must have been quite comical, but I asked to speak to my administrator in the hallway. She said, "Right now, in the middle of your observation?" I pleaded "Yes!" in both English and Italian. In the hallway, I said, "I can't do this!" I told her that I felt like I was a failure and I was faking it the whole time. She told me I was doing just fine and she actually liked my accent! She was very gentle and compassionate towards me and helped to calm me down. As you might imagine, it's tough to find an Italian teacher, so the leadership team was able to adjust the course to be more of an Italian culture course and then I eventually ended up teaching science, anyway!

I share that story for several reasons: What you don't think will be OK will turn out OK. Things will work out for you if you continue to put your best foot forward. Yet, you might be thinking: "But, Andrew, I can't stop worrying about being evaluated. It's in my head and I know something, just something will go wrong!" Don't worry about worrying. Here are some quick tips to get you in a better, more positive mindset.

1. You Will Always Have Another Chance

It is now or never, do or die, this is it, or this is the only chance. Even though those numbers from your evaluation mean a lot to you, there are so many other opportunities to show your colors and your true strengths. You will always have another chance. It is not all or nothing; it is a journey. While on that journey, this is just a short snapshot in time. If you keep moving on your journey with a positive mindset and love students, your body of work will shine through versus thinking that just forty-five minutes of your teaching defines you. I've told many a teacher that the numbers that pop up on that evaluation form will not have much to do with your success or lack of success in the school.

2. Teach Every Day Like You are Being Observed

I used to referee Division One college basketball and my supervisor always told me that you never know who is watching or who is in the stands. Maybe it's a Tuesday night and there are not a lot of people in the stands and you are tired from your day job or from refereeing a game the night before.

Maybe you don't work as hard or give it your all. There might be an NBA officiating scout in the stands who is there looking for talent or the coach of your next game sees you dogging it. What I used to do when I officiated was pick somebody out in the stands whom I could see their face and say to myself, "That is the supervisor and I'm gonna do a great job today!" I then took this strategy with me into the classroom and I used to tape a stick figure on the back wall (I'm not much of an artist!) and for me, in my own mind, that was the administrator. I knew someone was there every day watching my every move. Then, in the moment when they did come in to observe or just visit my class, I was used to him watching me.

3. Invite a Colleague in to Give You Critical Feedback

There is no better way than a friendly person that you can trust to offer you real, honest feedback. Ask your trusted colleague to give you at least three things they liked and three things they didn't like or that you can improve upon during the lesson. Be open and ready to receive feedback and do not be defensive. After all, trusted colleagues are important. Their eyes and ears can do a lot for you!

4. Digitally Record Your Lesson

Another tip is to video record yourself, whether it be audio, only, or both video and audio. Review what you did, how it looked and how it sounded. Just like inviting someone in to see your live lesson, sit with a few colleagues and ask for their feedback. Did they see what you saw or did they see other things? You will see things from a different vantage point when you record yourself.

5. Think about your "ZONEfulness"

I learned this term from my friend Joe, a mental strength coach at the University of Pennsylvania. He wrote a book entitled *ZONEfulness: 4 Techniques to Access and Master your Zone*. He describes ways to "zone in" and then defines "zone blockers" that can hurt us or block us from being successful. While he is describing methods and strategies for top Division 1 athletes, the same techniques can be used for educators--especially those who are psyching themselves out by getting worried about their upcoming formal observation. Joe shares these ZONE-ins: Extreme self-support, a focus on personal history of success and to see future memories of success. These are ZONE-blockers: fears and anxieties that stop you from being successful, such as self-criticism, "what-ifing" and "why-ning."

I love the movie *For the Love of the Game* starring Kevin Costner. He plays a pitcher for the Detroit

Tigers who is over the hump and at the end of his career. There's a scene in the movie while pitching against the Yankees and right before he pitches the ball, he tells himself: "Clear the mechanism." After he says these words to himself, the crowd silences and blurs in the background and he just focuses just on the catcher. I use this strategy in my own career as a principal.

6. Invite Administrators in Even When it is Not Your Formal Observation

I love when teachers do this. It makes me feel welcome and lets me know they want me in their room. It also lets me know that they are proud of the work they are doing and want some validation. It also takes any formality out of regular observations when they are actually conducted. Choose a few things each year to make you shine and don't be shy about inviting your administrators into your classroom. This will help you get more accustomed to them or anyone being in the room with you. Just like anything, the more you do it, the more comfortable you will get.

7. Know the Rubric

Familiarize yourself with what you are being "scored" on. Know what your school leaders are looking for. It is almost like an open book test and you just have to fill in the answers. This reminds me of Rory, one of our veteran teachers, in my own school. At the beginning of Rory's lesson, he emphatically yelled out the learning target while moving his open palm underneath the words that he sandwiched together. He knew I was looking for that and he gave it to me on a silver platter; yet, I also know he made it part of his daily routine. Rory gave his lesson a little extra mustard that day because he was familiar with the expectations of the school regarding solid instruction.

8. Train Your Students

I've had many students lean over to me during an observation and say, "She never does that. She's just doing it because you are here." I found this very telling and made sure I was back in that teacher's room more often. Train your students on your expectations and routines in the room because that way when the administrator is there, not much is different than what normally is going on. You can't fake being someone you are not just because there is a building principal or assistant principal in your classroom.

9. Include Your Administrator

I always like it when a teacher includes me in their lesson. I feel connected to the activity and I think the students enjoy it, as well. It shows everyone in the room, including you, that you are being inclusive of the leader of the building and not just leaving them on the outside looking in. While some administrators might prefer that they be left alone, I like the line from the musical *Hamilton*: "I wanna be in the room where it happens!" Ask for feedback or tips from the administrator and students. Ask questions, such as "What makes a great teacher in your opinion?" or "What are some of the go-to strategies that you see in other classrooms that work?" or "If I could do three things during each class period, what should those three things be?" Then do them and feel empowered to do them with your administrative team!

10. Ask Your Students

Give a survey to your students after each marking period. Asking for students' input, anonymously, shows them that you really care about your performance as well as their opinions. If the principal asks why you might have done a certain thing in a certain way, you can share the results of your student survey; that's a great piece of evidence that shows that you are caring, thoughtful and respectful to your students. It also gives you an opportunity to change some things that you don't even know you might be doing. How is this going to help you to stop worrying about your evaluation or formal observation? You will be so dialed into your students that a divine harmony and rhythm of your class will be recognized very easily by anyone who visits your classroom.

11. Success Leaves Clues

Ask the best teachers to see copies of their evaluations. My friend, Rob, who is a sports psychologist from Montclair State University always says, "Success leaves clues." Ask your successful colleagues what they do. Observe their classes. Ask if you can see several of their written observations to see what the comments said. The best teachers will be happy to share this with you, so don't be afraid to ask.

12. Ask for a Do-Over

Will there be some hardnose administrators that live and die by the rules that an observation is an observation? Sure. Hopefully, that's not the case for you, but if you don't ask for a redo will they just offer one without you asking? There's no shame in asking for a redo. I included this strategy in my book, *The Principal: Surviving and Thriving* as I called the "write-up" a "rip up." If I felt that there was a teacher, whom in my opinion, I thought could do better, I would write up the evaluation and give them the feedback. Then, during our post-observation, I would rip up the evaluation in front of them and say, "I believe you're better than this snapshot in time and I'd like to come in again."

13. Remember the 5 SW's

This is from a typical sales training mindset, but it has helped me greatly over the years. I try to remember The 5 SW's, which are:

- Sometimes it Will [go well].
- Sometimes it Won't [go well].
- So What?
- Someone's Waiting.
- So, Stick With it.

To me, this says it all and really sums up how we need to dispel our fears about formal observations. Last, but not least, my friend, Rob, taught me this strategy:

- Take your thumb and touch it to your pointer finger/1st finger and say, "I."
- Then repeat with your thumb and touch it to your middle finger and say "can."
- Next, touch your thumb to your ring finger and say "do."
- Lastly, touch your thumb to your pinky and say "this."

"I can do this."

Repeat this action three, four, or even five times. If you start to get nervous again, breathe deeply and slowly and do it again. This short exercise is simple, yet powerful. You are telling yourself in your mind and out loud that you got this, you are capable of anything and will be able to do it and get through it. You might think self-talk feels a little silly. No way! I find it quite effective and it helped me many a time.

Go get 'em and good luck. Remember, YOU CAN DO THIS!

Andrew Marotta is a longtime principal in the Port Jervis City School District in New York. He is the author of The School Leader and The Partnership. He is an education leadership expert and enthusiastic speaker who brings his message of surviving and thriving to school leaders everywhere. You can follow Andrew's blog at #ELBlog and his podcast at #ELB and learn more about him at www.andrewmarotta.com and #survivethrive.

(100)

Stop Teaching if You Don't Love the Profession any Longer

ERIK FRANCIS

Disclaimer:

This chapter should be read and not skipped over if you love your job and career as a teacher because at some point in your life, who knows, you might feel differently.

Why do you stay in education? Take a moment, pause and deeply and authentically reflect upon this question before responding. There are so many reasons to leave the profession. The obstacles keep piling up between misguided legislatures, the underfunding of schools, societal pressures, applying pedagogy to virtual learning situations and societal disarray. There are legitimate and viable reasons to justify throwing in the towel on the teaching profession, altogether. However, many of us continue to remain in education—be it as a classroom teacher, a school leader, or district administrator. As Simon Sinek asks us, "What's your WHY?"

What's Your Purpose and Reason Why You are a Teacher?

This question was probably easier for you to answer when you started teaching. Think back to how excited you were when you were earning your teaching degree and learning about education methods and theories. Think back to when you did your student teaching and had the opportunity to apply not only your education, but also your endowments and gained the initial experience and credentials that you needed to become a teacher. Think back to when you were given your own classroom and first student roster. Think back to how you looked forward to not only teaching but planning for and working with your students.

Do You Still Feel That Way?

Maybe these feelings have changed or evolved for you. Maybe you have become more practical or wiser in your career, recognizing and realizing the realities of being an educator. Maybe your first year or your first three years provided you with the expertise you needed to continue in this career. You could have left during those first three years, but something made you stay and continue. What was your reason WHY you became a teacher? Is that still your reason today or has it changed? It's acceptable and realistic that your reasons for staying in education have changed or evolved. But, more importantly, is your WHY today still a good enough reason to remain a teacher?

Education has Changed and Evolved, but Have You?

The education profession certainly has changed and evolved since you first started teaching and even throughout the course of your career. However, what goes into the profession? Pedagogy and politics permeate education and those have changed and evolved over time. Education is no longer just about academia and being an educator is not just about teaching literacy, numeracy and deeper thinking. It is about addressing the whole child by being aware of their academic needs and being sensitive to their socioemotional needs. It's about receiving and seeking continuous professional development not only to hone your own craft and skills, but to also stay up to date with the latest education reforms, research and trends. It is about advocating for your students, your profession and yourself to ensure empathy and equity are promoted and supported, not only through pedagogical intentionality, but having to do so professionally and politically within systems that have let us down. This may not be what you thought you signed up for years ago.

So, the big question is: have *you* changed and evolved with the profession and system or are you clutching, fighting and struggling professionally, personally and physiologically to be the teacher you aspired to be years ago or want to be right now?

Do You Enjoy Education and Being an Educator?

Being in education and being an educator are two separate things. You can be a teacher, but you might not enjoy teaching any longer. Maybe your interactions with students have soured over time. Conversely, you might enjoy teaching, but maybe you do not enjoy being a teacher any longer.

Which do you enjoy *more*: the practice of teaching in school or the profession of being a teacher at a school? You can still do and be both. But, maybe a lack of enjoyment is not about you at all. Maybe you no longer enjoy your *position*.

Have You Conducted a Health and Wellness Check?

The biggest indicator of whether there is joy in your teaching career is to conduct a health and wellness check–not only for yourself, but also for the betterment of the students you serve.

How do you feel when you wake up in the morning and head to your classroom? Do you feel a sense of excitement or dread for what the day may bring? Do you find yourself smiling or crying at the start or at the end of the school day? How often do you find yourself smiling versus crying?

Do you count down the days until the breaks, days off, winter or spring holidays and summer vacation? Do you look forward to a three or four-day weekend driven by the school calendar that showcases your upcoming days off? Do you hope and pray for inclement weather so school will be cancelled? Are you counting the days until you can retire? Does your pension keep you in the profession?

Now, think about your students and colleagues. Do you find yourself helping them or criticizing them more often than not? How do your students respond to you? Do they respect you? Do they feel safe and secure in your classroom? If someone asked them of their impression of you, how would they respond? I am not saying whether they like or dislike you. Would they say that they feel as if you care about them and enjoy teaching them? These questions are not only for you. These are also questions you could ask a colleague or a staff member whom you recognize and realize may be struggling in their own career journey. Life is too short to be miserable or make anyone else feel that way and that's all you are doing if you are in career atrophy.

A New Beginning and a New-Found Success

If you realize that you DO want to bail on your current position or teaching career, altogether, that is OK! You are not giving up or quitting. If your profession or your position does not bring you the enjoyment or enrichment it once did, then it's perfectly fine to accept and admit that and decide that it's time to move on. However, it doesn't mean that you need to stop teaching or being a teacher. There are a number of other avenues and opportunities for you to transfer to, share within your profession and use your skills for other opportunities which will help others. Here are a few pathways that you might want to consider.

Transition from Teacher to Administrator

Maybe one of the reasons why you are discouraged and disenfranchised with being a teacher is because of how you see and feel about the way the system is being run. Maybe you are frustrated with the leadership (or lack of leadership) not only in your school but also in the system of education, as a whole, and believe you could do better. If you become more frustrated with how schools and the system are being run, then maybe consider shifting your focus and seeking a career in school leadership and administration in order to make the changes that you feel will correct the missteps of others that you are witnessing.

Transition from Teacher to a Trainer of Teachers

Maybe you enjoy teaching but have become disillusioned or discouraged with teaching the curriculum or how children are being taught. Maybe you would like to teach or work with other teachers in order to demonstrate your expertise by showing them how they could work with their students effectively. If you are disheartened by the curriculum or with how children are being taught, then maybe consider looking into how you could become a trainer of teachers by working as an academic or instructional coach. You could also look into how you could expand your career and become an independent trainer who goes to schools and works with other teachers in the field.

Transition from Educator to Advocate

Maybe you are proud to be an educator and take pride in your profession, but you feel educators are not given the respect they should receive. Maybe you find yourself not only championing your students but also your colleagues by speaking and standing up when needed or when necessary. If your interests in education have shifted from instruction to advocacy, look into how you could take a leadership position in your local education union or association or even through volunteerism in a state or national organization. You may find a renewed sense of passion and pride in the profession by speaking and standing up for not only for yourself, but for your colleagues and children in large numbers of schools across your region or the nation.

Transition from Educator to Author

Maybe you have a talent in developing and delivering educational experiences that are engaging, enriching and enjoyable. Maybe you have strong ideas and opinions about education and want to share them with others. Maybe you want to share your experiences and showcase the experience of others and maybe you enjoy writing. If you want to express yourself and extend your voice in education, consider writing a regular blog or a full-length book in which you could share and showcase experiences, ideas, or perspectives about the profession or for helping the profession.

Transition beyond Education

Robert Marzano says, "Teaching is an art and a science. For some, it's a natural skill. For others, it is a strategy they learn. For a few, it's both." However, education is not the only field in which you could be an educator. All aspects of the workforce need teachers as advisers, coaches, or trainers to help others succeed and survive. If you aspire to extend your expertise beyond education, consider how you could use your personal skills and the professional strategies you have learned in a different profession.

Transition Outside of Education

Maybe you just do not enjoy education any longer, at all. Maybe it's time for a change, then. Change and the realization to make a change can be both difficult and frightening. However, what is more difficult or frightening: the unknown consequence of the change that you make or the feelings that you are experiencing about being in education as an educator? What if a change could help you professionally, personally, emotionally and physiologically? You just don't know. However, here's something you *can* feel secure about: you could always come back to teaching if that is what you really want to do even after a change is made.

Realize and Respond to Your Why

If you have lost the passion for education as a profession or because of your current position, then the best thing you could do, not only for yourself but also your students, is to ask yourself why you stay. If you have an immediate response that is more negative than positive or more counter-productive than productive, then it is time to consider other options and opportunities. You are not a failure if you pack it up. In fact, you will have made the brave and bold realization that what you are doing in education is no longer enriching or enjoyable for you and it is time to make a change right away. Perhaps, happiness is somewhere else for you. Whatever you decide, I wish you the very best.

Erik Francis is the owner of Maverik Education and an international author and presenter with over 25 years of experience working in education as a classroom teacher, site administrator, education program specialist with a state education agency and a trainer who provides professional development for teachers and school leaders. He is the author of ASCD's top selling book, Now That's a Good Question and Knowing is Half the Battle. Eric is also ranked #12 in the World's Top 30 Global Gurus in Education for 2021.

The Buck Stops Here:
A Final Plea to Abandon Practices with No Merit
JON CORIPPO

When I joined my first school district in 1996, I heard this aphorism often in the first two years of my career: *Doing things over and over without a different outcome–that's a form of insanity.*

Twenty-five years later, the district that taught me this adage is largely doing things in the very same exact ways! Meanwhile, I've facilitated a lot of professional development all over the world and what I have sadly learned is that this flawed kind of thinking and pedagogy is *everywhere. Even worse, this ineffective teaching has been identified by writers, leaders, researchers, TED Talkers and thinkers, repeatedly, time and time again!*

CAUTION: Don't Be Offended, but We are Doing Education ALL Wrong

My first mind blowing moment about how wrong we are was during the summer after my first year of teaching. I literally went to the education section at Barnes & Noble and located a skinny book entitled *Dumbing Us Down* by John Taylor Gatto. *He argued that school is actually succeeding.*

It's succeeding at making students who are docile, materialistic and unconcerned about any time in history other than the present. I had tears in my eyes when I read the first section of a book, entitled, *The Seven Lesson Teacher*. After reading those first few pages, *I realized that I had been an unwittingly co-conspirator against children in my own classroom and I resolved to change my behavior right away from that day forward and forever!*

In 2003, I read a book entitled, *17 Reasons Football is Better than High School*. It was written by a social ethnographer, named Herb Childress, who went into grand detail about how students were disengaged in classrooms, but at the same time, still deeply engaged in their activities *outside* of the classroom. Childress made it clear that kids are not to be blamed for their lack of engagement. We are the adults, we are the "experience designers" and it is our job to be the pied piper and draw students into the content by the artistic whistling of a humanistic flute that will activate pure joyful learning. *I realized that I had been an unwittingly co-conspirator against children in my own classroom and I resolved to change my lesson planning right away from that day forward and forever!*

TTWWADI

In my classroom in the early 2000's, I downloaded a file on my orange iMac computer (that's how long ago this was). The name of the file was, *That's The Way We've Always Done It*, or TTWWADI. This classic writing by Ian Jukes blew my mind with amazing historical examples of what hasn't changed (Aside: Did you know that today railroad tracks are the same width as a Roman oxcart? It was the way they always did it!) Jukes goes on to report that the mindset for the structure of our schools is based on decisions that were made in the days of the horse, buggy, kerosene lamp, factory floor and production line. It's a system in which most students are still released for three months each summer so that they can harvest the crops based on some European agricultural cycle. (Aside #2: Seven computers later, this PDF from Jukes et al. is still on my desktop). I realized then that we did not need to limit our thinking based on old systems. *I realized that I had been an unwittingly co-conspirator against children in my own classroom and I resolved to change my classroom management right away from that day forward and forever!*

Daily, we manage to extricate ourselves from many examples of the way we used to do it (TTWWADI) with great success. We migrated from Denny's Restaurant coffee to Starbucks as a destination. The city of Detroit has been supplanted by Tesla and there are a handful of other brand-new car startup companies as we speak, replacing the paradigm of the "big three." The phone went wireless and then became ubiquitous while Steve Jobs went ahead and removed all the buttons from phones so that we could use the screen for *what we needed it for and when we needed it right away*. The handheld Blackberry was no longer "in" or "cool."

Maybe it's Because We Are Doing "The Same Thing" So Well

I was lucky to meet Dr. Sonny Magana at ISTE in 2018. Sonny is an amazing researcher and educator that has done Oxford Library level research, showing that the addition of technology to the classroom actually has a subtractive effect on learning (from a typical .40 effect size related to student growth compared to a .34 effect size with poorly implemented Ed-tech initiatives). There are many reasons that this is the case in Sonny's research, but I would like to point out the fact that most teachers usually teach with the exact same pedagogical approach that they always have, even if content or materials/resources change. Teachers use a screen instead of a chalkboard; they hand out digital worksheets instead of mimeos. Teachers give students feedback in about the very same manner and within almost the very same time frame that they always have provided feedback. Why would we expect a different outcome, then?

Malpractice is STILL Manifesting

To reiterate: the classroom practices condemned in research and in this book, itself, are *still* manifesting in classrooms today while we proceed to carry out about the same practices we always have and then get just about the same results we always have, as well. In turn, students respond to us in about the same manner and respond to school in about the same way.

If we want different results, we are going to have to change the way that we work with students and behave as teachers. In addition to the earlier seminal documents that I mentioned, one of my favorite blog posts of all time was written by a good friend of mine, Sam Patterson. Sam had a simple exhortation for his readers: "Don't raise your hand; I'm calling on everybody". Sam was encouraging educators to use technology in order to democratize the classroom. Instead of using demeaning Popsicle sticks to get convergent answers, Sam advocated for the idea that all students should be getting feedback in almost real-time ways via the use of technology. Nothing spurs growth like rapid quick, meaningful feedback.

Poor technology integration is also a huge factor in our failing systems: Billions of dollars have been spent on "interactive" whiteboards, "sit and listen" professional development while *Teachers Pay Teachers* is making some teachers incredibly wealthy by mass distributing what are basically a series of "dolled-up" worksheets. If there was a magic worksheet that could raise scores, we would have found it by now. News flash: It does not exist.

SLOOOOWWWW FEEDBACK is killing student growth. Students adapt and learn nearly almost immediately in sports, video games and social media. But, in class, students can wait days or weeks for a score on a simple multiple-choice quiz. Without feedback, students lose momentum and interest and, most importantly, their trust in the process of education corrodes. Lessons continue to lack collaborative elements (beyond simplistic things like "shoulder partners") and lessons delivered are still mostly produced by corporate lesson planners who may have no classroom experience whatsoever.

How Do We Fix Education?

What I love about the 100 ideas and concepts in this book is that they provide real, actual and articulated ways for us to step away from the old practices. The worst thing about what we do in education is that we do not properly imagine new outcomes and new futures for our students. We are always aiming for a convergent and static approach even when our own school experience as children and all the research and all of these readings demonstrate that such an approach [to anything] has never really worked, anyway. The goal of this book is to be the proverbial grain of sand in an oyster. The goal of this book is to grow a pearl, to help educators understand practices and behaviors that replace the ones that we have had *within our own failure of imagination* in eliminating them.

Dr. Magana's research shows that we can create experiences for students that more than *quadruple* their academic output. But, we won't do that by memorializing the old systems at a higher tempo or at a higher volume. We must achieve those results by using new systems in better ways that are brain-friendly and student-centered. These practices should also not lead to teacher burnout as we strive to fill their hearts with stories and victories about student success and feelings of satisfaction that, frankly, has been missing from our profession for so long. Look to basic science: change the input, change the result. It is not about Ed-tech; it's about feedback, creating and collaborating. We educate human children: let's revel in that. What will really change 20 years from now?

STOP doing these 100 things that DON'T work for really anyone. If your goal is to become a five-star classroom, a school with synergistic school culture, or a magnetic off-the-charts dynamic success, then STOP the recommended nonsense that we so boldly put together for you.

Jon Corippo has served as a classroom teacher, high school principal, director and assistant principal while leading educational nonprofits for 25 years. Jon's passion for student learning led to the development of the bestselling book: Eduprotocol Field Guide Series. Jon loves interacting with all types of educators for professional development and is famous for his offer of "free lifetime tech support" both inside and outside of where he resides in California.

References

Adverse Childhood Experiences (ACES). "Nearly 35 Million U.S. Children have Experienced One or More Types of Childhood Trauma." Retrieved at: https://acestoohigh.com.

Bravata, et. al. (2020). Prevalence, Predictors, and Treatment of Impostor Syndrome: A Systematic Review. Journal of General Internal Medicine, 35(4), pages 1252–1275.

Child Mind Institute. 2016 Mental Health Report. Retrieved at: https://childmind.org/report/2016-childrens-mental-health-report/.

Childress, H. (1998). "Seventeen Reasons Why Football is Better than High School." *Phi Delta Kappan, 79(8)*, pages 616-619.

Crowley, M. C. (2011). Lead from the Heart: Transformational Leadership for the 21st Century. Indiana: Balboa Press.

Donohoo, J. (2018). "The Power of Collective Efficacy." *Educational Leadership*, 75 (6), pages 40-44.

Freire, P. (1972). Pedagogy of the Oppressed. 1968. Trans. Myra Bergman Ramos. New York: Herder.

Gatto, J. (2005). Dumbing Us Down: The Hidden Curriculum of Compulsory Schooling. British Columbia: New Society Publishers.

Hargreaves, A. and O'Connor, M. (2018). "Solidarity with Solidity: The Case for Collaborative Professionalism." Phi Delta Kappan Online. Available at: https://journals.sagepub.com/doi/pdf/10.1177/0031721718797116.

Marotta, A. (2020). The School Leader: Surviving and Thriving, 2nd Edition. New York: Routledge.

Marzano, R. (2017). The New Art and Science of Teaching. Indiana: Solution Tree Press.

Matas, C. (1993). Daniel's Story. New York: Scholastic.

Siciliano, M. (2016). "It's the Quality Not the Quantity of Ties that Matters: Social Networks and Self-Efficacy Beliefs." *American Educational Research Journal, 53, (2)*, pages 227-262.

Vygotsky, L. S. (1980). Mind in Society: The Development of Higher Psychological Processes. Massachusetts: Harvard University Press.

Wilcox, K. et al. (2012). Are Close Friends the Enemy? Journal of Consumer Research, Columbia Business School Research Paper, pages 12-57. Available at: https://ssrn.com/abstract=2155864.

Youngman, E. (2020). 12 Characteristics of Deliberate Homework. New York: Routledge.

What's Coming Next in the 100 Series?

100 No-Nonsense Things that ALL School Leaders Should STOP Doing

100 No-Nonsense Things that ALL Parents Should STOP Doing

100 No-Nonsense Things that ALL Students Should STOP Doing

Bring the 100 STOP series to your school, district, or organization! Through powerful content and stories that will rejuvenate your staff and get everyone on the same page, and depending on where you are located, we will deploy one or more of our 100+ presenters to offer no-nonsense guidance on transforming your school culture into a dynamic, synergistic, a five-star community. You can follow the hashtag #100StopSeries on most social media channels in to stay up to date on the following books within the 100 STOP Series. You may also subscribe to our free e-newsletter at www.pushboundconsulting.com and become part of the 100 STOP series "Crumpled-Up-Paper Movement." This project is designed to get all stakeholders of your school community on the same page BECAUSE . . .

"Uncontrolled variation is the enemy of quality."
–Dr. W. Edwards Deming

**PUSHING
BOUNDARIES**
CONSULTING, LLC

What's Coming Next for Pushing Boundaries?

Pushing Boundaries Junior

PBJ (Junior) books invite kids to think, empathize and stand up for what is right. PBJ books refuel kids' hearts just like a peanut butter and jelly sandwich refuels their bodies.

Violet Goes to Snapping School

You won't want to miss this inspirational story of adversity, perseverance and belonging. Violet, and her alligator siblings hatched in the bayou, but they couldn't find their mommy. Indigo, an alligator that was passing by, saw the hatchlings and knew she must take care of them. She nurtured them, adopted them and raised them as her own. This newly formed family grew up in the bayous and rivers of Louisiana. On her first day of school Violet discovered that learning was very difficult for her. She didn't like school until her teachers created a plan that would ensure her success at Snapping School. Follow Violet's journey as she discovers her talents and sense of belonging in this world.

Close Reading | Content Integrated | SEL | Special Education | Adoption

PUSHING
BOUNDARIES
CONSULTING, LLC

$23.75
ISBN 978-1-7370390-0-6
52375>

9 781737 039006

Made in the USA
Las Vegas, NV
05 June 2021